Active Business Tracks

Anglais ➡ B2

BTS 1re et 2e années

Claire Delarocque

Marie-Hélène Fougeron

Nathan
TECHNIQUE

Cet ouvrage permet d'organiser la préparation sur les deux années : les chapitres sont conçus comme des dossiers thématiques dans lesquels on puise d'une année sur l'autre parmi les nombreux supports, selon les parcours différenciés, les activités de groupes ou le travail individuel. Il permet une grande souplesse d'usage.

DÉCOUVRIR UN CHAPITRE

Ouverture

Entrée dans le thème par un document, une vidéo et des questions.

Entrée dans le thème

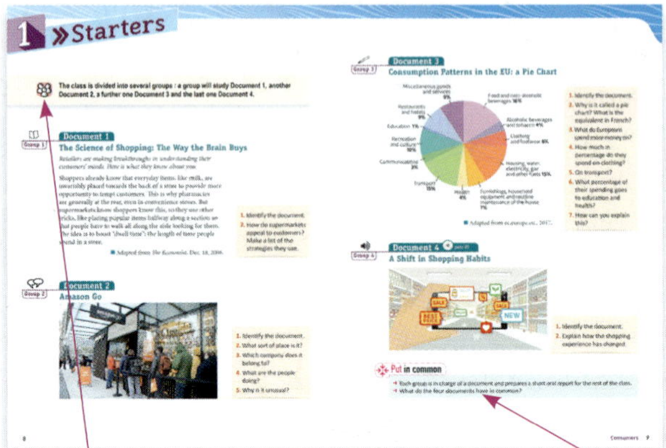

Travail en groupe

Objectifs de mise en commun

Parcours différenciés sur des supports variés

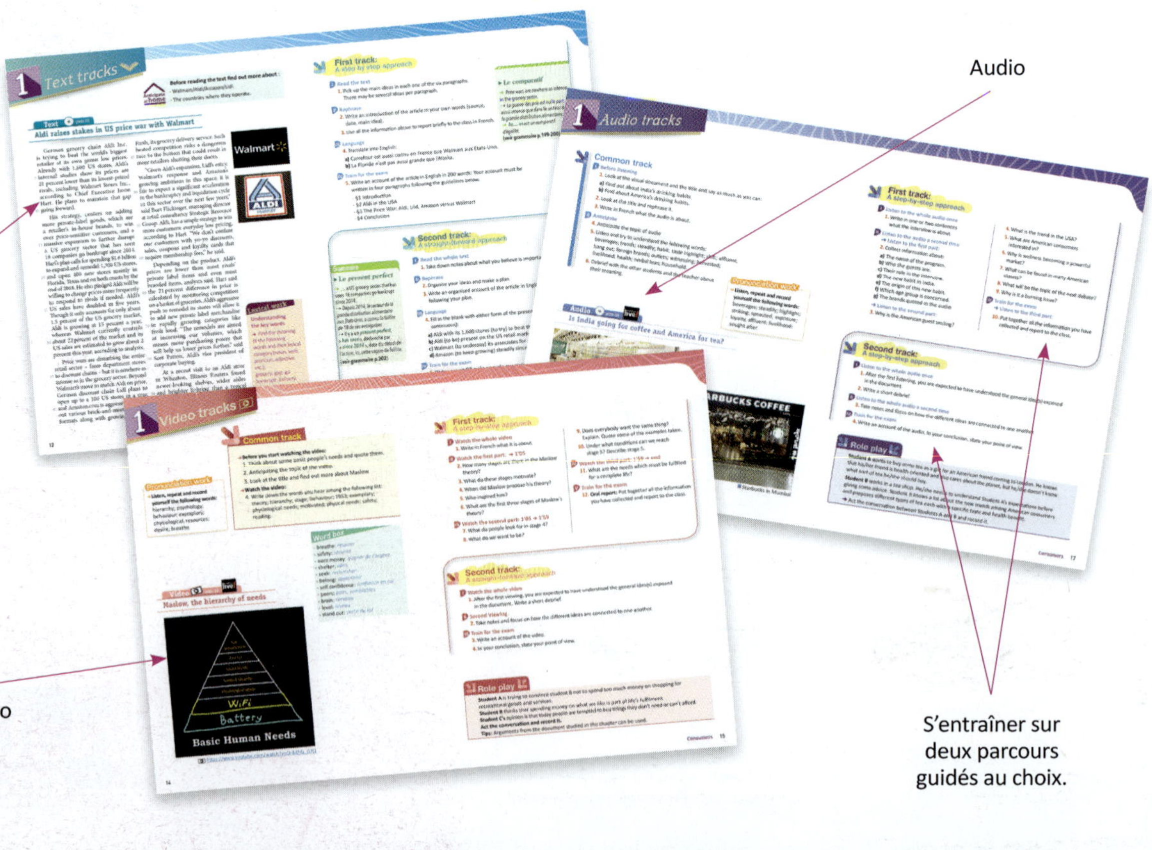

Texte

Audio

Vidéo

S'entraîner sur deux parcours guidés au choix.

Du français à l'anglais : apprendre à reformuler

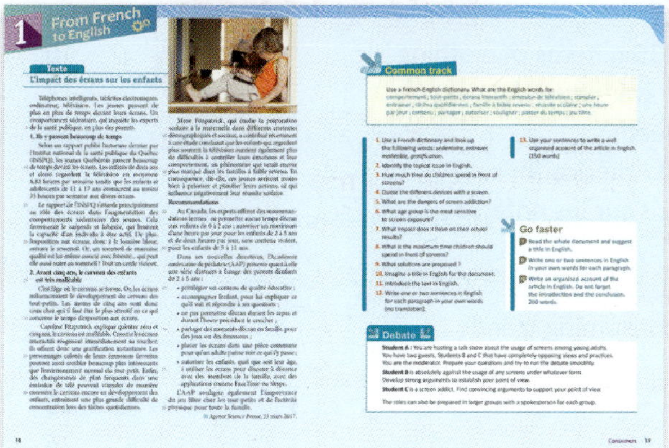

Des tâches pour travailler l'écrit et l'oral

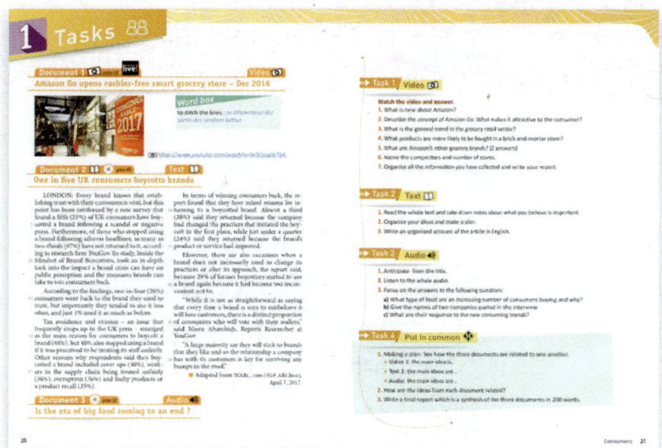

Acquérir des connaissances sur la thématique du chapitre

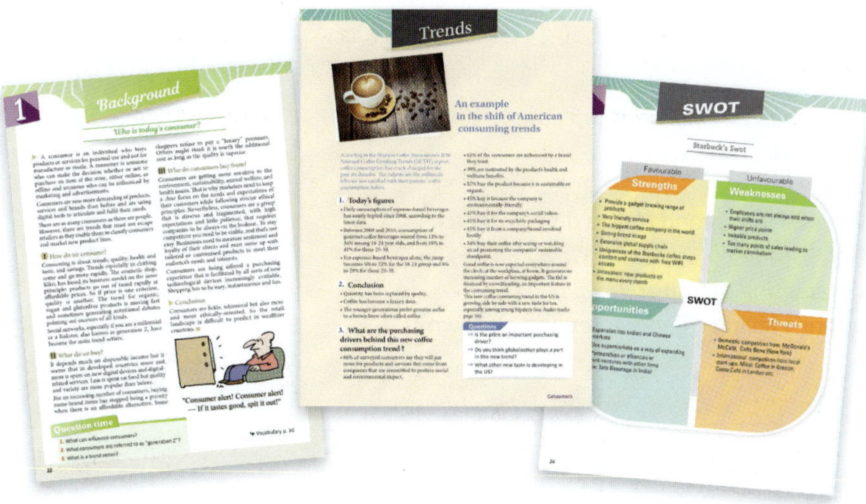

Auto-bilan

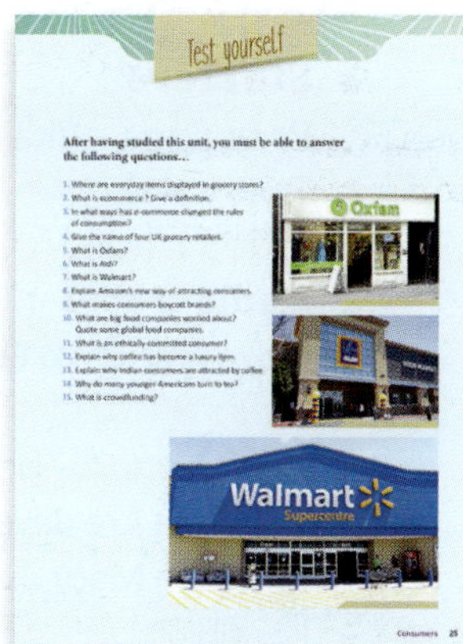

S'entraîner à l'examen

Vocabulaire du chapitre

Grâce à l'appli Nathan Live, accédez au fil des pages aux audios et vidéos !

Comment faire ?

1. Téléchargez l'application gratuite Nathan Live disponible dans tous les stores sur votre smartphone ou votre tablette (Appstore, GooglePlay).
2. Ouvrez l'application. Flashez les pages de votre manuel où le logo apparaît. Visionnez ou écoutez les ressources !

⚠ **L'application nécessite une connexion internet.**

4 Work 79

5 Passengers and commuters 103

6 Freight transport 127

Édition : Aude Benkaki
Conception maquette et couverture : David Bart
Mise en page : Graph'M
Relecture : Anne Andrault
Infographie : David Bart
Cartographie : Légendes Cartographie
Iconographie : Catherine Barbotte
Fabrication : Maria Pauliat

ISBN : 978-2-09-165096-8

1 Consumers

Question

What is Black Friday?

Word box

- consumer spending: *les dépenses des consommateurs*
- mid-priced brands: *marques à prix moyens*
- customer's loyalty cards: *cartes de fidélité*

Anticipate at home

Consumers VIDÉO 01

Nathan live!

https://www.youtube.com/watch?v=_BO94gH2IlE

? What information do consumers want when they buy food?

1 » Starters

The class is divided into several groups : a group will study Document 1, another Document 2, a further one Document 3 and the last one Document 4.

Group 1

Document 1

The Science of Shopping: The Way the Brain Buys

Retailers are making breakthroughs in understanding their customers' minds. Here is what they know about you.

Shoppers already know that everyday items, like milk, are invariably placed towards the back of a store to provide more opportunity to tempt customers. This is why pharmacies are generally at the rear, even in convenience stores. But supermarkets know shoppers know this, so they use other tricks, like placing popular items halfway along a section so that people have to walk all along the aisle looking for them. The idea is to boost "dwell time": the length of time people spend in a store.

■ Adapted from *The Economist*, Dec. 18, 2008.

1. Identify the document.
2. How do supermarkets appeal to customers? Make a list of the strategies they use.

Group 2

Document 2

Amazon Go

1. Identify the document.
2. What sort of place is it?
3. Which company does it belong to?
4. What are the people doing?
5. Why is it unusual?

Group 3

Document 3
Consumption Patterns in the EU: a Pie Chart

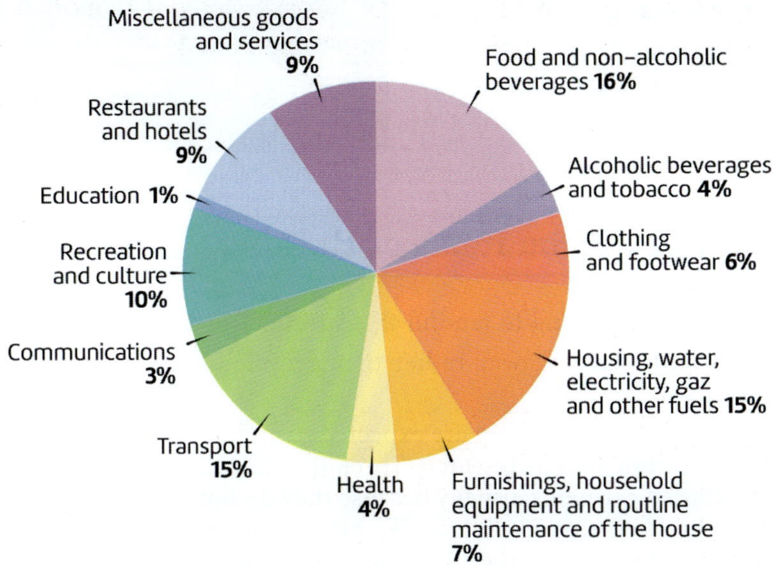

■ Adapted from ec.europe.eu., 2017.

1. Identify the document.
2. Why is it called a pie chart? What is the equivalent in French?
3. What do Europeans spend more money on?
4. How much in percentage do they spend on clothing?
5. On transport?
6. What percentage of their spending goes to education and health?
7. How can you explain this?

Group 4

Document 4 piste 01
A Shift in Shopping Habits

1. Identify the document.
2. Explain how the shopping experience has changed.

Put in common

→ Each group is in charge of a document and prepares a short oral report for the rest of the class.
→ What do the four documents have in common?

1 Prep page

Anticipate at home

Before reading the text, investigate:

- Who are the Britons? Where do they live? How many people live there? How big is the country?
- Find information about Sainsbury's/ Marks & Spencer; Oxfam.

Text piste 02

Britons expected to throw away 235m items of clothing

Britons expected to send 235m items of clothing to landfill this spring.

Study finds three-quarters of consumers throw away rather than recycle or donate unwanted garments.

A predicted 235m items of Britons' unwanted clothing are expected to end up in landfill unnecessarily this spring, according to new research. Three-quarters of consumers admit to binning their discarded garments, usually because they do not realise that worn-out or dirty clothes can be recycled or accepted by charities, a survey of 2,000 people commissioned by the supermarket Sainsbury's has found.

Consumers are expected to get rid of 680m pieces of clothing as they spring-clean their wardrobes, the survey shows. However, the annual fashion detox will be damaging for the environment, with a staggering 235m of the garments expected to end up in landfill. People will dispose of an average of 19 items, with seven going straight in the bin.

Over the past 10 years, clothing has been the fastest growing waste stream in the UK. In partnership with the charity Oxfam, Sainsbury's is urging consumers to donate unwanted clothes to its collection points alongside the traditional recycling bins in its store car parks. The study also uncovered the reasons people do not donate or recycle clothing, with 49% saying they did not think they could because the clothes were worn out or dirty. A further 16% said they did not have time to visit a charity shop, or could not be bothered to sort items, while 6% did not realise clothing could be recycled.

Men are more likely to send clothes to landfill, with 82% saying they would bin items this spring compared with 69% of women.

"If clothes go out with the rubbish, they'll end up in landfill, so we've teamed up with Oxfam to help Britons become more charitable and environmentally savvy this spring," said Paul Crewe, head of sustainability at Sainsbury's. "No matter if they're worn out or grubby, we're calling on shoppers to donate their unwanted clothes at recycling points in our stores across the UK."

Marks & Spencer also has a partnership with Oxfam, which began in January 2008. Donors handing old M&S clothing in to Oxfam stores receive a £5 M&S voucher, while its "shwopping" scheme encourages customers to hand over an old or unwanted garment whenever they buy a new one. Figures show that 27m garments have been "shwopped" since 2008.

Adapted from *The Guardian*, April 6, 2017.

Lexical work

Understanding the key words

→ Find the meaning of the following words and their lexical category (noun, verb, pronoun, adjective, etc.): item; landfill; consumer; donate; garment; discard; charity; survey; sustainability.

Rephrase the tittle with your own words.

I Read the whole text

1. Pick up the Figures in the text and find what they correspond to.
2. Write a sentence about the two companies and the charity quoted in the text.
3. What kind of garments/clothes are referred to in the article?

II Rephrase

4. Rephrase the key ideas in each paragraph in one or two sentences.
5. Translate into French:
   a) Consumers were asked to recycle their clothes.
   b) People were told to give their unwanted clothes to charities.
6. Translate into English:
   a) Aujourd'hui, on encourage les gens à recycler leurs vêtements.
   b) On s'attend à ce que les consommateurs changent leurs habitudes.

III Language

7. Why are the words "shwopped" and "shwopping" between inverted commas?
8. Can you guess the meaning of these words?
9. Find other examples either in English or in French.
10. Complete the translation: Consumers are expected to get rid of 680m pieces of clothing... → *On s'attend à...*

IV Train for the exam

11. Write an account of the document in French. (140 words)
12. What role should charities play in making consumption habits more sustainable?

V Branching out

13. Find out if "shwopping" exists in France, and if it's the case, find which retailers propose it. What do you do with the clothes you don't wear any more? Do you think "Shwopping" is a good idea? Can you think of other items which could be recycled?

Grammaire

▸ Le passif impersonnel

→ Britons are expected to send 235m items of clothing to landfill → ***On s'attend à*** *ce que les Britanniques envoient 235 millions d'articles vestimentaires à la décharge.*

→ Consumers are expected to get rid of 680m pieces of clothing → ***On s'attend à*** *ce que les consommateurs se débarrassent de 680 millions d'articles vestimentaires.*

(voir grammaire p.200)

Role play

Work in pairs: Student A tries to convince his/her/neighbour to recycle his/her old garments. **Student B** does not want to bother and throws them away.

Tips for Student A:
You should/shouldn't; If I were you, I would; I advise you to...

Tips for Student B:
no time to waste; it is no use; don't believe in recycling...

Anticipate at home

Before reading the text find out more about :
- Walmart/Aldi/Amazon/Lidl.
- The countries where they operate.

Text piste 03

Aldi raises stakes in US price war with Walmart

German grocery chain Aldi Inc. is trying to beat the world's biggest retailer at its own game: low prices. Already with 1,600 US stores, Aldi's internal studies show its prices are 21 percent lower than its lowest-priced rivals, including Walmart Stores Inc., according to Chief Executive Jason Hart. He plans to maintain that gap going forward.

His strategy, centers on adding more private-label goods, which are a retailer's in-house brands, to win over price-sensitive customers, and a massive expansion to further disrupt a US grocery sector that has seen 18 companies go bankrupt since 2014. Hart's plan calls for spending $1.6 billion to expand and remodel 1,300 US stores, and open 400 new stores mainly in Florida, Texas and on both coasts by the end of 2018. He also pledged Aldi will be willing to change prices more frequently to respond to rivals if needed. Aldi's US sales have doubled in five years. Though it only accounts for only about 1.5 percent of the US grocery market, Aldi is growing at 15 percent a year, whereas Walmart currently controls about 22 percent of the market and its US sales are estimated to grow about 2 percent this year, according to analysts.

Price wars are disturbing the entire retail sector – from department stores to discount chains – but it is nowhere as intense as in the grocery sector. Beyond Walmart's move to match Aldi on price, German discount chain Lidl plans to open up to a 100 US stores in a year, and Amazon.com is aggressively testing out various brick-and-mortar grocery formats along with growing Amazon Fresh, its grocery delivery service. Such heated competition risks a dangerous race to the bottom that could result in more retailers shutting their doors.

"Given Aldi's expansion, Lidl's entry, Walmart's response and Amazon's growing ambitions in this space, it is fair to expect a significant acceleration in the bankruptcy and liquidation cycle in this sector over the next few years," said Burt Flickinger, managing director at retail consultancy Strategic Resource Group. Aldi, has a simple strategy to win more customers: everyday low pricing, according to Hart. "We don't confuse our customers with yo-yo discounts, sales, coupons and loyalty cards that require membership fees," he said.

Depending on the product, Aldi's prices are lower than most rivals' private label items and even most branded items, analysts said. Hart said the 21 percent difference in price is calculated by monitoring competition on a basket of groceries. Aldi's aggressive push to remodel its stores will allow it to add new private label merchandise in rapidly growing categories like fresh food. "The remodels are aimed at increasing our volumes, which means more purchasing power that will help us lower prices further," said Scot Patton, Aldi's vice president of corporate buying.

At a recent visit to an Aldi store in Wheaton, Illinois Reuters found newer-looking shelves, wider aisles and brighter lighting than a typical Aldi store. There was also a bigger assortment of fresh, organic, gluten-free products and antibiotic-free meats.

Adapted from *Business News*, May 11, 2017.

Lexical work

Understanding the key words

→ Find the meaning of the following words and their lexical category (noun, verb, pronoun, adjective, etc.):
grocery; gap; go bankrupt; delivery; discounts; fees; organic; gluten-free.

→ Rephrase the title with your own words.

First track:
A step-by-step approach

I Read the text

1. Pick up the main ideas in each one of the six paragraphs. There may be several ideas per paragraph.

II Rephrase

2. Write an introduction of the article in your own words (source, date, main idea).
3. Use all the information above to report briefly to the class in French.

III Language

4. Translate into English:

a) Carrefour est aussi connu en France que Walmart aux États-Unis.
b) La Floride n'est pas aussi grande que l'Alaska.

IV Train for the exam

5. Write an account of the article in English in 200 words: Your account must be written in four paragraphs following the guidelines below.

- §1 Introduction
- §2 Aldi in the USA
- §3 The Price War: Aldi, Lild, Amazon versus Walmart
- §4 Conclusion

Grammaire

▸ Le comparatif

→ Price wars are nowhere as intense as the grocery sector.
→ *La guerre des prix est nulle part aussi intense que dans le secteur de la grande distribution alimentaire.*
→ **As… as** *est un comparatif d'égalité.*
(voir grammaire p.199-200)

Second track:
A straightforward approach

I Read the whole text

1. Take down notes about what you believe is important.

II Rephrase

2. Organise your ideas and make a plan.
3. Write an organised account of the article in English in 200 words, following your plan.

III Language

4. Fill in the blank with either form of the present perfect (simple/continuous):

a) Aldi with its 1,600 stores (to try) to beat the world's biggest retailer.
b) Aldi (to be) present on the US retail market since 1976.
c) Walmart (to underpay) its associates for ages.
d) Amazon (to keep growing) steadily since 1994.

IV Train for the exam

5. Write a report OR make an oral presentation. Use the research you carried out before and during the study of the text. Investigate further to answer the following questions: Define the concept of hard discount. Why would consumers turn to hard discounters? Why would consumers also turn to online retailers ? What is the situation in the French grocery sector ?

Grammaire

▸ Le present perfect

→ … a US grocery sector that has seen 18 companies go bankrupt since 2014.
→ *Depuis 2014, le secteur de la grande distribution alimentaire aux États-Unis, a connu la faillite de 18 de ses entreprises.*
→ Il y a un ***present perfect***, « ***has seen*** », déclenché par « ***since 2014*** », date du début de l'action, ici, cette vague de faillite.
(voir grammaire p.202)

1 Video tracks

Common track

→ **Before you start watching the video:**

1. Think about some basic people's needs and quote them.
2. Anticipating the topic of the video.
3. Look at the title and find out more about Maslow.

→ **Watch the video:**

4. Write down the words you hear among the following list: theory; hierarchy; stage; behaviour; 1953; exemplary; physiological needs; motivated; physical needs; safety; reading.

Pronunciation work

→ **Listen, repeat the following words and record yourself:** hierarchy; psychology; behaviour; exemplary; physiological, resources; desire; breathe.

Word box

- breathe: *respirer*
- safety: *sécurité*
- earn money: *gagner de l'argent*
- shelter: *abris*
- seek: *rechercher*
- belong: *appartenir*
- self confidence: *confiance en soi*
- peers: *pairs, semblables*
- brain: *cerveau*
- level: *niveau*
- stand out: *sortir du lot*

Video vidéo 02 Nathan live!

Maslow, the hierarchy of needs

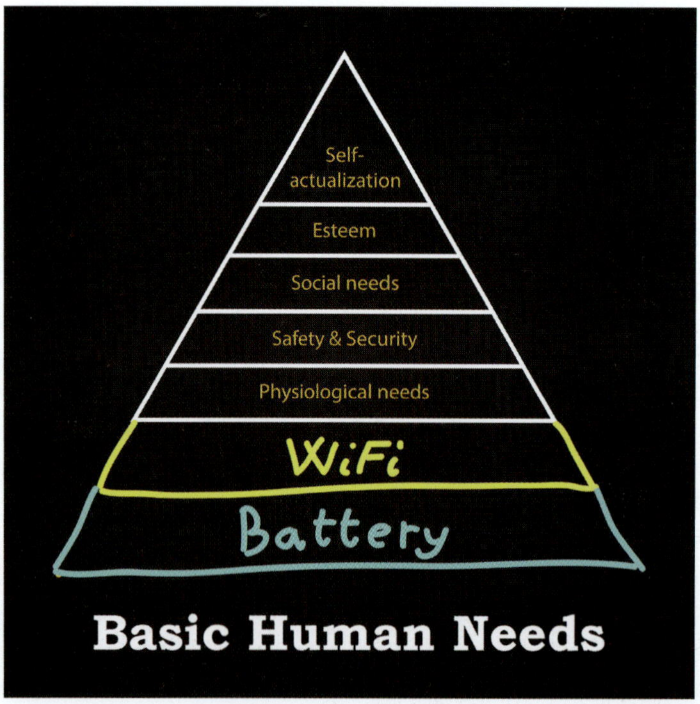

https://www.youtube.com/watch?v=O-4ithG_07Q

First track:
A step-by-step approach

I Watch the whole video

1. Write in French what it is about.

II Watch the first part: → 1'05

2. How many stages are there in the Maslow theory?
3. What do these stages motivate?
4. When did Maslow propose his theory?
5. Who inspired him?
6. What are the first three stages of Maslow's theory?

III Watch the second part: 1'05 → 1'59

7. What do people look for in stage 4?
8. What do we want to be?
9. Does everybody want the same thing? Explain. Quote some of the examples taken.
10. Under what conditions can we reach stage 5? Describe stage 5.

IV Watch the third part: 1'59 → end

11. What are the needs which must be fulfilled for a complete life?

V Train for the exam

12. **Oral report:** Put together all the information you have collected and report to the class.

Second track:
A straightforward approach

I Watch the whole video

1. After the first viewing, you are expected to have understood the general idea(s) exposed in the document. Write a short debrief.

II Second Viewing

2. Take notes and focus on how the different ideas are connected to one another.

III Train for the exam

3. Write an account of the video.
4. In your conclusion, state your point of view.

Role play

Student A is trying to convince student B not to spend too much money on shopping for recreational goods and services.
Student B thinks that spending money on what we like is part of life's fulfilment.
Student C's opinion is that today people are tempted to buy things they don't need or can't afford.
Act the conversation and record it.
Tips: Arguments from the document studied in the chapter can be used.

1 Audio tracks

Common track

I Before listening

1. Look at the visual document and the title and say as much as you can:

   a) Find out about India's drinking habits.
   b) Find about America's drinking habits.

2. Look at the title and rephrase it.
3. Write in French what the audio is about.

II Anticipate

4. Anticipate the topic of the audio.
5. Listen and try to understand the following words:
   beverages; trends; steadily; habit; taste highlight; shift; affluent; hang out; foreign brands; outlets; witnessing; harvested; livelihood; health; herbal teas; household.
6. Debrief with the other students and the teacher about their meaning.

Pronunciation work

→ **Listen, repeat the following words and record yourself:**
beverages; steadily; highlight; striking; sprouted; exposure; loyalty, affluent; livelihood; sought after.

Audio piste 04 Nathan live!

Is India going for coffee and America for tea?

A Tea Store in New York

Starbucks in Mumbaï

First track:
A step-by-step approach

I Listen to the whole audio once

1. Write in one or two sentences what the interview is about.

II Listen to the audio a second time

➜ Listen to the first part:

2. Collect information about:

a) The name of the program.
b) Who the guests are.
c) Their role in the interview.
d) The new habit in India.
e) The origin of this new habit.
f) Which age group is concerned.
g) The brands quoted in the audio.

➜ Listen to the second part:

3. Why is the American guest smiling?
4. What is the trend in the USA?
5. What are American consumers interested in?
6. Why is wellness becoming a powerful market?
7. What can be found in many American closets?
8. What will be the topic of the next debate?
9. Why is it a burning issue?

III Train for the exam

➜ Listen to the third part:

10. Put together all the information you have collected and report to the class.

Second track:
A straightforward approach

I Listen to the whole audio once

1. After the first listening, you are expected to have understood the general idea(s) exposed in the document.
2. Write a short debrief.

II Listen to the whole audio a second time

3. Take notes and focus on how the different ideas are connected to one another.

III Train for the exam

4. Write an account of the audio. In your conclusion, state your point of view.

Role play

Student A wants to buy some tea as a gift for an American friend coming to London. He knows that his/her friend is health-oriented and also cares about the planet, but he/she doesn't know what sort of tea he/she should buy.

Student B works in a tea shop. He/she needs to understand Student A's expectations before giving some advice. Student B knows a lot about the new trends among American consumers and proposes different types of tea each with a specific taste and health benefit.

➜ Act the conversation between Students A and B and record it.

Texte

L'impact des écrans sur les enfants

Téléphones intelligents, tablettes électroniques, ordinateur, télévision. Les jeunes passent de plus en plus de temps devant leurs écrans. Un comportement sédentaire, qui inquiète les experts de la santé publique, en plus des parents.

1. Ils y passent beaucoup de temps

Selon un rapport publié l'automne dernier par l'Institut national de la santé publique du Québec (INSPQ), les jeunes Québécois passent beaucoup de temps devant les écrans. Les enfants de deux ans et demi regardent la télévision en moyenne 8,82 heures par semaine tandis que les enfants et adolescents de 11 à 17 ans consacrent au moins 35 heures par semaine aux divers écrans.

Le rapport de l'INSPQ s'attarde principalement au rôle des écrans dans l'augmentation des comportements sédentaires des jeunes. Cela favoriserait le surpoids et l'obésité, qui limitent la capacité d'un individu à être actif. De plus, l'exposition aux écrans, donc à la lumière bleue, entrave le sommeil. Or, un sommeil de mauvaise qualité est lui-même associé avec l'obésité... qui peut elle aussi nuire au sommeil ! Tout un cercle vicieux.

2. Avant cinq ans, le cerveau des enfants est très malléable

C'est l'âge où le cerveau se forme. Or, les écrans influenceraient le développement du cerveau des tout-petits. Les moins de cinq ans sont donc ceux chez qui il faut être le plus attentif en ce qui concerne le temps d'exposition aux écrans.

Caroline Fitzpatrick explique qu'entre zéro et cinq ans, le cerveau est malléable. Comme les écrans interactifs réagissent immédiatement au toucher, ils offrent donc une gratification instantanée. Les personnages colorés de leurs émissions favorites peuvent aussi sembler beaucoup plus intéressants que l'environnement normal du tout-petit. Enfin, des changements de plan fréquents dans une émission de télé peuvent stimuler de manière excessive le cerveau encore en développement des enfants, entraînant une plus grande difficulté de concentration lors des tâches quotidiennes.

Mme Fitzpatrick, qui étudie la préparation scolaire à la maternelle dans différents contextes démographiques et sociaux, a contribué récemment à une étude concluant que les enfants qui regardent plus souvent la télévision auraient également plus de difficultés à contrôler leurs émotions et leur comportement, un phénomène qui serait encore plus marqué dans les familles à faible revenu. En conséquence, dit-elle, ces jeunes arrivent moins bien à prioriser et planifier leurs actions, ce qui influence négativement leur réussite scolaire.

Recommandations

Au Canada, les experts offrent des recommandations fermes : ne permettre aucun temps d'écran aux enfants de 0 à 2 ans ; autoriser un maximum d'une heure par jour pour les enfants de 2 à 5 ans et de deux heures par jour, sans contenu violent, pour les enfants de 5 à 11 ans.

Dans ses nouvelles directives, l'Académie américaine de pédiatrie (AAP) présente quant à elle une série d'astuces à l'usage des parents d'enfants de 2 à 5 ans :

- privilégier un contenu de qualité éducative ;
- accompagner l'enfant, pour lui expliquer ce qu'il voit et répondre à ses questions ;
- ne pas permettre d'écran durant les repas et durant l'heure précédant le coucher ;
- partager des moments d'écran en famille, pour des jeux ou des émissions ;
- placer les écrans dans une pièce commune pour qu'un adulte puisse voir ce qui s'y passe ;
- autoriser les enfants, quel que soit leur âge, à utiliser les écrans pour discuter à distance avec des membres de la famille, avec des applications comme FaceTime ou Skype.

L'AAP souligne également l'importance du jeu libre chez les tout-petits et de l'activité physique pour toute la famille.

Agence Science Presse, 23 mars 2017.

Common track

Use a French-English dictionary. What are the English words for:
comportement ; tout-petits ; écrans interactifs ; émission de télévision ; stimuler ; entraîner ; tâches quotidiennes ; famille à faible revenu ; réussite scolaire ; une heure par jour ; contenu ; partager ; autoriser ; souligner ; passer du temps ; jeu libre.

1. Use a French dictionary and look up the following words: *sédentaire, entraver, malléable, gratification*.
2. Identify the topical issue in English.
3. How much time do children spend in front of screens?
4. Quote the different devices with a screen.
5. What are the dangers of screen addiction?
6. What age group is the most sensitive to screen exposure?
7. What impact does it have on their school results?
8. What is the maximum time children should spend in front of screens?
9. What solutions are proposed ?
10. Imagine a title in English for the document.
11. Introduce the text in English.
12. Write one or two sentences in English for each paragraph in your own words (no translation).
13. Use your sentences to write a well organised account of the article in English. (150 words)

Go faster

I Read the whole document and suggest a title in English.

II Write one or two sentences in English in your own words for each paragraph.

III Write an organised account of the article in English. Do not forget the introduction and the conclusion. 200 words.

Debate

Student A : You are hosting a talk show about the usage of screens among young adults. You have two guests, Students B and C that have completely opposing views and practices. You are the moderator. Prepare your questions and try to run the debate smoothly.

Student B is absolutely against the usage of any screens under whatever form. Develop strong arguments to establish your point of view.

Student C is a screen addict. Find convincing arguments to support your point of view.

The roles can also be prepared in larger groups with a spokesperson for each group.

Document 1 vidéo 03 — Video

Amazon Go opens cashier-free smart grocery store – Dec 2016

Word box

to ditch the lines : *se débarrasser de/ sortir des sentiers battus*

https://www.youtube.com/watch?v=SV5DqxgW764

Document 2 piste 05 — Text

One in five UK consumers boycotts brands

LONDON: Every brand knows that establishing trust with their customers is vital, but this point has been reinforced by a new survey that found a fifth (21%) of UK consumers have boycotted a brand following a scandal or negative press. Furthermore, of those who stopped using a brand following adverse headlines, as many as two-thirds (67%) have not returned to it, according to research firm YouGov. Its study, Inside the Mindset of Brand Boycotters, took an in-depth look into the impact a brand crisis can have on public perception and the measures brands can take to win consumers back.

According to the findings, one-in-four (26%) consumers went back to the brand they used to trust, but importantly they tended to use it less often, and just 1% used it as much as before.

Tax avoidance and evasion – an issue that frequently crops up in the UK press – emerged as the main reason for consumers to boycott a brand (48%), but 40% also stopped using a brand if it was perceived to be treating its staff unfairly. Other reasons why respondents said they boycotted a brand included cover ups (40%), workers in the supply chain being treated unfairly (36%), corruption (36%) and faulty products or a product recall (35%).

In terms of winning consumers back, the report found that they have mixed reasons for returning to a boycotted brand. Almost a third (28%) said they returned because the company had changed the practices that initiated the boycott in the first place, while just under a quarter (24%) said they returned because the brand's product or service had improved.

However, there are also occasions when a brand does not necessarily need to change its practices or alter its approach, the report said, because 29% of former boycotters started to use a brand again because it had become too inconvenient not to.

"While it is not as straightforward as saying that every time a brand is seen to misbehave it will lose customers, there is a distinct proportion of consumers who will vote with their wallets," said Nasra Aharchich, Reports Researcher at YouGov.

"A large majority say they will stick to brands that they like and so the relationship a company has with its customers is key for surviving any bumps in the road."

Adapted from WARC.com *(Web ARChive)*, April 7, 2017.

Document 3 piste 06 — Audio

Is the era of big food coming to an end ?

Task 1 Video

Watch the video and answer.

1. What is new about Amazon?
2. Describe the concept of Amazon Go. What makes it attractive to the consumer?
3. What is the general trend in the grocery retail sector?
4. What products are more likely to be bought in a brick-and-mortar store?
5. What are Amazon's other grocery brands? (2 answers)
6. Name the competitors and number of stores.
7. Organise all the information you have collected and write your report.

Task 2 Text

1. Read the whole text and take down notes about what you believe is important.
2. Organise your ideas and make a plan.
3. Write an organised account of the article in English.

Task 3 Audio

1. Anticipate from the title.
2. Listen to the whole audio.
3. Focus on the answers to the following questions:
   a) What type of food are an increasing number of consumers buying and why?
   b) Give the names of two companies quoted in the interview.
   c) What are their response to the new consuming trends?

Task 4 Put in common

1. Making a plan: See how the three documents are related to one another.
   - Video 1: the main idea is...
   - Text 2: the main ideas are...
   - Audio: the main ideas are...
2. How are the ideas from each document related?
3. Write a final report which is a synthesis of the three documents in 200 words.

1 Background

Who is today's consumer?

A consumer is an individual who buys products or services for personal use and not for manufacture or resale. A consumer is someone who can make the decision whether or not to purchase an item at the store, either online, or offline and someone who can be influenced by marketing and advertisements.

Consumers are now more demanding of products, services and brands than before and are using digital tools to articulate and fulfil their needs.

There are as many consumers as there are people. However, there are trends that must not escape retailers as they enable them to classify consumers and market new product lines.

I How do we consume?

Consuming is about trends, quality, health and taste, and savings. Trends especially in clothing come and go more rapidly. The cosmetic shop, Kiko, has based its business model on the same principle: products go out of trend rapidly at affordable prices. So if price is one criterion, quality is another. The trend for organic, vegan and glutenfree products is moving fast and sometimes generating nutritional debates pointing out excesses of all kinds.

Social networks, especially if you are a millennial or a linkster, also known as generation Z, have become the main trend-setters.

II What do we buy?

It depends much on disposable income but it seems that in developed countries more and more is spent on new digital devices and digital-related services. Less is spent on food but quality and variety are more popular than before.

For an increasing number of consumers, buying name-brand items has stopped being a priority when there is an affordable alternative. Some shoppers refuse to pay a "luxury" premium. Others might think it is worth the additional cost as long as the quality is superior.

III Who do consumers buy from?

Consumers are getting more sensitive to the environment, sustainability, animal welfare, and health issues. That is why marketers need to keep a clear focus on the needs and expectations of their customers while following stricter ethical principles. Nevertheless, consumers are a group that is diverse and fragmented, with high expectations and little patience, that requires companies to be always on the lookout. To stay competitive you need to be visible, and that's not easy. Businesses need to measure sentiment and loyalty of their clients and must come up with tailored or customised products to meet their audience's needs and interests.

Consumers are being offered a purchasing experience that is facilitated by all sorts of new technological devices increasingly available. Shopping has to be easy, instantaneous and fun.

Conclusion

Consumers are fickle, whimsical but also more and more ethically-oriented. So the retail landscape is difficult to predict in wealthier countries.

"Consumer alert! Consumer alert!
— If it tastes good, spit it out!"

Question time

1. What can influence consumers?
2. What consumers are referred to as "generation Z"?
3. What is a trend setter?

↳ Vocabulary p. 30

An example in the shift of American consuming trends

According to the National Coffee Association's 2016 National Coffee Drinking Trends (NCDT) report, coffee consumption has much changed for the past six decades. The culprits are the millennials who are not satisfied with their parents' coffee consumption habits.

1. Today's figures

- Daily consumption of espresso-based beverages has nearly tripled since 2008, according to the latest data.
- Between 2008 and 2016, consumption of gourmet coffee beverages soared from 13% to 36% among 18-24 year olds, and from 19% to 41% for those 25-39.
- For espresso-based beverages alone, the jump becomes 9% to 22% for the 18-24 group and 8% to 29% for those 25-39.

2. Conclusion

- Quantity has been replaced by quality.
- Coffee has become a luxury item.
- The younger generations prefer genuine coffee to a brown brew often called coffee.

3. What are the purchasing drivers behind this new coffee consumption trend ?

- 66% of surveyed consumers say they will pay more for products and services that come from companies that are committed to positive social and environmental impact.
- 62% of the consumers are influenced by a brand they trust.
- 59% are motivated by the product's health and wellness benefits.
- 57% buy the product because it is sustainable or organic.
- 45% buy it because the company is environmentally-friendly.
- 43% buy it for the company's social values.
- 41% buy it for its recyclable packaging.
- 41% buy it from a company/brand involved locally.
- 34% buy their coffee after seeing or watching an ad promoting the companies' sustainable standpoint.

Good coffee is now expected everywhere around the clock: at the workplace, at home. It generates an increasing number of brewing gadgets. The fad is financed by crowdfunding, an important feature in the consuming trend.
This new coffee consuming trend in the US is growing side by side with a new taste for tea, especially among young hipsters (see Audio tracks page 16).

Questions

→ Is the price an important purchasing driver?

→ Do you think globalisation plays a part in this new trend?

→ What other new taste is developing in the US?

Starbuck's Swot

	Favourable	Unfavourable
Internal	**Strengths** • Provide a gadget brewing range of products • Very friendly service • The biggest coffee company in the world • Strong brand image • Extensive global supply chain • Uniqueness of the Starbucks coffee shops comfort and cosiness with free WIFI access • Innovation: new products on the menu every month	**Weaknesses** • Employees are not always told when their shifts are • Higher price points • Imitable products • Too many points of sales leading to market cannibalism
External	**Opportunities** • Expansion into Indian and Chinese markets • Use supermarkets as a way of expanding • Partnerships or alliances or joint-ventures with other firms (ex: Tata Beverage in India)	**Threats** • Domestic competition from McDonald's McCafé, Caffe Bene (New York) • International competition from local start-ups: Mikel Coffee in Greece, Costa Café in London, etc.

SWOT

Test yourself

After having studied this unit, you must be able to answer the following questions…

1. Where are everyday items displayed in grocery stores?
2. What is ecommerce ? Give a definition.
3. In what ways has e-commerce changed the rules of consumption?
4. Give the name of four UK grocery retailers.
5. What is Oxfam?
6. What is Aldi?
7. What is Walmart?
8. Explain Amazon's new way of attracting consumers.
9. What makes consumers boycott brands?
10. What are big food companies worried about? Quote some global food companies.
11. What is an ethically-committed consumer?
12. Explain why coffee has become a luxury item.
13. Explain why Indian consumers are attracted by coffee.
14. Why do many younger Americans turn to tea?
15. What is crowdfunding?

Cosmetics : A shake-up in make-up

Kiko is applying fast-fashion principles to the cosmetics business

COPYING can be a form of innovation when a company pinches ideas from a different industry and applies them to its own. This is what Kiko, a Milanese cosmetics company, is doing. It is adopting the principles already used to great success by "fast-fashion" clothing chains such as Zara and H&M: constantly changing the line-up of products in its stores to encourage customers to visit frequently; responding rapidly to the latest consumer trends; and keeping prices low. Its success is encouraging some of the industry's bigger brands to rethink their distribution model.

Worldwide, the cosmetics market (including cleansers and skin creams as well as make-up) grew by 3.6% to €181 billion ($240 billion) in 2014; it is expected to double over the next 10-15 years, according to EY, a consulting firm. Thus far, the industry has essentially been divided in two. More expensive brands tend to be sold in specialist beauty-store chains or in concessions in department stores, where shoppers can try them and get beauty tips before buying. Cheaper brands are sold in chemists' shops or supermarkets, with little customer service. Kiko's chain of own-label stores offers the best of both worlds: cheap prices plus make up advice.

Kiko's revenues have risen to €432m since it was founded in 1997 by Percassi, an Italian retail group. According to Kantar Worldpanel, a research firm, French 15-24-year-olds now buy as much from Kiko, in volume terms, as they do from Sephora, a cosmetics multi-brand retailer with revenues said to be around €4.6 billion which is part of LVMH, a luxury-goods giant.

Much of Kiko's success draws on Percassi's experience in fashion retail. Antonio Percassi, the group's boss, who also owns several other brands, a restaurant and a football club, began working with Benetton, an Italian clothing chain, in the 1970s to develop its shops around the world. In 2001 he entered a joint venture with Inditex, the Spanish group which owns Zara, to bring its brands to Italy. This year Percassi partnered with Victoria's Secret, an American underwear firm which has driven sales of lingerie out of department stores and into its smaller shops, to open its first Italian outlets.

Kiko operates all the outlets where its products are sold, which all have the same modern design. This makes it easier to provide a consistent level of service, says Mr Percassi. Being vertically integrated also makes it easier to ensure the shops remain well-stocked. The chain has two distribution centres: one in Bergamo, Italy, for European outlets, and one opened recently in New Jersey for North America.

Kiko's growth seems to be encouraging other firms in the cosmetics and beauty business to reconsider their business models. Higher-end brands like Benefit (part of LVMH) and L'Occitane (which is mostly in the skincare end of the business) are putting more emphasis on their own outlets and less on selling through other retailers. Nocibé, a big French retailer, last year began testing stores that stock mainly its own cosmetics brand, which it developed two years earlier. L'Oréal, the world's largest cosmetics group, is opening "dermacentres", outlets which sell its skincare brands, such as Vichy and La Roche Posay. It is also developing the retail network of Nyx, a Los Angeles-based cosmetics firm with annual sales of $200m, which it bought last year.

So far most customers of Kiko, as at other cosmetics firms, are women. But men who moisturise are becoming less rare, and in South Korea there is a brisk trade in masculine make-up. Kiko's parent company has taken a cautious step towards this market, opening a chain called Womo (as in *uomo*, "man" in Italian), which sells men's clothes and toiletries. It would be no problem for these stores to slip in a few discreet lines of cosmetics for men.

Adapted from *The Economist,* Dec.5, 2015.

I Compréhension de l'écrit

Après avoir lu attentivement le texte, vous en ferez un compte rendu en français, en faisant apparaitre les idées essentielles (minimum 210 mots – maximum 250 mots). Indiquez précisément le nombre de mots.

II Expression écrite

Traitez les deux sujets en anglais :

a. South Korea's biggest cosmetics firm IOPE is targeting its male customers. How would you market male products in a macho, socially conservative culture? (200 words + or – 10%.)

b. Some companies became global and did not make it: Walmart in Germany or in Japan, Tesco in the USA. What is the key to a successful development abroad? (100 words, + or – 10%.)

III Interaction écrite

Rédigez une lettre commerciale en anglais selon l'usage commercial courant en tenant compte des informations ci-dessous.

Expéditeur : Institut Alexia, Charline Brin, Directrice des ventes, 5 rue Bugeaud, 69006 Lyon, France

Destinataire : Thomas Richmond, Directeur, AJUNE, 45 Dibden Road, Bristol, B594QB United Kingdom

Date : le 15 mars 2018

Objet : réponse à la demande de renseignements

Corps de la lettre :

- L'entreprise était heureuse de recevoir cette demande de renseignements au sujet du matériel de coiffeur et autres produits que l'entreprise fabrique.
- Elle envoie un catalogue, les prix, des échantillons des shampoings et colorants.
- Par ailleurs, l'entreprise offre aussi des cosmétiques bio.
- Quel que soit le produit que vous choisirez, nous avons assez de stock pour vous livrer sous une semaine après réception de votre bon de commande.
- Si votre commande est supérieure à 7 000 euros, vous aurez une réduction de 5 % sur le montant au-delà de cette somme.
- Les conditions de paiement sont indiquées sur l'exemplaire de la facture pro-forma.
- L'entreprise sera heureuse de lier des liens commerciaux avec votre entreprise.
- Salutations.

➥ Tools p. 214

1 Present danger: trading standards' battle against deadly Christmas gifts

From unsafe dolls to exploding hoverboards, the festive period is busy for officers inspecting goods in UK ports.

Her name, according to the cheap cardboard label, is "Shu Yi Baby", but the large plastic doll in a green outfit will not be welcomed into any UK households as a gift on Christmas Day: the imported toy has been declared unsafe after undergoing tests and will be destroyed.

In a warehouse on the edge of Felixstowe, the UK's busiest port and commercial gateway for the Far East, officers are stepping up their fight against dangerous goods that flood the Christmas gift market. They are focusing on what they consider high risk products such as toys, electrical items, cosmetics and power tools.

"The doll came in a large consignment from the Far East and probably cost a few cents, or pence," declares Phil Reed, an import surveillance officer with the National Trading Standards, tugging at the doll's clothing and soft plastic feet. Tests on the dolls were carried out last month after the container that delivered them was impounded*. Reed has now received the test results and they are alarming. They reveal that the toy's feet contain harmful levels of chemicals that can cause long-term health problems.

The use of phthalates, which can disrupt children's hormones, is tightly restricted across Europe. But the laboratory tests show that the levels in this toy – destined for pre-Christmas markets breach regulations. In addition, the doll has a false CE mark that suggests that she meets recognised EU safety standards.

"This is purporting to be a stamp of approval and appears to be a deliberate attempt to mislead consumers," says Reed.

Also tested from the same consignment* were "plush" dolls, made from a furry synthetic fabric, where weak zips and easy access to battery compartments failed the safety assessment and were deemed to be dangerous choking hazards* for young children.

Reed is surrounded by piles of bulging cardboard boxes on pallets in Shed 70 – a warehouse the size of a football pitch, where the selected contents of some containers are inspected.

More than 40% of all imported goods coming into the UK do so via Felixstowe, where it typically takes three days to unload the up to 19,224 containers on the world's biggest capacity cargo ship, the 395m MSC Oscar.

A staggering 4m full containers come through the port every year, and Reed is responsible for organising and carrying out regular inspections. "It would be difficult for any agency to examine anything but a very small proportion of the containers arriving at the port each year," says Reed. "Therefore we base our examinations on those which we consider to pose the greatest safety risk to consumers. Or we might be focusing our attention on those importers or traders who have a history of importing non-compliant and unsafe products." Reed opened some boxes and found electrical products that are proving popular for Christmas, including hair straightening brushes, steam facial cleansers and portable chargers. He is constantly on the lookout for products with faulty plugs and chargers that can overheat and cause fires.

"One particular trend we have spotted is the growth in 'micro-importers' – consumers in the UK who order half or even a whole container of goods to import for onward sale," adds Reed. "They have no idea what they are buying and are not interested in finding out. This can lead to fake, and often dangerous, products such as hoverboards ending up in people's homes."

Adapted from *The Guardian*, Nov. 28, 2017.

*Impounded : *confisqué/ saisi.*

*Consignment : *envoi.*

*Choking hazards : *risques d'étouffement.*

2 Behind the battle against counterfeit goods

vidéo 4

https://www.youtube.com/watch?v=5YrflmjOBfo

I Compréhension de l'écrit

Write an account of the article in French (200 words +/-10%).

II Expression écrite

Write a paragraph about both the attractivity and the dangers of counterfeit goods. Should consumers of counterfeit goods be sanctioned? (150 words minimum)

III Vidéo

- Watch the video twice and take notes.
- Take 10 minutes to prepare an oral report.
- Report and discuss with the examiner.

Vocabulary

after-sale service: *service après-vente*
appeal (vb)/appeal (n): *attirer/attrait*
average (adj): *moyen(ne)*
bargain (n): *affaire (faire une affaire)*
brand awareness: *reconnaissance de la marque*
brick-and-mortar store: *magasin phsysique "en dur"*
buying/purchasing/spending power: *pouvoir d'achat*
cashier-free (adj): *sans caissier*
check-out (n): *caisse*
compulsive spender: *acheteur compulsif*
consumer behavior: *comportement du consommateur*
consumer spending: *dépense des consommateurs*
consumption (n): *consommation*
consumption patterns: *habitudes de consommation*
convenience foods: *plats préparés*
coupons (n): *bons d'achat/ de réduction*
crowdfunding (n): *financement participatif*
customer service: *service client*
disposable (adj): *jetable*
e-commerce: *commerce en ligne*
expenditure (n): *dépense*
fulfill their basic needs: *répondre à leurs besoins élémentaires*
go mainstream: *devenir majoritaire*
go on a shopping spree: *avoir la fièvre acheteuse/faire des folles dépenses*
go to waste: *aller au rebus (à la poubelle)*
groceries (n): *courses alimentaires*
home delivery: *livraison à domicile*
household (n): *ménage/foyer*
impulse buying: *achat impulsif*
income (n): *revenu*
item (n): *article/produit*
loyalty card: *carte de fidélité*
luxury brand: *marque de luxe*
meet consumers' needs: *répondre aux besoins des consommateurs*
mid-priced brand: *marque de moyenne gamme*
non-processed foods: *nourriture non industrielle*
online review: *critique en ligne*
pitch the company's products: *faire l'éloge des produits d'une entreprise*
popup ad: *fenêtre publicitaire sur Internet*
purchase decision-making process: *processus de décision d'achat*
purchasing behavior: *comportement d'achat*
retail/store brand: *marque de magasin*
sales (n): *soldes/ventes*
scheme (n): *dispositif/programme*
spending patterns: *habitudes de dépenses*
take-away: *à emporter*
tap a market: *pénétrer un marché*
the grab-and-go culture of eating: *la culture de la nourriture à emporter*
rate: *évaluer*
trend (n): *tendance*
upscale brand: *marque haut de gamme*

2 Marketing & distribution

Tesco in Malaysia

Question

What do you know about Tesco ?

Word box

- increase sales: *augmenter les ventes*
- make a purchase: *effectuer un achat*
- be competitive: *être compétitif*
- ideal features: *caractéristiques idéales*
- customer demand: *demande du client*
- supermarket aisles: *allées de supermarché*
- shelves : *linéaires*

Anticipate at home

What is marketing ? VIDÉO 05

https://www.youtube.com/watch?v=MoQz3SaWY9s

1. What is the purpose of marketing?
2. Who does marketing hope to convince?
3. What are the 4 Ps?

2 » Starters

The class is divided into several groups: a group will study document 1, another document 2, a further one document 3 and the last one document 4.

Group 1

Document 1

Membership Programs

Sephora, a luxury cosmetic retailer leading the way in the industry, is one of the best examples of B2C marketing strategies. Sephora has an extremely effective membership program dubbed "Beauty Insider". The membership program is a merit-based program that separates consumers into three different member tiers: Beauty Insider, VIB and VIB Rouge. Each tier hosts its own set of exclusive rewards. The reason this B2C marketing strategy is so effective is that they put in place certain yearly-spend-determined thresholds* that need to be reached in order to increase a membership status. The rewards in the highest tier (VIB Rouge) are so appealing to consumers that it provides heightened incentive to spend more so they can breach the price threshold.

www.ermarsys.com, 2018.

* thresholds: *seuil.*

1. Identify the document.
2. What is a B2C marketing strategy?
3. What does Sephora do to attract customers and turn them into loyal customers?
4. Why do customers want to become members?

Group 2

Document 2 piste 07

Aldi

1. Identify the document.
2. How many stores does Aldi plan to open in the US?
3. How would you describe Aldi and what products does it sell?

2 Marketing & distribution

Tesco in Malaysia

Question

What do you know about Tesco ?

Word box

- increase sales: *augmenter les ventes*
- make a purchase: *effectuer un achat*
- be competitive: *être compétitif*
- ideal features: *caractéristiques idéales*
- customer demand: *demande du client*
- supermarket aisles: *allées de supermarché*
- shelves : *linéaires*

Anticipate at home

What is marketing ? VIDÉO 05

https://www.youtube.com/watch?v=MoQz3SaWY9s

1. What is the purpose of marketing?
2. Who does marketing hope to convince?
3. What are the 4 Ps?

2 » Starters

The class is divided into several groups: a group will study document 1, another document 2, a further one document 3 and the last one document 4.

Group 1

Document 1

Membership Programs

Sephora, a luxury cosmetic retailer leading the way in the industry, is one of the best examples of B2C marketing strategies. Sephora has an extremely effective membership program dubbed "Beauty Insider". The membership program is a merit-based program that separates consumers into three different member tiers: Beauty Insider, VIB and VIB Rouge. Each tier hosts its own set of exclusive rewards. The reason this B2C marketing strategy is so effective is that they put in place certain yearly-spend-determined thresholds* that need to be reached in order to increase a membership status. The rewards in the highest tier (VIB Rouge) are so appealing to consumers that it provides heightened incentive to spend more so they can breach the price threshold.

www.ermarsys.com, 2018.

* thresholds: *seuil.*

1. Identify the document.
2. What is a B2C marketing strategy?
3. What does Sephora do to attract customers and turn them into loyal customers?
4. Why do customers want to become members?

Group 2

Document 2 piste 07

Aldi

1. Identify the document.
2. How many stores does Aldi plan to open in the US?
3. How would you describe Aldi and what products does it sell?

Group 1

Document 3
Cooking, Heating, Lighting Fire

"Product diversification, I like that."

1. Identify the document.
2. Who are these sellers?
3. What are the products for sale?
4. What's the difference between the three products?
5. What do the consumers appreciate about them?
6. What does it reveal about some companies' marketing strategies?
7. What does it reveal about consumers' behavior?
8. What does this cartoon make fun of?

Group 4

Document 4 vidéo 06 Nathan live!
Brand Marketing

https://www.youtube.com/watch?v=LomLMdosYzM

Word box
- direct selling: *vente directe*
- word of mouth: *bouche-à-oreille*

1. Identify the document.
2. Have mothers a lot of free time?
3. How do they get to know new products?
4. Is it an efficient method?

Put in common

→ How are the three documents related?
→ What can you deduce from companies' marketing strategies?

2 Prep page

Anticipate at home

Before reading the text, investigate:

- Where do coconuts grow? Are there coconut farmers? What do we do with coconuts? Are there different types of coconuts depending on the country?
- Find information about Safeway; Target; All Market Inc.

Text piste 08

Vita Coco

Vita Coco, the world's largest coconut-water brand, expects to approach $1 billion in sales this year by expanding into new categories, raising its profile as a possible acquisition target.

"All Market Inc., the brand's parent company, has branched out into coconut milk, coconut oil and other products – a move that will bring the Vita Coco name into the dairy and personal-care aisles of supermarkets. The expansion also has brought interest from large beverage companies looking to tap into the growth", Chief Executive Officer Michael Kirban said.

"We're probably the largest independently owned natural-beverage company in the world," he said, adding that strategic acquirers have contacted him.

Shifting consumer tastes have brought upheaval to the beverage industry, prompting Coca-Cola Co., PepsiCo Inc. and Dr Pepper Snapple Group Inc. to seek acquisitions. They are looking for ways to diversify away from traditional soda and high-calorie juices, which are losing favor with many shoppers. Coca-Cola previously purchased Vita Coco's chief competitor, Zico, in 2013.

Vita Coco already has ties to a number of beverage giants: Dr Pepper was a US distribution partner, Red Bull China has a 25 per cent stake. As a startup it got its first major investment from Verlinvest, a firm controlled by the Belgian families. Kirban, 41, declined to discuss specific sales figures, but says the New York-based company is profitable. It paid a $30 million dividend to investors last year.

'Owning the Coconut'

Vita Coco plans to near $1 billion in sales by "owning the coconut in different areas of the store," said Kirban, who co-founded the company 13 years ago. In addition to selling coconut milk and oil, the company has added an artisanal line and a chilled 1.5-liter juice that comes in flavors like lemonade and grapefruit. The idea is to attract consumers who are ditching soda and looking for alternatives.

The global market for coconut water hit $2.2 billion in 2016, up from $533 million five years earlier, according to Euromonitor International. The industry's sales have grown more than 20 percent annually in the past nine years. Compare that with carbonated soft drinks, which have been growing in the low single digits.

Vita Coco accounted for 46 percent of the $889 million US market, more than triple the share of Zico, its next-closest competitor.

Milk Alternative

By offering flavored juices and coconut milk, the company aims to capitalize on consumers ditching traditional supermarket staples. Sales of regular milk declined in the US between 2011 and 2016, but plant-based alternatives – including coconut milk – have surged 61 percent.

Vita Coco Coconut Milk is launching in March, first at the Safeway supermarket chain and then at other grocers and independent retailers. The target audience is consumers drinking organic milk who want a non-dairy

Lexical work

Understanding the key words

→ Find their meanings and their lexical category (noun, verb, pronoun, adjective, etc.): aisles of supermarkets; to tap into; shifting; upheaval; ties; grapefruit; single digits; ditch; staples; watered down; chilled seek.

→ Find a suitable translation for: soft drinks; beverage; dairy products; to be in business; to be known for; soda-provider; sugar-laden; eventually.

→ Now, try to find another title for the article.

option that doesn't taste watered down.

The company's new lineup of chilled coconut water, meanwhile, will be on shelves next to brands like PepsiCo's Tropicana and Coca-Cola's Simply – an attempt to capitalize on the decline of once-popular juices. The 1.5-liter bottles launched in test markets in the second half of last year and are now being rolled out nationally in stores such as Target and Safeway.

Vita Coco also is spending $25 million on its first major ad campaign. Until now, the company has been relying on the star power of celebrity investors such as Rihanna.

Finding an Exit

Kirban expects to eventually sell the business to a strategic buyer. Indeed, beverage startups have been attracting investments from Big Soda such as Coca-Cola, PepsiCo, and Dr Pepper. Vita Coco could go that same route.

■ Adapted from *Bloomberg*, Feb. 14, 2017.

I Read the whole text

1. Write everything you know about Vita Coco:

a) Who owns it, how much money does it make, the name of its CEO, the type of products it sells, the name of the supermarkets that distribute them.

b) Vita Coco products can be found in two aisles of a supermarket. Which ones? Explain why?

II Rephrase

2. Rewrite what you have learned about consumer tastes and the role of celebrities.

3. Focus on potential buyers and find reasons for buying out the startup.

III Language

4. Translate into French:

a) Her environmentally-minded friend supported the COP 21.

b) They responded to her clearly-defined demand.

IV Train for the exam

5. Write an account in French of the document. (200 words)

6. **Go further:** How do consumers taste impact markets?

Grammaire

▶ Place de l'adverbe devant un adjectif

"We are the largest **independently owned** natural beverage company".

→ *Nous sommes la plus grande entreprise indépendante de boissons naturelles.*

Ex : her **beautifully** sophisticated dress

Their **technically** designed shoes

(voir grammaire p. 205)

Role play

Work in pairs: Student A tries to convince Student B that traditional dairy products should be replaced. **Student B** is hard to convince as he/she loves milk/cheese, yogurts and eats some with every meal.

Tips for Student A: List arguments, using link words such as: moreover; in addition to; unlike; etc. and start with: "It is medically proven that..."; "It is a well-known fact that..."; "Environmentalists strongly believe that..."

2 Text tracks

Anticipate at home

Before reading the text find out more about:
- Amazon/Whole Foods/Kroger/Sprouts Farmer Markets/Aldi/Lidl.
- The products they sell and where.
- What they have in common.
- What makes them different.

Text piste 09

Amazon slashes Whole Foods prices on first day after $13.7bn takeover

The companies signalled last week that they would selectively cut Whole Foods prices starting on Monday, and promised more discounts in the future. On its first day as part of Amazon, organic grocery chain Whole Foods slashed prices on popular items like avocados and apples on Monday by a third as it tries to shake off its reputation for high prices.

Major supermarket chains and grocery sellers, including Kroger, Sprouts Farmers Market, Supervalu, Costco and Walmart Stores, already were struggling with growing pricing pressure when Whole Foods and Amazon announced their $13.7bn merger deal on 16 June. And, shares in those food sellers have fallen on worries that Amazon could disrupt the grocery business in the same way it did with books and electronics…

Some analysts estimate that Whole Foods would have to cut prices by 10 to 15 per cent overall to truly compete with other food sellers. Nevertheless, its surgical cutting of prices on popular staples could force other retailers to follow. That would only add pressure on those retailers, who already were preparing for another step down in prices as German discounters Aldi and Lidl expand in the United States and intensify the price war historically led by Walmart.

As part of Amazon's putting its stamp on the grocer, Whole Foods stores displayed promotions for Amazon's Echo speaker in tongue-in-cheek fashion, with signs reading "Farm Fresh" and "Pick of the Season." The Echo plays a critical role in Amazon's burgeoning ambitions to popularize and dominate the market for voice-controlled computing. Echo speakers are equipped with Amazon's voice-controlled assistant Alexa, which competes with Apple Inc.'s (AAPL.O) Siri. Users can direct Alexa to set timers, play music, read recipes, order deliveries, and perform a host of other activities.

Shares of Amazon were up 0.1 percent at $946.01 in afternoon trading. Sprouts was the hardest hit of the food sellers. Its shares tumbled 9.8 percent on Monday, compared with the 2.7 per cent drop for Supervalu and the less than 1 per cent decline for the remainder of the group.

Adapted from *The Independent*, August 28, 2017.

Lexical work

Understanding the key words

→ Find their meanings and what each of them is (ex: a noun, a verb, an adjective, etc.): slash; takeover; organic; display; struggling; produce; merger; staple; stamp; retailer; share; compete; loyalty; deliveries.

→ Rephrase the title with your own words.

Price drop on avocados at Whole Foods Market after Amazon's acquisition of Whole Foods.

First track:
A step-by-step approach

I Read the text

1. Pick up the main idea(s) in each paragraph.

II Rephrase

2. Write an introduction to the article in your own words.

3. Use all the information above to report briefly to the class in French.

III Language

4. Translate into English :

a) Lidl a ouvert ses premiers magasins aux USA en juin dernier.
b) Amazon attendait le meilleur moment pour conquérir le marché de l'alimentaire.
c) Les parts de marché d'Amazon ont grimpé de 1 % dans l'après-midi.

IV Train for the exam

5. Write a 180 word account in English following the guidelines below.

- §1 Introduction
- §2 Whole Foods new pricing policy
- §3 The reasons why other grocery retailers worry about the merger
- §4 The German discounters' competition
- § 5 Amazon's ambition on the voice-computing market
- §6 Conclusion

Grammaire

▶ Le prétérit

→ "On its first day as part of Amazon, organic grocery chain Whole Foods **slashed** prices on popular items"

→ Le premier jour de son rachat par Amazon, la chaîne alimentaire bio Whole Foods ***a cassé*** les prix sur les articles les plus en vogue.

- Le prétérit (*simple past*) se caractérise par la terminaison *ed* à la fin des verbes dits réguliers.
- Le prétérit des verbes irréguliers (ils sont nombreux) sont à savoir par cœur.
- Le prétérit se réfère à un moment précis du passé, révolu. (ici *on its first day* représente le marqueur temporel).

(voir grammaire p. 201)

Second track:
A straightforward approach

Grammaire

→ "Some analysts estimate that Whole Foods **would have to cut** prices by 10 to 15 %."

→ *Certains experts estiment que Whole Foods serait obligé de baisser ses prix de 10 à 15 %.*

→ ***Have to*** remplace l'auxiliaire modal ***must*** (devoir) lorsque celui ci ne peut pas être utilisé au présent.

(voir grammaire p. 206)

I Read the text

1. Read the whole text and take down notes about what you believe is important.

II Rephrase

2. Organize your ideas a make a plan.

3. Write an account of the article in English in 190 words.

III Language

4. Fill in the blanks with **must** or **have** to at the required tense.

a) Consumers.....beware of credit card phishing when they buy online. (present)
b) Grocery retailers.....lower their prices if they want to remain competitive. (future)
c) This mall......close down for lack of customers. (simple past)

IV Train for the exam

5. Write a report or make an oral presentation. Use the research you carried out before and during the study of the document. Investigate further to discuss the following topics:

- What strategy could traditional retailers use to stand up against Amazon?
- Can the digital revolution make traditional marketing eventually disappear?

2 Video tracks

Common track

→ **Before you start watching the video:**
1. Anticipate on the title of the video.
2. Find out more about organic food.

→ **Watch the video:**
3. Watch and understand the following words: growth; grocer; labeled; fertilizers; genetically-modified organisms; meat; hormones; antibiotics; outdoors; nutritional benefits; worth; animal feed.

Pronunciation work

→ **Listen, repeat the following words and record yourself:**
agriculture; free of genetically-modified organisms; antibiotics; pesticides; healthier; exposure

Video vidéo 07 Nathan live!

Organic food

https://www.youtube.com/watch?v=81el7ocDTUo

Tips

→ **A definition of the term "organic food"**
Organic food is food produced by methods that comply with the standards of organic farming. Organizations regulating organic products may forbid the use of certain pesticides and fertilizers in farming. Special certification is required to market food as organic.

First track:
A step-by-step approach

I Watch the whole video

1. Name the website that posted the video.
2. What is required to make a produce organic?
3. Why is organic food becoming more popular?

II Second Viewing

4. Explain what the big retailers do to increase their sales.
5. How much money is spent by the consumer?
6. Explain national standards.

III Train for the exam

7. Write a report OR make an oral presentation following the guidelines below.

   I. Introduction: What is the topic? Give the source.

   II. Development

   a) Organic food is popular: reasons.

   b) Scientific research questions its healthy impact.

   III. Conclude

Second track:
A straightforward approach

I Watch the whole video

1. Answer the question of the title: Are organic foods really healthier?

II Second Viewing

2. Organic foods are popular: So what do retailers and farmers do?
3. What are the reasons for eating organic foods?

III Train for the exam

4. Write a report OR make an oral presentation following the guidelines below.

   I. Introduction

   II. Impact of consumers' shifting consuming habits

   III. Role of scientific research

   IV. Conclusion

Role play

Student A is a spokesperson for an industrial food company. He is debating with student B about the dangers of processed, industrialized food. Find arguments to defend the mainstream food industry.

Student B is a spokesperson for an environmental group called "Forks over Knives" defending organic food and veganism.

Tips for Student A: Price/availability/respect of new standards/efforts made by the industrial food companies to promote sustainability/the lack of scientific proofs/the danger of veganism, etc.

Tips for Student B: Sustainable farming/toxic components in industrial food/animal welfare/dangers of meat, etc.

2 Audio tracks

Common track

I Before listening

1. Find out about loyalty cards and give information about your own loyalty cards.
2. Do loyalty cards turn the customer into a loyal customer?
3. Don't loyalty cards compete with each other?
   How does a loyalty card make a customer really loyal?

II Anticipate

→ **Anticipate the topic of the audio**

4. Look at the title and say as much as you can.

→ **Words, expressions, ideas you may hear**

5. Listen and try to understand the following words:
   junk mail; schemes; cardholders; to be rewarded; bonus points; repeat business; marketing strategies; barcode; keytags/keyrings; application forms; to pay off.

Audio piste 10 Nathan live!

Loyalty cards

Loyalty cards

Pronunciation work

→ **Listen, repeat the following words and record yourself:**
loyalty card; patrons; discount; gathered; worrying; unfortunately; loyal; scheme.

First track: A step-by-step approach

I Listen to the whole audio

1. Write in French what it is about.

II Listen to the first part

2. Collect information on: place, time, names and figures.

III Listen to the second part

3. What is the new information we get?

IV Listen to the third part

4. What else do we learn?

V Train for the exam

5. Put together all the information you have collected and report to the class.

Second track: A straightforward approach

I Listen to the whole audio once

1. After the first listening, you are expected to have understood the general idea(s) exposed in the document. Write a short debrief.

II Listen to the whole audio a second time

2. Take notes and focus on how the ideas are connected to each other.

III Train for the exam

3. Write an account of the audio. In your conclusion, state your point of view.

Role play

Student A and Student B meet and want to find out if Student C and Student D have loyalty cards.

Student A and Student B meet to list 10 questions about loyalty cards.

TIPS:
You want to ask if they have a loyalty card, if it is free, what bonus it gives them, etc.
Think of how the shop contacts the loyalty cardholder.
Once you have your 10 questions, ask them to Student C and Student D and write down their answers.
Recap and report to the class.

Info

History of loyalty cards

Loyalty and rewards programs have become commonplace in today's society. Physical stores as well as online retailers are using them to boost their image by granting loyal customers all sorts of discounts.

But who started it? And have they always been so popular?

Stamps were given away at one time to turn shoppers into loyal customers. You would collect them and they would enable you to get at a discount price an item that appealed to you.

Then, there were also **"box tops"**: they were **coupons** printed directly on the product packages granting the customer a discount on his or her purchase either straight away or on his or her future purchase. Here individual brands were introducing ways to entice customers to buy what was not always on his or her shopping list. It is Betty Crooker who introduced this loyalty programme in 1929.

Frequent Fliers is another type of loyalty programme introduced by airline companies in 1981. It is a most popular programme that offers passengers free flights after having gathered a certain number of miles.

Retailers come up with new ideas all the time and we, customers, have so many loyalty cards in our wallet that it's almost impossible to find the right one when we need it.

2 From French to English

Texte

Le Net, grand traître du commerce

Repérer en magasin puis acheter en ligne est devenu une habitude pour nombre de consommateurs. Tout l'écosystème du secteur est ébranlé.

Toys'Rus abdique. L'enseigne américaine de jouets a annoncé jeudi 18 septembre s'être placée sous la protection du chapitre 11 de la loi américaine sur les faillites. La chaîne aux 1 600 magasins ne parvient plus à rembourser ses dettes. Comme d'autres ténors de la distribution américaine, dont le grand magasin Macy's, Toys'Rus est confronté à la concurrence du Net, qui, en quelques années seulement, a raflé 13,7 % des achats de jouets aux États-Unis.

La défaillance du numéro un mondial du jouet dit tout de la féroce concurrence qu'impose l'e-commerce à la distribution d'antan. Car, partout dans le monde, repérer en magasin le jouet dont rêve un enfant pour Noël, comparer son prix depuis son smartphone et l'acheter en ligne à moindre coût et se le faire livrer à temps est devenu un sport national.

Mode, produits électroniques, bricolage ou jouets : aucun secteur n'y échappe. Amazon, le numéro un mondial de la vente en ligne serait toujours le grand gagnant de ce comportement. Près de 60 % de ceux que l'on appelle les « showroomers » finissent par acheter en ligne à moindre coût sur la plateforme du géant américain aux 136 milliards de dollars (114 milliards d'euros) de chiffre d'affaires, selon une étude réalisée en 2013 aux États-Unis.

À Paris, depuis 3 ans, le magasin Zig et Puce avertit ses clients du risque de ce « showrooming* » qui cantonne un point de vente au seul rôle de salon d'exposition de modèles. Sur les étagères de cette petite boutique du 15e arrondissement, les gérants ont collé une affichette jaune. Ils l'ont intitulée « showrooming* » : « Profiter de nos compétences pour ensuite acheter sur Internet, c'est d'abord nous manquer de respect et aussi un mauvais calcul pour l'avenir » peut-on y lire.

L'affichette a été punaisée il y a trois ans. Pas question de l'enlever. « Il faut que les clients sachent les dommages qu'entraîne leur achat sur Amazon après avoir profité de notre conseil ! Moi, je ne vis pas d'amour et d'eau fraîche ! » s'agace le gérant. Car, plus que jamais, la pression du Net se fait sentir dans les allées des magasins. « C'est l'effet smartphone. Il est devenu naturel de consulter un site Web alors qu'on est en train de faire du shopping », observe un consultant en marketing.

Nouveau type de point de vente

Certains distributeurs multiplient les efforts pour inciter leurs clients à pousser la porte de leurs magasins. Boulanger est en train de développer un nouveau concept : l'enseigne propose à ses clients de tester des articles dans une petite boutique de 300 m² baptisée « Le Comptoir Boulanger ». Zadig & Voltaire cajole ses clients du Net : dans son nouveau magasin de la rue Cambon à Paris, une partie de son personnel est employée à leur accueil.

B. Demeure, consultant au sein du cabinet Oliver Wyman, spécialiste de la distribution, déclare : « Les transactions récentes démontrent également combien les commerçants ont pris conscience qu'il n'est plus possible de n'être que virtuels ou que physiques. Il leur faut être omnicanal. Amazon a mis la main sur Whole Foods, Walmart a passé un accord avec Google Shopping et les Galeries Lafayette rachètent la Redoute. Nous estimons d'autre part que 10 % des ventes alimentaires et 50 % des ventes non alimentaires se feront sur Internet dans cinq ans. »

Adapté du *Monde*, 22 septembre 2017.

* Le showrooming : pratique du consommateur qui consiste à se rendre chez un commerçant en magasin pour évaluer physiquement un produit qu'il finira par acheter en ligne à moindre prix grâce à des logiciels ou applications de comparateurs de prix.

Common track

Find the English translation of:

acheter en ligne; habitude; grand magasin; concurrence; faillite; jouet; livrer; chiffre d'affaires; étude; distributeur; allée (supermarché); commerçant; ventes alimentaires.

1. Read the whole document.
2. Use a dictionary. Look up the following words and find an equivalent in English: traître ; ébranlé ; abdiquer ; féroce ; moindre coût ; compétence ; vivre d'amour et d'eau fraîche ; omnicanal ; passer un accord.
3. Identify the main topic in English.
4. What makes the internet a traitor for other retailers?
5. Imagine a title in English for the document.
6. Introduce the text in English.
7. Write one or two sentences in English for each paragraph in your own words (no translation).
8. Use your sentences to write a well organized account of the article in English 180 words.

Go faster

I Read the whole document and suggest a title in English.

II Write one or two sentences in English in your own words for each paragraph.

III Write an organized account of the article in English. Do not forget the introduction and the conclusion. (200 words)

IV Branching out: Give your own point of view on the different categories of points of sales explaining how they hope to attract customers.

V Write a 150 word essay developing why "Showrooming" will force retailers to change their strategies.

Debate

Group A : Students from group A are in favour of e-commerce , of show rooming and they believe the new retail landscape does not threaten traditional shopping.

Group B : Students from group B are against the spreading of e-commerce and show rooming because they believe consumers are only looking for the best bargains and are going to stop going to high street stores and shopping malls

Tips Group A

E-commerce advantages: available 24/7-home delivery-secure payment-lower prices- time sparing –etc.

Tips group B

-High street shops closing down-city centers and shopping malls deserted – job cuts – multi channel distribution – the pleasure of shopping with friends etc.

One student from each group is responsible for organizing the debate and allocating speaking time.

Document 1 piste 11 — Text

Guinot, the French cosmetics company, bets on tennis underdogs

Sweden's Robin Soderling, who was ranked 25th in 2009, stuns No. 1 Rafael Nadal at that year's French Open, where he had been undefeated. At the same tournament three years later, the 111th-ranked Virginie Razzano of France beats Serena Williams in the first round. At this year's Australian Open, the 117th-ranked Denis Istomin of Uzbekistan defeats Novak Djokovic.

Besides rocking the tennis world with their upset victories, all of these long-shot winners had another thing in common: each wore sponsored patches from the French cosmetics company Guinot on their outfits, as have hundreds of other winners and (mostly) losers in high-profile matches.

Guinot has developed an approach to maximize exposure at the world's tennis events by making endorsement deals with lower-ranked players who are scheduled to face the biggest stars. Though other companies occasionally enter similar short-term deals – the high-end grocer Dean & DeLuca has tried it at the United States Open this year – Guinot is the most prominent practitioner in tennis. Roughly eight to 10 deals are struck at each Grand Slam event.

Players are offered a few thousand dollars per patch, which are pre-made and bear the corporate logo. The amount increases based on the player's ranking and round of the tournament, stopping around $10,000. Three players have won Grand Slam titles wearing Guinot patches: Svetlana Kuznetsova, the 2004 US Open and 2009 French Open champion; Samantha Stosur, who won the 2011 US Open; and the 2013 Wimbledon champion Marion Bartoli.

Rules for the size and placement of corporate logos on tennis outfits are strict, especially at Grand Slam events. Only two patches are allowed, neither of which can exceed six square inches. When a Guinot-sponsored player has room for just one logo, they wear the Guinot brand patch. When they have room for two, a patch for Guinot's brand Mary Cohr is added. Players iron or sew them on themselves, or take their outfits to the on-site tournament tailor to have them applied.

Adapted from *New York Times*, Sept. 3, 2017.

Document 2 piste 12 — Audio

Ruby Chocolate is the new black

Document 3 vidéo 08 Nathan live! — Video

Coca marketing campaign in Australia

https://www.youtube.com/watch?v=2X8Bd3-G6IU

Task 1 Text

Read the whole text.

1. Take down notes about what you believe is important.
2. Organize your ideas and make a plan.
3. Write an organized account of the article in French.

→ **Be critical:** Write in French what you did not learn and would have liked to learn, or what is missing.

Task 2 Audio

Listen to the whole audio.

1. Listen to the whole audio and take down notes about what you believe is important.
2. Organize your ideas and make a plan.
3. Write an organized account of the article in French.
4. How do you understand the expression "the new black"?

Word box

- concoction: *préparation/mélange/ concoction*
- shade: *teinte*
- a trade secret : *un secret de fabrication*
- skeptical : *sceptique*

Task 3 Video

Anticipate from the title.

1. Write how you consume and then compare.

Watch the video.

2. Watch the whole video and collect the main ideas, the examples, and write a report.

Task 4 Put in common

1. Making a plan: see how the three documents are related to one another.
   - Text 1: the main idea is...
   - Audio 2: the main ideas are...
   - Video 3: the main ideas are...
2. How are the ideas from each document related?
3. Write a synthesis of the three documents in French starting with the plans carried out in Task 4, question 1.

2 Background

How does marketing operate?

Marketing is a process based on multiple activities to sell a product to consumers referred to as the 4 Ps of the marketing mix: Product Place Price Promotion (see video p. 31).

- The product or service must be designed to satisfy and attract its targets audience. Audiences are not targeted at random. Marketers should know who their core targets are according to age group, gender, social background, etc.

- The place where the product will be sold to the customers must also be decided after a thorough study on how the company wants its product to be positioned. That is the reason why customers cannot find luxury brands at huge retailers' stores. If luxury goods were marketed in a superstore, it would greatly damage the brand image of the companies they belong to.

- The price has to correspond to the product's features and to the image it is supposed to convey. A too low price has the same negative impact as a too high price.

- Promotion. To make their products known to their audience, marketers generally communicate through advertising although an increasing number of high profile companies rely on word of mouth.

- Packaging is sometimes considered as the 5th P of the marketing mix in an increasingly competitive market where each brand's goal is to stand out.

I Retailing

Without retailing manufacturers would not be able to reach the customers, which makes of retailing the final but essential link between companies and consumers.

The retailing landscape has undergone tremendous changes ever since high technology has allowed customers to make their purchase in one click. Smartphones' cutting edge technology allowing their users to compare, buy, and pay in one device is aggravating the pressure on retailers. In order to fight back, traditional brick-and-mortar retailers have to wrack their brains to find how they can attract customers again and keep them loyal.

II How do retailers fight back?

Pop up stores have been multiplying ever since the first pop up store opened in Los Angeles in 2000. The aim is to offer customers an original experience where the point of sales becomes a place for short lasting events.

III Multi format stores/multi channel retail

Mainstream grocery stores such as Carrefour in France, Tesco in the UK and Walmart in the US have developed multi format stores allowing them to open small and medium sized points of sale in the center of cities and towns.

IV Click and Collect

In an effort to counter the growing power of online retailers such as Amazon, mainstream grocery stores around the world have developed a Click and Collect service. Customers are invited to shop online and drive to collect their prepaid and prepacked groceries directly delivered in their cars' boots by members of the staff.

Conclusion: the price war

Retailers are doing their best to satisfy their customers' needs for a specific product by making it available almost instantaneously either in the point of sales or at their doorsteps. And yet, some realize they cannot compete with giants like Amazon which are able to deliver at their customers' doorstep a branded product for almost half the price they would have paid in a point of sale.

Now that Amazon has tapped the grocery market, mainstream grocery retailers find themselves threatened by two enemies: the online giant on one side and the German hard discounters on the other side. We can wonder what place will be left for them in the years to come.

Question time

1. Give a short definition of marketing.
2. Quote the 5 Ps of the marketing mix.
3. What has changed in today's retail landscape?
4. How do high street retailers try to fight back?

Vocabulary p. 54

Are developed nations facing a general retail meltdown?

For the past couple of years, many retailers have been having a difficult time, and the end of the tunnel isn't yet to be seen. The bad retail results are particularly hard felt in the United States where some of the most iconic retailers such as Macy's and Sears have announced over 100 store closures for 2017. Ralph Lauren itself is closing its flagship store on Fifth Avenue. These figures are all the more surprising that the US economy is healthy, with rising wages and unemployment at its lowest. Experts are relating this phenomenon to a revolution in the retail landscape originating from many changes occurring in consumers' buying patterns. Here are some of them:

1. People are simply buying more items on line than they used to

The simplest explanation for the decline of brick-and-mortar shops is that Amazon is eating up retail. Between 2010 and 2016, Amazon's sales in North America quintupled from $16 billion to $80 billion; half of all US households today are Amazon subscribers.

2. Amazon is not the only one responsible for traditional retailers'

decline. The unprecedented growth of mobile phones savvy apps allows customers to enjoy a more complete shopping experience, keeping them away from high street stores and malls.

3. America built far too many malls

There are about 1,200 malls in America today. Ten years from now there might be about 900 The number of malls in the US grew more than twice as fast as the population between 1970 and 2015. Mall visits declined by 50% between 2010 and 2013, and they have kept up falling ever since.

4. Consumers have become bargain hunters,

more attracted by discounters, fast fashion outlets and club stores than by department stores.

5. Americans are shifting their spending from materialism to meals out with friends

Clothing stores have dwindled as consumers shifted their spending away from clothes toward travelling and dining out. Travel is booming, the rise of restaurants is even more remarkable. In 2016, for the first time, Americans spent more money in restaurants and bars than at grocery stores.

6. Young people's influence

Many young people are driven by the experiences that will make the best social media content. It could be anything, from a beach picnic, to beautifully arranged organic food display. Better food, entertainment and even fitness options might bring teens and families back to malls and their brick-and-mortar stores, provided they know how to anchor this new breed of consumers.

Conclusion

If traditional retailers wish to recapture consumers' interest and trust, they will have to find innovative strategies proposing enough incentives enabling them to compete with the giant online retailers like Amazon which for the time being are gaining ground at an unprecedented pace.

Questions

- How are Americans changing their spending habits?
- What do young people appreciate today?
- What should brick-and-mortar retailers do to attract consumers again?

2 SWOT

Macy's Swot

Favourable | Unfavourable

Internal

Strengths

- One of the largest chain stores in the US operating more than 800 stores across various states.
- Excellent brand recognition.
- Wide variety of products.
- Ships products to over 100 countries across the world.
- Quality customer services.
- Excellent updated and high-profile stores.
- Strong market share.

Weaknesses

- Does not generate enough revenue.
- The company has limited global brand recognition. No international scope.
- The market share is decreasing due to fierce competition.
- The company should plan to invest and spread and operate more subsidiaries.

SWOT

External

Opportunities

- The company's reputed brand name could be marketed across the globe.
- E-commerce is another opportunity that the company has to develop
- The company should open new stores to boost sales.
- With the promotional events such as environmental causes the company can create more awareness.

Threats

- The company should focus on the competitors and counter their moves.
- Low prices offered by the major brands such as Walmart.
- Massive attacks by the giants of e-commerce.
- Slowdown of economy makes people spend less.

Test yourself

After having studied this unit, you must be able to answer the following questions…

1. Quote four different types of retailers.
2. Why is marketing necessary for companies?
3. Why is online retailing increasingly popular?
4. What is “showrooming”?
5. What new market has Amazon tapped?
6. Is the rise of online retailing the only cause for the decline of malls in developed countries?
7. What are Macy’s and Sears?
8. What are their equivalents in France?
9. What are *Whole Foods, Guinot* and *Vita Coco*?
10. What is brand endorsement? Give examples.
11. What can explain the decline of malls and department stores in developed countries?
12. Name two hard discounters and explain their strategies.

Tips

Reasons for shopping at your local shops:

- Customer service is good; the retailer knows you; the retailer makes you feel loved; the retailer is more flexible, more knowledgeable, more innovative, and will go out of her/his way to find what you want; it benefits the local community.

Reasons for not shopping at your local shops:

- The shop has limited business hours; has a limited selection; does not market its goods; might have high prices and its building might look dated or/and dated.
- However, the new general consumer trend is to shop small. Small is Beautiful. Here is the point of view of famous humorist David Sedaris:
  “I’d rather go to an actual shop — preferably a small one — than to a harshly lit superstore, or, worse still, a website,” Sedaris said. “I don’t want to buy my books and my toilet paper and my clothing all under the same roof. I want beauty in my life. I want charm. I want contact with actual people. It is, for me, a large part of what makes life worth living.”

Millennial 'influencers'

Beauty vloggers and cult celebrities are being courted by luxury brands.

Seven years ago, Chiara Ferragni was a fledgling 23-year-old fashion blogger, studying law at university in Milan. She never finished her degree, but now lives in a $3.5m Los Angeles mansion packed with antiques, and spends her days travelling the world in midriff-revealing tops, Gucci sweatshirts, cut-off jeans and a collection of Louis Vuitton. How do we know this?

Every day, the "Blonde Salad" shares images of her gilded lifestyle with her 9.6 million followers on Instagram, making her one of the cult celebrities of the social media world. Unlike Taylor Swift, Beyoncé et al, who have all made their names elsewhere and maintain fanbases on the photo-sharing platform, Ferragni has found fame and fortune solely by publishing photographs of herself wearing a variety of designer ensembles in a range of glamorous locations. Now worth a reputed $12m, with a line of branded shoes selling at up to $500 a pair, and a contract with Pantene as a global ambassador, Ferragni is a role model to a generation of digital natives who have established a viable career as social media "influencers".

In just a few years, the power of blogs and platforms such as Instagram has created a new marketing genre that has seen brands investing heavily in collaborations with the big names in the online space. Beca Alexander, founder and president of the social media casting and management agency Socialyte Collective, represents about 100 influencers, each with between 30,000 and 2 million followers.

"One of our top influencers did about $1m last year and the average for those on our books is around $200,000 a year," says the digital entrepreneur from her New York office.

Alexander developed a programme two years ago known as "product bombing", whereby a co-ordinated campaign saw numerous, carefully selected micro-influencers paid to talk about a new product at a specified time, thus saturating the social media space within the target demographic. "That worked really well, and created huge awareness and demand, seeing stock sellout rapidly," she says.

"We have no issue with social influencers working with brands, as long as consumers aren't misled," says Guy Parker, chief executive of the Advertising Standards Authority, which is working with the Federal Trade Commission in the US and the newly formed International Council of Advertising Self-Regulation to develop some kind of oversight of influencer marketing. "We define advertising as a tweet, vlog, blog or Instagram post where the influencer has been paid and there has been some control over the content. We therefore expect the post to have #ad on it in a prominent position. "Many millennials believe this isn't necessary as they claim to be able to see whether content is 'sponsored', but we believe it is imperative to protect consumers who aren't that savvy, and ensure they know."

Callum McCahon, strategy director at the social media agency Born Social, says the industry needs to be self-regulating, and that Instagram must take some responsibility for protecting consumers using their platform. "Users scroll through feeds fast and are trained to skip past hashtags. I believe Instagram needs to have its own mandatory labelling system for a 'paid-for' post, which Facebook – which owns Instagram – has launched recently as branded content."

There is no doubt that a generation of style-conscious entrepreneurs are making a good living – in some cases a fortune – by building their own personal brands online with fan bases to rival many established global businesses. The challenge will be for newcomers to join a crowded market, and for those with a substantial following to keep them loyal.

"The reason a brand is using an influencer is the trusting relationship they have with their followers," says McCahon. "When it is done properly it is a very effective method of building a brand and selling product."

The Observer, Sun. 28 May 2017.

I Compréhension de l'écrit

Après avoir lu attentivement le texte ci-contre, vous en ferez un compte rendu en français, en faisant apparaître les idées essentielles (environ 200 mots – maximum 250 mots). Indiquez précisément le nombre de mots.

II Expression écrite

Traitez en anglais du sujet suivant :
→ What makes social medias attractive for many people? Can they always be trusted?

III Interaction écrite

Rédigez une lettre commerciale en anglais selon l'usage commercial courant en tenant compte des informations ci-dessous.

Expéditeur: Jamie Carlson, Snow & Flower,
13 rue de la Cambre, 50160 Saint Lo, France.

Destinataire : Riokan Katsutaro Annex, 3-8-4 Yanaka – Taito-Ku, Tokyo, Japon

Objet : réservation d'une chambre double

Date : 31 octobre 2018

Corps de la lettre :

- Conversation téléphonique ce jour-même pour réserver une chambre double pour deux personnes du 25 avril au 1er mai.
- L'heure exacte d'arrivée n'est pas encore connue car nous arrivons de Kyoto.
- À combien s'élève la nuitée ? Comment désirez-vous être réglé ?
- Avez-vous besoin d'un numéro de carte bleue pour réserver la chambre ?
- Offrez-vous un petit déjeuner ? Est-il japonais ou occidental ? Quel en est son coût ?
- Salutations d'usage.

↳ Voir Tools p. 214

1 Black Friday lifts UK retail sales despite income squeeze

Official data suggests shoppers are defying inflation increase, weak wage growth and slump in sterling since Brexit vote.

Black Friday discounts encouraged British consumers to increase their spending on the high street and online in November, despite the most protracted squeeze on household income in memory. Officials at the Office for National Statistics said the American-inspired promotional event had helped drive a 1.1% increase in the number of goods bought last month compared with October, with sales of electrical household appliances making the biggest contribution to growth. City economists had forecast growth of 0.4%.

The figures suggest consumers are willing to keep spending despite the sharpest rise in inflation for almost six years, driven by the higher cost of importing goods to the UK as a consequence of the pound's weakness since the Brexit vote. Households are also coming under pressure from weak wage growth, despite recordlow levels of unemployment in the UK and falling net migration, which should be acting to drive up the bargaining power of British workers to demand higher wages as firms face labour shortages. According to the Resolution Foundation thinktank, average annual pay when taking account of inflation may not return to its pre-financial crisis peak until at least 2025.

Economists have previously warned that stronger spending growth may be coming at the expense of household savings as a result of rising prices and weaker earnings growth. Households also run the risk of borrowing more to keep up with the rise in the cost of living. Still, the sales figures are encouraging for the health of the economy, providing some relief for retailers hit by higher inflation driving up their costs and potentially discouraging shoppers. Economists said the sales increase would help boost GDP* growth in the final three months of the year.

Non-food sales rose 1.5% in November from the previous month, while household goods sales – which includes electrical appliances in hot demand over Black Friday – were up 2.9%. There was a 1.4% rise in sales of textiles, clothing and footwear, while food sales increased by 0.6%. The monthly sales figures also show the increasing importance of online shopping in the UK, with an increase in average weekly spending of 10.2% compared with a year ago. Internet sales account for 17% of the retail sector, excluding automotive fuel, compared with 16.1% a year ago.

There are, however, warnings that the Black Friday lift could be short-lived because the sales encourage consumers to finish their Christmas shopping earlier in the year, which could lead to weaker sales in the traditional boom month of December.

Ruth Gregory, a UK economist at the consultancy Capital Economics, said: "Black Friday discounting has generally led consumers to do their Christmas shopping earlier than usual, rather than making many additional purchases. So some weakening in December seems likely."

Adapted from *The Guardian*, Dec. 14, 2017.

* GDP: PIB *(produit intérieur brut)*

I Compréhension de l'écrit

Write an account of document 1 in French. (180 words)

II Expression écrite

When do the peaks in consumer spending occur in France? Explain and give examples.

III Interaction écrite

You are launching a new fashion clothes brand. Write a mailing offering incentives to the 30 first buyers. (100 words)

2 Thrills for no frills

piste 13

IV Audio

1. Listen to the whole document once and answer the questions:
- **a)** What sort of document is it?
- **b)** What is the name of the program?
- **c)** Where does it take place?
- **d)** What is the main topic?

2. Listen to the document a second time and answer the following questions:
- **e)** What is "court circuit"?
- **f)** Where can it be found?
- **g)** What happens every Thursday evening?
- **h)** Who is Irene Glamour?

3. Listen to the document a third time.
- **i)** How are the meals organized?
- **j)** Why is it a unique experience for Irene Glamour?
- **k)** How does the reporter conclude the program?
- **l)** Explain the name of the program.
- **m)** Explain what the "new marketing trend" mentioned by the reporter refers to.

4. Reporting on what you have undestood
- **n)** Now report to the class or to a group about the audio and give your own opinion on the topic.

Vocabulary

address needs (vb): *répondre à des besoins*
advertisement/ad/advert (n): *spot publicitaire, annonce*
advertising (n): *publicité*
apparel (n): *vêtement*
bargain (n), (vb): *bonne affaire, marchander*
batch (n) : *lot*
brand (n): *marque*
brick-and-mortar store (n): *magasin physique*
buy in bulk (vb): *acheter en gros*
celebrity endorsement(n): *marque représentée par une célébrité*
click-and-mortar store (n): *magasin à la fois physique et en ligne*
commercial (US) (adj): *spot publicitaire*
competition (n): *concurrence*
competitor (n): *concurrent*
consumer behavior/pattern (n): *comportement du consommateur*
corner shop/convenience store (n): *magasin de proximité*
department store (n): *grand magasin (Galeries Lafayette, etc.)*
digital marketing (n): *marketing numérique*
display (vb): *présenter*
flagship store (n): *magasin pilote, navire amiral*
grocery shopping (n): *courses alimentaires*
handle (vb): *manipuler*
high street store (n): *magasin de centre-ville*
hit the shelves (vb): *arriver sur les rayons (être mis en vente)*
item (n): *article* (product, good)
label (n): *étiquette*
labelling (n): *étiquetage*
layout (n): *agencement, disposition*
loyalty card (n): *carte de fidélité*
low end (n): *bas de gamme*
mall (US) (n): *centre commercial*
market products (vb): *commercialiser des produits*
market research (n): *étude de marché*
midrange (adj): *milieu de gamme*
multi format store (n): *magasin décliné en plusieurs formats (i.e Carrefour)*
niche (n): *créneau*
packaging (n): *conditionnement/emballage*
pop up store (n): *magasin éphémère*
premium (adj/n): *avantage, privilège*
price tag (n): *étiquette de prix*
product packaging (n): *conditionnement du produit*
product/brand/company endorsement (n): *utilisation d'une personnalité ou d'une célébrité pour véhiculer l'image d'un produit, d'un événement, d'un service ou d'une marque*
provide (vb): *fournir*
pure player (n): *magasin exclusivement sur Internet*
retailer (n): *détaillant, commerçant*
retailing (n): *commerce de détail*
sample (n): *échantillon*
shoe-box store (n): *magasin rectangulaire en tôle dans les zones commerciales à l'entrée des agglomérations*
showcase (n): *vitrine*
showrooming (n): *consulter les produits en magasin pour les acheter ensuite en ligne*
the spending/consuming power/purchasing power (n): *pouvoir d'achat*
supply (vb): *fournir*
target (n): *cible*
target consumer segments (vb): *cibler des catégories de consommateurs*
trend (n): *tendance*
trade secret (n): *secret commercial*
upscale/high end (adj): *haut de gamme*
warehouse store (n): *magasin, entrepôt*
wholesaler (n): *grossiste*
word of mouth (n): *bouche-à-oreille*
wrapping material (n): *papier/matériel d'emballage*
youth-targeted promotions (n): *des promotions destinées aux jeunes*

3 Companies

Info

Un lobby est un groupe d'intérêts qui fait pression sur les instances gouvernementales.
Le lobbying se réfère aux actions menées par ces groupes pour augmenter leur influence.

Who lobbies the most?

Question

What companies try to have the most influence? Can you think of a reason?

Word box

- get a raise: *obtenir une augmentation*
- be paid fairly: *avoir un salaire correct*
- quality products: *produits de qualité*
- be challenged at work: *avoir un emploi qui présente des défis*
- get valuable feedback: *avoir des retours pertinents*
- do good work: *faire du bon travail*
- promote talent: *promouvoir le talent*
- ensure a strong company culture: *s'assurer d'une veritable culture d'entreprise*

Anticipate at home

What are the biggest companies in the world? VIDÉO 09

Nathan live!

https://www.youtube.com/watch?v=svEG3kwmuRg

?

1. Which is the biggest company in the world?
2. Two companies are compared: which ones?

3 » Starters

The class is divided into several groups: a group will study document 1, another document 2, a further one document 3 and the last one document 4.

Group 1

Document 1

Bayer and Monsanto: a $66 billion merger

The second-largest deal of the year 2016 was announced by German pharmaceutical and chemicals giant Bayer, which said it would buy US seed* and agricultural chemical company Monsanto. The combined company would control over a quarter of the global supply of seeds and pesticides, assuming the merger is completed. Monsanto shareholders accepted the deal in December, though it still requires regulatory approval.

Both companies have struggled to expand their market shares while coping with low grain prices and decreased spending on crop sprays.

*seed: semence, graine

■ Adapted from http://fortune.com

1. Identify the document.
2. What do Monsanto and Bayer sell?
3. What will the consequences of the merger be?

Group 2

Document 2 piste 14

What are "chaebols" and why are they controversial?

■ Demonstration in Seoul against corruption

1. Identify the document.
2. What is a chaebol? Give examples.
3. What happened with the election of the new president and the appointment of the new fair trade commissioner?
4. What is this type of company organisation criticised for?

Group 3

Document 3
Samsung and Apple

1. Identify the document.
2. What are these companies famous for?
3. Do they work together? Why?
4. Do they cooperate with each other?
5. What would they both like to be?
6. Which one appears as the strongest in the visual?
7. Do you think this could change? Why?

Group 4

Document 4
What is a start-up ?

1. Identify the document.
2. List all the elements necessary to launch a start-up.
3. Is money the most important element?
4. Why are teamwork and innovations essential?
5. Is it true also for other types of companies?

Put in common

→ Each group reports to the class, while the others take notes.
→ Use your notes and recapitulate: What are the common links between the four documents?
→ What can you deduce?

↳ Vocabulary p. 78

3 Prep page

Anticipate at home

Before reading the text, investigate:
- What type of company is Ikea?
- When and where was it founded?
- List the types of goods you can buy at Ikea.
- Where are the Ikea stores located? Why?

Text piste 15

Ikea undertakes some home improvements

The furniture giant is belatedly deepening its presence in e-commerce.

On a Sunday afternoon, shoppers participate in the ritual that is a trip to Ikea. This experience has changed remarkably little since the late 1950s when Ikea, which is still privately owned, set up its first store in southern Sweden and found that people would travel long distances for low-cost, self-assembled goods. Ikea has become the world's largest seller of furniture, with over 400 shops around the world and €38bn ($42bn) of revenue.

But now it is acknowledging that customers might want to shop in new ways. In what Torbjörn Lööf, chief executive of Inter Ikea, which owns the brand, has described as its biggest change in interacting with customers since the Ikea concept was founded, he has said it will experiment with selling furniture on third-party online platforms (it already sells items on its own website). It is not yet known whether it will sell on Amazon or China's Alibaba, the biggest names in e-commerce.

The firm also recognises that DIY labour does not always make people fonder of their purchases. In September Ikea Group, which runs most of the retail outlets, announced its acquisition of Task Rabbit, an app that, among other things, connects handymen to customers with odd jobs to be done. Taken together with other changes introduced in recent years—such as a handful of click-and-collect sites in some city centers, home delivery and a new augmented-reality app for smartphone to help customers visualise furniture in their homes—it is clear that the company is keen to create alternatives to its vast suburban outlets.

Such steps seem overdue. According to a survey of 29 countries by PwC, a consulting firm, around 30% of respondents would rather buy furniture on the internet than in shops. Although footfall at individual Ikea stores has been falling since 2015, the number of visits to the group's website has increased by over a fifth. Yet in 2016 online sales accounted for only 4% of the firm's total revenue. Ikea has doubtless noticed that an American competitor, Ashley Furniture, successfully sells its goods on Amazon, and that Alibaba, too, carries several ranges of furniture.

The new strategy carries the usual risks faced by firms going online. Customers are not shifting entirely to e-commerce, notes Marc-André Kamel of Bain & Company, a consulting firm, but wish to mix and match channels. Mr. Lööf therefore has little choice but to offer customers both physical and digital options, which could raise costs.

Lexical work

Understanding the key words

→ Find the meaning of the following words and their lexical categories (noun, verb, adjective, pronoun, adverb, etc.): flat-pack furniture; awaits; acknowledging; brand; handymen; odd jobs; suburban outlets; a brick-and-mortar shop.

→ Now, try to rephrase the title in your own words.

"Its plan to experiment with using big third-party online sellers such as Amazon is surprising," says Mr. Kamel, "because it would need to cede some control over its branding." Being on Amazon or Alibaba would also invite direct comparison with other furniture manufacturers. The Swedish giant is betting that it can win new customers online who would never trek to its superstores. But will it succeed?

■ Adapted from *The Economist*, Nov. 2, 2017.

I Read the whole text

1. Write everything you know about Ikea:
- Who owns the company?
- How many shops are there worldwide?
- What is the name of the CEO?
- What are the three online services Ikea offers its clients?
- Which other competitive company is mentioned?

2. Who are Alibaba and Amazon? What online services do they offer?

II Rephrase

3. What you have learned about what consumers needs and how they shop?

4. Give the key ideas in each paragraph in one or two sentences.

III Language

5. Try to find the root of the following words and classify them in their lexical category. Use a dictionary.

	verb	adverb	adjective	translation in French
deepening				
belatedly				
frictionless				

6. Compare deepen to shorten; whiten, broaden: what do you understand?

7. Compare frictionless to tireless; worriless; shoeless.

8. Compare belatedly to handsomely; hesitantly.

IV Train for the exam

9. Write an account in French of the document. (200 words).

V Branching out

10. Go further: What made the Ikea business model so successful among consumers? Do you think it has to be changed?

Role play

Student A hates buying furniture at Ikea because he/she prefers to have it delivered and assembled by professionals at home.
Student B is in favour of self delivered and assembled furniture because it lowers costs.
Student C interferes to explain that thanks to Ikea's new partnership with Task Rabbit, customers can have their Ikea furniture assembled by handymen.

You can play the scene, record it and debrief on it with the class.

3 Text tracks

Anticipate at home

Before reading the text find out more about :

- Aldi/Lidl/Sainsbury's/Tesco
- their nationalities;
- the products they sell and where;
- what makes them different from one another.

Text piste 16

Aldi and Lidl grow despite ignoring the internet

It hasn't stopped the discount grocers from thriving.

The aisles are wide, the lights bright and shelves low. Most obviously, however, the apples shine and the broccoli beckons. For those used to the cramped, dimly lit Aldi stores, the new supermarket in Herten, Germany, is almost shocking.

Opened in April this is the prototype for a vast new renovation and expansion programme across Europe, Britain and America. It is the discount giant's big bet on the future of shopping, all the more daring as the money is going almost entirely on bricks and mortar. Defying the conventional wisdom that customers want both in-store and online shopping ("omnichannel" in the jargon) Aldi wants to conquer the retail world by ignoring the internet. As too, to a lesser extent, does its great German rival Lidl. Plenty of other grocers reckon this may be the miscalculation that eventually brings them down.

Founded in 1945 and 1973 respectively, Aldi (split into two legally separate companies, Aldi Nord and Aldi Süd) and Lidl have been eating up the competition, especially since the financial crash of 2008. In the cut-throat British market, Aldi (owned by Süd) increased its groceries share to 6.8%, from 6.2% just a year ago; Lidl's jumped from 4.6% to 5.2%. At home in Germany, Aldi Nord's market share has reached 12.9%, and Lidl's 8.9%.

However, Aldi acknowledges that it must change to keep growing at this pace. Kay Rueschoff, Aldi Nord's director of marketing, concedes that low prices, the discounters' hallmark, are no longer enough. To lure middle-class shoppers, Aldi has to focus on quality too, hence the shiny store in Herten. In all, Aldi Nord is spending €5.2bn ($6.1bn) on revamping its 4,800 stores in Europe (excluding Britain and Ireland) and opening hundreds of new ones. Besides ambient interiors, there is more fruit, veg and wine.

Mr. Rueschoff bristles at any suggestion that Aldi is changing too much. The new stores still sell only about 1,400 items, as opposed to the 50,000 or so on many rivals' shelves, enabling big economies of scale. At Lidl, a new generation of senior managers last year began to upgrade their stores in a similar way.

The discounters reason that they will not make much money out of it. Britons buy 7.3% of their groceries online, up from 6.7% a year ago, second only to South Koreans. Tesco, Sainsbury's and others have spent hundreds of millions of pounds on sophisticated internet operations. Yet, these stores are merely "cannibalising themselves", driving most of their shoppers from their most profitable channel (the store) to the least profitable (online).

For the moment, Aldi's decision to spend its money on physical stores is working. In less developed e-commerce markets, like America, they may have even more of an advantage. But the proportion of people shopping online can only go one way, so the strategy carries risks.

■ Adapted from *The Economist*, October 26, 2017.

Lexical work

Understanding the key words

➜ Find their meanings and their lexical categories (noun, verb, adjective, adverb, etc.): thriving; aisles; shelves; beckons; cut-throat; groceries; to lure; preserve; deemed; revamped; economy of scale.

➜ Rephrase the title in your own words and write an introduction (source and date).

First track: A step-by-step approach

I Read the text

1. Pick up the main idea(s) in each paragraph.

II Rephrase

2. Rephrase the idea(s) you have found in each paragraph.

III Language

3. Translate into English:

a) It must change to keep growing at this pace.
b) Aldi Nord is spending a lot on revamping its 4,800 stores.
c) Lidl has just begun operating in America.

IV Train for the exam

4. Use all the information above to report briefly to the class in French.

5. Write a account in English following the guidelines below (200 words):

§1 Introduction (source, date and main idea)
§2 A brief history of Aldi and Lidl
§3 Aldi Süd and Lidl in Britain
§4 Aldi's new strategy and Lidl's new strategy
§5 Point of view on Tesco's strategy
§6 Conclusion

Grammaire

▸ Le gérondif

Après certains verbes comme **to start, to continue, to finish** et des postpositions, **le verbe est en -ing.**

→ *(***voir grammaire p. 200** *avec une liste non exhaustive des verbes qui sont suivis d'un V-ing)*

Second track: A straightforward approach

I Read the text

1. Take down notes about what you believe is important.

II Rephrase

2. Organise your ideas a make a plan.

III Language

3. Use hundred or hundreds:

a) He bought 3 .... T-shirts.
b) .... of people were at his funeral.

IV Train for the exam

4. Write an account of the article in French in 200 words.

5. Write a report OR make an oral presentation. Use the research you carried out before studying the text and investigate further to discuss the following topics:

- What strategies should discount companies have to target upscale customers?
- What should a European company do to set its business in the USA?

Grammaire

▸ Quelques nombres

→ Tesco, Sainsbury's and others have spent **hundreds** of **millions** of pounds on sophisticated internet operations.
→ Aldi Nord is spending €5.2 **billion**.
→ *Tesco, Sainsbury's et d'autres enseignes ont dépensé des centaines de millions de livres sterling.*

- La phrase 1 : **hundreds** et **millions** sont des noms, donc au pluriel.
- La phrase 2 : **billion** est un adjectif, donc invariable.

3 Video tracks

Common track

→ Before you start watching the video:

1. Anticipate on the title of the video.
2. Explain who is Mark Zuckerberg and what you know about his company.
3. Look at the title and think about what sorts of "painful moments" a company may face.

→ Watch the video:

4. Listen and try to hear and understand the following words: low points; connect; offer; management; bets; acquisitions; crazy; oculist; team; talented; CEO; stuff; move; pride.
5. Debrief with the other students and the teacher about their meaning.

Pronunciation work

→ Listen, repeat the following words and record yourself: beyond; expertise; pride; incrementally; thought; bought; bigger bets.

Video vidéo 10 Nathan live!

Zuckerberg shares painful moments in the history of Facebook

https://www.youtube.com/watch?v=y74cdtfl4Oo

Tips

What is required to run a company well?

- Have effective communications skills.
- Be able to assess people.
- Have talented people who trust you and your values.
- Focus on what really matters.
- Screen out unnecessary noise.
- Take risks.
- Be obsessed with excellence.
- Have values.
- Create something that outlasts you.
- Deal swiftly with conflicting demands.
- Take unpleasant decisions.

First track: A step-by-step approach

I Watch the whole video once

1. Write in French what it is about.

II Watch the video a second time

- Watch the first part ('53 s):

2. What did Yahoo want to do some time ago?
3. Did Zuckerberg accept the offer? Why not?
4. Did all the executives agree with him?
5. What were the consequences of his decision?

- Watch the second part ('53 s → end):

6. What question is the host asking Zuckerberg about?
7. According to Zuckerberg, does a CEO sometimes have to do "crazy things"?
8. What company did Facebook buy?
9. Does he regret buying it? Why?
10. Explain what he says about being a good CEO: "being able to make big moves is better than have pride."

III Train for the exam

11. **Oral report:** Put together all the information you have collected and report to the class.

Second track: A straightforward approach

I Watch the whole video

1. After the first viewing, you are expected to have understood the general idea(s) exposed in the document. Write a short debrief.

II Watch the video a second time

2. Take notes and focus on how the different ideas are connected to one another.

III Train for the exam

3. Write an account of the video. In your conclusion, state your point of view.

Role play

Student A comes up with a new idea of a product or service. He/she is convinced that it will work.

Student B needs convincing. He/she is not quite sure.

→ Imagine a dialogue in which Student A has to explain the project and Student B wants to understand if it is the right product, at the right time, at the right price for their consumers.

Help yourself

appealing, engaging, target a consumer, market the product, advertise, the age group, social media, launch the product, meet a need, be trendy

3 Audio tracks

Common track

I Before listening

1. Find out about Alibaba and Amazon and give information about them.

Alibaba.com

amazon

II Anticipate

→ Anticipating the topic of the audio

1. Before listening to the audio, look at the visual and the title and say as much as you can.

→ Words, expressions, ideas you may hear

2. Listen and try to understand the following words:
efficient; empower; fulfillment; insight; headquarters; model; network; tariffs; trade; warehouse.

3. Debrief with the other students and the teacher about their meaning.

Pronunciation work

→ Listen, repeat the following words and record yourself:
exclusive; empire; first and foremost; percentage; storefront; philosophy to empower.

Audio piste 17 Nathan live!

Alibaba

New York City, September 2014.

First track:
A step-by-step approach

I Listen to the whole audio

1. Write in French what it is about.

II Listen to the first part

2. Collect information on:

a) The location of the interview, the person interviewed, his name and position in his company.
b) The description he makes of Amazon's business model.
c) Alibaba's philosophy.
d) The number of sellers they work with.

III Listen to the second part

3. What strategy does Alibaba use to be able to satisfy all of its customers?
4. How did Jack Ma persuade the American president that Alibaba was good for the US economy?
5. How many people are directly employed by Alibaba?
6. What is the American point of view on Chinese trade?
7. What did many people think of Jack Ma when he adopted a different business plan?
8. What is Jack Ma's point of view on the two different business models?
9. Which company will the next programme focus on?

IV Train for the exam

10. **Oral report:** Put together all the information you have collected and report to the class.

Second track:
A straightforward approach

I Listen to the whole audio once

1. After the first listening, you are expected to have understood the general idea(s) exposed in the document. Write a short debrief.

II Listen to the whole audio a second time

2. Take notes and focus on how the different ideas are connected to one another.

III Train for the exam

3. Write an account of the audio. In your conclusion, state your point of view.

Role play

Student A explains his/her consuming habits online and offline. **Student B** does the same. Then, they compare their notes to see what reasons make them buy online or not, and stores where they buy online and offline.

3 From French to English

Texte

Le japonais Uniqlo impose son vestiaire partout en France

Uniqlo entame une série d'ouvertures en France. L'enseigne japonaise d'habillement inaugurera, jeudi 2 novembre, un nouveau point de vente à Paris, au sein du grand magasin Printemps, récemment rénové, place de la Nation, dans le 20e arrondissement. Il occupera 840 m². À la fin novembre, Uniqlo s'installera aussi dans la ville de Metz (Moselle), au sein du centre commercial Muse. Ce magasin-là sera plus grand encore (925 m²) pour présenter tous les jeans, chemises, doudounes et autres tee-shirts manga que la marque vend à petits prix, grâce à une production à moindre coût en Asie.

Ces deux inaugurations – l'une à Paris, l'autre en province – illustrent la nouvelle offensive de la chaîne japonaise de mode dans l'Hexagone. Dix ans après son entrée en Île-de-France, à Paris, à la Défense, dans les Hauts-de-Seine, Uniqlo accélère, pour convertir le plus grand nombre de Français à sa mode de pulls de couleurs et de jeans pour hommes, femmes et enfants. « *Tout passera par l'ouverture de nouveaux magasins et l'accélération de la vente en ligne* », explique Hidenori Nishino, directeur général d'Uniqlo en France. Car, dans les agglomérations françaises où l'enseigne n'est pas présente, le numérique peut être un palliatif ou un laboratoire, pour estimer le potentiel d'une grande surface avec pignon sur rue.

La France fait partie des priorités du numéro trois mondial de l'habillement, derrière l'espagnol Inditex, propriétaire de Zara, et le suédois H&M. Avec des ventes qui ont atteint 13,9 milliards d'euros pour l'exercice 2016-2017, clos fin août, soutenues par un bond de 8,1 % à l'étranger, le groupe a l'ambition d'ouvrir 180 magasins dans le monde, dont une centaine en Chine, en 2018. À cette date, sa maison mère, Fast Retailing, présente dans 18 pays, devrait réaliser la majorité de son chiffre d'affaires à l'étranger. La holding espère alors exploiter 3 502 points de vente, dont 1 246 Uniqlo à l'étranger et 831 au Japon. Il le faut. Sur son marché domestique, le distributeur, fondé en 1963 par Tadashi Yanai, est confronté à la déflation et au manque de dynamisme de la consommation. Dès lors, il doit trouver des relais de croissance à l'étranger.

En France, l'ambition de M. Yanai redouble alors que le marché traverse une crise sans précédent depuis 2008. L'enseigne s'en moquerait presque. « *À la fin du printemps 2018, Uniqlo disposera de 25 magasins au total en France, dont 11 en dehors de Paris et de l'Île-de-France* », précise M. Nishino.

Mais le nippon est encore loin derrière les grandes enseignes de mode en France. Entré en 1998 dans l'Hexagone, H&M, autre spécialiste de la mode pour toute la famille, aligne plus de 200 magasins sur le territoire. Uniqlo, lui, est encore assez jeune sur le marché français. Il a fait ses premiers pas en province dans la ville de Marseille […] en 2014. Depuis, il s'est installé à Strasbourg, Lyon, Bordeaux, Nice, Lille et Toulouse. Il a également étendu son réseau en Île-de-France […].

Ce n'est pas fini. Au printemps 2018, la chaîne ouvrira les portes d'un magasin de 560 m² rue de Passy, dans le 16e arrondissement. Il entrera aussi dans deux centres commerciaux majeurs qu'Unibail exploite en région parisienne. Ce sera à Parly 2, au Chesnay (Yvelines), et à Carré Sénart à Lieusaint (Seine-et-Marne).

Uniqlo fait figure de locomotive propre à attirer de nouveaux visiteurs.

Car, désormais, le secteur des centres commerciaux et les propriétaires de pieds d'immeubles en centres-villes l'attendent avec impatience. Le marché de l'habillement traverse une crise sévère depuis une dizaine d'années. Les enseignes qui ouvrent de nouveaux magasins en France se font rares. Tous les acteurs du secteur espèrent que, comme à Lyon lors de son inauguration le 29 septembre, l'enseigne attirera la foule des grands jours et relancera la consommation de mode.

D'après *Le Monde Économie*, 28 octobre 2017.

Common track

1. What do the following words mean? Look for them in the dictionary if necessary and note the appropriate definition:
   offensive; l'Hexagone; palliatif; la holding; déflation.
2. Find their lexical categories (noun, verb, adjective, adverb, etc.).
3. Rephrase in a few lines the main idea of the article in French.
4. What are the English words for:
   enseigne; habillement; centre commercial; numérique; vente en ligne; région parisienne; mode.

1. Use a dictionary: look up the following words and find equivalents in English:
   fréquenter; faire figure de locomotive; la foule des grands jours; son vestiaire.
2. Identify the main topic in English.
3. What makes Uniqlo different from the other retailers?
4. Imagine a title in English for the document.
5. Introduce the text in English.
6. Write one or two sentences in English for each paragraph in your own words (no translation).
7. Use your sentences to write a well-organised account of the article in English. (180 words)

Go faster

I **Read the whole document and suggest a title in English.**

II **Write one or two sentences in English in your own words for each paragraph.**

III **Write an organised account of the article in English. (200 words) Do not forget the introduction and the conclusion.**

Debate

Students from group A believe in Uniqlo's expansion in France. They also think this expansion will help its competitors. Prepare your arguments.

Students from group B don't believe in Uniqlo's ability to expand further on the French market. Prepare your arguments.

Branching out

- Give your own point of view on the number of garment retailers and their prices.
- Write a 150 word essay developing why Uniqlo will or will not succeed and why bricks-and mortar shops are where consumers want to buy.

Document 1 vidéo 11 Nathan live! — Video

Getting to the bottom of Samsung's Galaxy Note 7 crisis

https://www.youtube.com/watch?v=ui29CoxavBM

Document 2 piste 18 — Text

What does it take to destroy a company's brand name?

What changes a corporate branding disaster from being a costly and damaging affair, to one with fatal consequences for the company concerned? How is it some firms have been able to bounce back while others are unable to survive? Both the German car giant Volkswagen and South Korean mobile phone maker Samsung have been subject to controversy in recent times. VW is still dealing with its diesel emissions scandal, and Samsung has had to face overheating phone batteries. Yet both have put these corporate disasters behind them. VW has just seen its pretax profits rise 44.3%, while Samsung's operating profits have gone up by 48%. Other firms have not been so fortunate.

Emissions scandal

In 2015, it emerged that Volkswagen had fitted illegal software to its diesel vehicles allowing them to cheat on emissions tests. It meant VW's diesel vehicles were able to emit up to 40 times the legally allowable pollution level. The revelations came as a shock to many. VW has so far agreed to pay about $25bn (£19bn) to address US claims.

Yet this public relations disaster has not stopped VW from overtaking Toyota as the world's largest carmaker.

As the scandal broke, VW put together a comprehensive plan to deal with it. It has acknowledged its wrong-doing, pleading guilty in the USA. At the same time, the group has embarked on a significant cost-cutting exercise. The scandal has cost VW billions, but could have cost it even more if it had mishandled things. What VW did was clearly wrong but it has had a positive effect on the group.

Burning batteries

If you're one of the world's leading smartphone sellers, the last thing you want is to have to recall one of your flagship products.

Yet that is just what South Korea's electronics giant Samsung was forced to do amid reports of inflammable batteries. Last September, Samsung recalled 2.5 million Galaxy Note 7 smartphones after complaints of overheating and exploding batteries. The debacle cost Samsung about $5.3bn, and has been hugely damaging to its reputation. Samsung has said it takes "responsibility for our failure to ultimately identify and verify the issues arising out of the battery design and manufacturing process." That acceptance is a crucial part of its crisis management strategy, says Wayne Lam, analyst at IHS Market.

Adapted from www.bbc.com, 2017.

Document 3 piste 19 — Audio

When sailing becomes easy, time-saving and cheap

Task 1 Video

Watch the video and answer:

1. Explain what you know about Samsung and the problem they had with their flagship product.
2. What do you know about the smartphone market today?
3. What should smatphone companies focus on to establish and keep their customers' trust?
4. Organise all the information you have collected.
5. Write your report.

Task 2 Text

Read the whole text and answer:

1. Which companies is the text about?
2. Describe the mistakes they made.
3. Do mistakes and frauds always damage a company's brand name?
4. Organise your ideas and make a plan.
5. Write an organised account of the article in English.

Task 3 Audio

Listen to the whole audio

1. Anticipate from the title.
2. Collect key words, key data, key ideas.
3. Write an organised report.

Task 4 Put in common

1. Making a plan: See how the three documents are related to one another.
   - Video 1: the main idea is...
   - Text 2: the main ideas are...
   - Audio: the main ideas are...
2. How are the ideas from each document related?
3. Write a final report which is a synthesis of the three documents.

3 Background

What is a company today?

The word company is a general term which can be replaced by firm or corporation, according to the context. The word business can also be used to refer to a company.

Companies can be small, **medium sized (SME)** or big. They can be **global**, meaning they are present in many parts of the world. A new breed of companies, called **start-ups**, are innovative and fast growing businesses generally launched by one person or a small team from a simple computer on a table corner.

Companies **manufacture** and **market** goods and services. They are managed by an executive team headed by the **Chief Executive Officer** (**CEO**), sometimes called the **chairman**.

Companies are made of several **departments** (i.e. the **sales department**, the **human resources department**, the **accounting department**, the **R&D → research and development department** etc.) and generally have their **headquarters** in their hometown (i.e Coca Cola in Atlanta, Georgia, USA).

Companies manufacturing products often operate their own factories, but they can also **outsource** the manufacturing process (i.e. Renault's Dacia is manufactured in Romanian factories). Companies can outsource any department when operating internally would increase the costs.

The GAFAM: Google, Apple, Facebook, Amazon and Microsoft are called the "big" five or the GAFAM. They represent the most active and innovative global US companies focused on high technology and artificial intelligence (AI).

The BATX: The GAFAM's domination is being challenged by the Chinese BATX, along with the South Korean consumer electronics company Samsung. These initials stand for four Chinese companies similar to the GAFAM:

– Baidu (the Chinese Google)
– Alibaba (the equivalent of Amazon)
– Tencent (a social network like Facebook)
– Xiomi (the Chinese equivalent of Apple)

I External problems

- Companies depend on the general economic and political context which can have a disastrous impact on their bottom lines. For example, the economic downturn triggered by the subprime crisis of 2008 forced many companies of goods and services to file for bankruptcy.
- They also depend on the cost of raw materials.
- Natural disasters such as floods, earthquakes, hurricanes, tsunamis, droughts can seriously damage a company.
- Climate change and environmental change can **transform the demand for goods**: for example, if global temperatures rise, demand for cold weather products such as heating might decline.
- Massive social unrest can also pose a threat to companies. When strikes affect the transport network, employees are late or stuck at home.
- New legislation imposing new standards can force companies to abruptly change the manufacturing of their products, or their strategy. This type of changes can come with huge financial cost.

There are no real solutions to avoid external problems except being constantly on the watch to be able to prevent a disaster.

II Internal problems

Companies also have to face internal problems although they should be easier to prevent than external ones:

- Problems in the managing team may have negative consequences on a company, affecting its profitability.
- Lack of trust between the employer and the employees can constitute an obstacle for the company's growth.
- A wrong strategic move may also have long lasting consequences.
- A bad public image due to a company's mistreatments of its workforce, at home or abroad.
- A bad public image because the company has betrayed consumers' trust.
- Faulty products can also damage a company's image with consequences on its sales.

Question time

1. What are the Chinese BATX? How do these Chinese companies operate and where?
2. Explain what external and internal problems a company may face.

➥ Vocabulary p. 78

Trends

Social work? Is it still the province of charities and government programmes?

Companies are social and economic structures providing goods or services to customers. But next to companies, whether they are (1) small and medium-sized companies (SMCs), (2) single or sole proprietorship like Ikea, (3) partnerships, (4) private limited companies (Ltd) with shareholders but not quoted on the stock exchange or (5) public limited companies (Plcs), there are charities playing a bigger part in our societies as well as public benefit corporations (PBCs).

1. What is a charity?

A charity is a social enterprise whose goal is to complete a social mission. Charities do not make profits, or reinvest their profits into good things in order to continue doing good deeds that will benefit society as a whole. Charities often fund their good work through donations and fundraising, but can also sell products or services. But charities have become much more professionalised. For instance, the Emmaus megastore on the outskirts of Preston, a northern English city, the biggest charity shop in the UK, resembles other retail outlets. Indeed, non-profit organisations operate more and more like businesses with goals to reach, effective marketing techniques, trained volunteers and a business plan.

2. Reasons for this major shift

Governments in the USA, in the UK, and the EU keep on funding charities but do it through contracts. Charities now need to bid for contracts with performance targets, such as finding work for 100 jobless people within a month, and compete therefore with rivals.
Moreover, British charities provide welfare assistance to recipients in exchange of "vouchers" given by the British government. Food banks, for instance, provide a few days' worth of meals to people who have received a voucher by their local council. For instance, the Trussell Trust, the biggest food bank organisation, which has more than 400 food banks across the country, gets vouchers and not subsidies. It also helps people access other sources of help.
Finally, charities have increased their retailing department when the crisis hit. They offer a wider range of goods with even brand-new goods, and therefore compete with for-profit organisations.

3. Charitable businesses and public benefit corporations (PBCs)

There are 165,000 registered charities in England and Wales alone. By comparison, the UK has nearly 30 times as many companies. Some may think there are too many but it shows that charities fill in a social gap. They may differ in size and in goals but provide a service that the state has abandoned.
In the USA the new business structure, the PBC, has introduced "public good" in the company's charter. In other words, PBCs are for-profit organisations with a charitable purpose but are taxed like any other corporations. For example, Patagonia decided to donate all 2016 Black Friday sales ($10 million in total) to non-profit organisations. Today, there are almost 4,000 public benefit corporations (PBCs) across the USA, including well-known brands such as Patagonia, Kickstarter, and This American Life. This corporate structure exists across 31 American states.
So are companies turning charitable work into a corporate principle? Have charities led the way to committing companies to be financially involved? It is certainly a sign that earning money should serve the better good.

Questions

1. What is the difference between a company and a charity?
2. Why has the border between companies and charities become confused?

EasyJet's SWOT

Favourable | Unfavourable

Internal

Strengths

- **Network:** huge network in Europe, carrying more than 73 million passengers, second biggest airline carrier in Europe by number of passengers carried
- **Pricing:** average fares somewhere around 50% lower than those of the major carriers on short haul routes and 20% to 40% below those of most other lower cost competitors
- **Fleet:** average fleet age is around four years, versus 9-11 years for European flag carriers, giving advantages in terms of fuel efficiency, maintenance costs and customer perception

Weaknesses

- **Competition:** cost per seat is around 50% higher than Ryanair's, so it is vulnerable to direct competition
- **Earnings:** highly seasonal hence vulnerable to any unexpected problems in the summer

SWOT

External

Opportunities

- **Market growth:** a significant market player in the growing aviation industry in years to come
- **Cost cuttings:** have defined areas for cost reduction, such as airports, ground handling, engineering and fuel

Threats

- **Brexit:** the consequences of Brexit still unknown → decided to move to Vienna after Brexit to remain in the euro zone
- **Climate change:** increasing number of periods of bad weather across Europe disrupting air carriers

Test yourself

After having studied this unit, you must be able to answer the following questions…

1. What is a merger? Give an example.
2. What are the positionings of Aldi and Lidl?
3. What company has Ikea bought?
4. What is a chaebol?
5. What problems did Samsung have?
6. What are the internal problems a company may face?
7. What are the external problems a company may face?
8. What is a start-up?
9. Why is Tiwal a promising company?
10. What is a socially responsible company?
11. What do the initials GAFAM mean?
12. What do the initials BATX mean?
13. Who is Alibaba's CEO?
14. What differences are there between Amazon and Alibaba?
15. What is a charity?
16. Ho do charities operate?

Tips

➡ BATX is the New GAFA

Chinese tech giants, Baidu, Alibaba, Tencent and Xiaomi, are expanding dramatically and are getting to the West. Some think the BATX are the Chinese twins of the GAFA (Google, Amazon, Facebook and Apple).

They are not very well-known in the West, except for Alibaba and Jack Ma. These giants are, however, behind almost every digital innovation in China. The BATX have been able to grow fast as they started copying the GAFA without having to compete with them as the Chinese authorities made it hard for Facebook or Amazon or Google to expand there. Like the GAFA, they have revolutionised every single industry, whether in financial services, in transport, or in retail. Every industry is being disrupted by them.

Today, the Chinese tech Dragons are preparing their development in the West. In fact, they already have a foot there as Tencent bought 12% of Snap (Snapchat), Alibaba and Tencent invested in Taxify to compete with Uber, and Baidu acquired Kitt.ai, an American start-up specialised in Artificial Intelligence. Soon, the BATX will be household names. Watch out.

1 Samsung unveils new management to quell leadership crisis

HONG KONG – Samsung Electronics, the South Korean tech giant, announced a new slate of executives on Tuesday in an effort to bring stability to its top ranks. The company, a global name in smartphones and microchips, has been suffering from a leadership vacuum. The crown prince of its controlling family was sent to prison this year on bribery charges. The family's patriarch has been in a coma since 2014. Three weeks ago, a senior executive responsible for one of its most successful businesses abruptly resigned.

The troubles at Samsung's management have not diminished its status as an innovative – and highly profitable – powerhouse in the technology world. That point was underscored on Tuesday when the company reported a record-high profit for the second quarter in a row. But the newly appointed executives, who have been drawn from Samsung's deep ranks of professional managers, could help ensure the company can run while the fate of the powerful family that built the Samsung empire remains under a cloud.

But in mid-October, Samsung said Mr. Kwon[1] planned to retire. Explaining his decision, Mr. Kwon said the company was "confronted with unprecedented crisis" and needed new leadership.

Samsung also said on Tuesday that its chief financial officer, S.H. Lee, would become chairman of the board starting in March.

Mr. Kwon currently holds that position, too, but Samsung said it would separate the two roles for the first time. Mr. Lee, who is no relation to the Lees who founded Samsung, will leave his post as finance chief.

Lee Kun-hee, the family patriarch who fell into a coma in 2014, remains chairman of Samsung Electronics, a different position from chairman of the board.

C.W. Chung, an analyst at Nomura, said the leadership reshuffle was supposed to have taken place last year but was delayed when the heir to the Samsung conglomerate, Lee Jae-yong, was implicated in a political scandal.

In that scandal, Lee Jae-yong and other executives were charged with paying millions of dollars in bribes and other inducements to win the backing of Park Geun-hye, then South Korea's president, for a corporate deal. Ms. Park[2] was eventually impeached and ousted. Mr. Lee was sentenced in August to five years in prison; an appeal is underway.

Samsung's dominance in many of the fastest-growing areas in tech have kept it afloat despite all that – and despite last year's disastrous recall of the company's fire-prone Galaxy Note 7 phone. No company sells more smartphones than Samsung. But Samsung also makes many of the chips and display panels that go into its rivals' devices. And its chips power the data centers and servers that are in high demand, thanks to the rapid expansion of cloud computing and services powered by artificial intelligence.

Adapted from *The Guardian*, October 31, 2017.

1. The Samsung Electronics chief executive officer.
2. Président.

I Compréhension de l'écrit

Rédigez un compte rendu en français de 150 mots (+/– 10 %).

II Expression écrite

Quel genre de problèmes une entreprise peut-elle avoir à affronter ?
Donnez des exemples. (150 mots ou plus)

4 Work

Questions

1. What type of document is it?
2. When was it released?
3. What does it feature?
4. What letter appears in the background? Why?
5. Debrief on the title, the subhead and the body copy.

Anticipate at home

Gender equality in the workplace VIDÉO 12

https://www.youtube.com/watch?v=75g8nBPrUZ8

1. What are these women's positions (jobs) in their companies?
2. What are they complaining about?

The workplace in 1944.

4 » Starters

The class is divided into several groups: a group will study document 1, another document 2, a further one document 3 and the last one document 4.

Group 1

Document 1

70% of employers are searching candidates' social media profiles

When looking for candidates via social networking sites, employers search for a few key items giving them good reasons hire them:

- Information that supports their qualifications for the job (61%)
- If the candidate has a professional online identity at all (50%)
- What other people are posting about the candidate (37%)
- For any reason at all not to hire a candidate (24%)

69% are using online search engines such as Google, Yahoo and Bing to research candidates as well, compared to 59% in 2016.

Over half of employers find contents on social media stopping them from hiring a candidate. Here are a few examples:

- Candidate posted information about them drinking or using drugs: 38%
- Candidate had discriminatory comments related to race, gender or religion: 32%
- Candidate had poor communication skills: 27%
- Candidate was linked to criminal behavior: 26%
- Candidate's screen name was unprofessional: 22%
- Candidate lied about an absence: 17%
- Candidate posted too frequently: 17%

■ Adapted from https://www.careerbuilder.com

1. Identify the document.
2. What do many employers do before hiring employees? Why?

4 Work

Questions

1. What type of document is it?
2. When was it released?
3. What does it feature?
4. What letter appears in the background? Why?
5. Debrief on the title, the subhead and the body copy.

Anticipate at home

Gender equality in the workplace VIDÉO 12

https://www.youtube.com/watch?v=75g8nBPrUZ8

1. What are these women's positions (jobs) in their companies?
2. What are they complaining about?

The workplace in 1944.

4 » Starters

The class is divided into several groups: a group will study document 1, another document 2, a further one document 3 and the last one document 4.

Group 1

Document 1

70% of employers are searching candidates' social media profiles

When looking for candidates via social networking sites, employers search for a few key items giving them good reasons hire them:

- Information that supports their qualifications for the job (61%)
- If the candidate has a professional online identity at all (50%)
- What other people are posting about the candidate (37%)
- For any reason at all not to hire a candidate (24%)

69% are using online search engines such as Google, Yahoo and Bing to research candidates as well, compared to 59% in 2016.

Over half of employers find contents on social media stopping them from hiring a candidate. Here are a few examples:

- Candidate posted information about them drinking or using drugs: 38%
- Candidate had discriminatory comments related to race, gender or religion: 32%
- Candidate had poor communication skills: 27%
- Candidate was linked to criminal behavior: 26%
- Candidate's screen name was unprofessional: 22%
- Candidate lied about an absence: 17%
- Candidate posted too frequently: 17%

Adapted from https://www.careerbuilder.com

1. Identify the document.
2. What do many employers do before hiring employees? Why?

Group 2

Document 2 piste 22

The worst thing about working at Facebook

1. Identify the document.
2. Explain why Facebook employees are spoiled and why it can have a negative impact.

Group 3

Document 3 vidéo 13 Nathan live!

Why more companies should be teleworking: from Calgary, Alberta (USA)

https://www.youtube.com/watch?time_continue=22&v=FOLVoRp3q3U;

1. Identify the document.
2. Watch the video and take down notes.
3. Write a few lines to sum up what you have understood.

Group 4

Document 4

The importance of workplace diversity

1. Identify the document.
2. Can you read all the words on the document?
3. What do they refer to?
4. What word is the most visible?
5. Explain the title of the document with your own words.
6. What is the purpose of this document?
7. Do you think it is important? Why?

Put in common

- Each group reports to the class while the others take notes.
- Use your notes and recapitulate: What are the common links between the four documents?
- What can you deduce?

4 Prep page

Anticipate at home

Before reading the text, investigate:
- Why do people need to work?
- How do you understand the expression a "living wage"?
- What is for you the opposite of a fair society?

Text piste 23

A fair, decent society needs a real living wage for its workers

Tia's appeal was simple and direct. If her mother Sandra was paid the living wage, she wouldn't have to work around the clock to make ends meet, Tia would be able to see her in the evenings, they could have a family life.

Tia Sanchez made her plea as she stood alongside her mother and her grandmother Martha – both cleaners in Whitehall, both obliged to travel to work at dawn each morning – before hundreds of members of Citizens UK, a community organisation, and guest speakers Gordon Brown, then prime minister, and the leader of the opposition, David Cameron, both coming to the end of a general election campaign.

Brown was visibly moved by Tia's testimony. And Cameron responded positively. That was 2010. A year later the first living wage week was held, given cross-party support, and the Living Wage Foundation was established to advise, encourage and give accreditation to companies paying the voluntary living wage, then set at £8.30 in London, £7.20 outside the city, compared to a national minimum wage of £6.08 for over-18-year-olds.

By 2012, 432 companies had signed up to pay the living wage. The number had grown to more than 1,000 by 2014, including local authorities, unions and universities. Last week, Liverpool became the third Premier League club to commit to paying all employees, including casuals on match days, the real living wage, costing the club around £1m extra a year. (Chelsea and Everton also pay the living wage. The Premier League has a staggering £3.6bn turnover, so the shame is that the entire league isn't doing what is decent.)

Today, 3,600 companies have signed up, including Ikea, Oliver Bonas, Lidl and Lush, and a third of FTSE 100 companies are paying a real living wage of £8.45 an hour to everyone over 18 outside London and £9.75 in London.

The Observer has campaigned for the living wage for five years. The quiet heroes of the movement are the chambermaids, cleaners, security guards, carers, cooks and shop staff who have told their stories, battling to stretch a pitiful wage, often subjected to bullying and intimidation in the workplace, rotten conditions, stress and exhaustion. That's why the Real Living Wage campaign has never been simply about wage packets but always, also, about the rules of commitment that ought to prevail in a decent, fair society.

The national living wage is calculated at 55% of the median wage; it is compulsory on employers, it offers no London weighting, it excludes younger earners – and it is not enough. By contrast, the real living wage is calculated on the cost of living. Last year the Living Wage Commission reported that spiralling rents and snail-like wage growth mean that the national living wage is "failing to provide basic needs for the lowest paid."

Adapted from *The Guardian*, Sunday 5 November 2017.

Lexical work

Understanding the key words

→ Find the meaning of the following words and their lexical categories: living wage; around the clock; make ends meet; family life; cleaner; dawn; minimum wage; cross party support; give accreditation; unions; casuals; sign up; carers; shop staff; bullying; rotten; rules of commitment; median wage; compulsory; cost of living; rents.

→ Now, try to rephrase the title in your own words.

■ Boycott Cineworld Living wage protest, London, 25 Feb 2017.

I Read the whole text

1. Focus on the meaning of the following:
- living wage §1.
- minimum wage §3.
- median wage §7.

2. What is the difference between the three notions? Write and explain.

II Rephrase

3. Give the key ideas in each of the seven paragraphs in one or two sentences.

4. Focus on the last paragraph and explain the difference between the national living wage and the real living wage.

III Language

5. Translate into English:

a) Si les employés étaient mieux payés, la société serait plus juste.

b) Si les salaires étaient plus élevés, les employés pourraient payer leur loyer sans difficulté.

c) Si le salaire minimum était calculé sur le coût de la vie, les salariés seraient plus heureux.

d) Si sa mère ne travaillait pas 24 heures sur 24, sa fille la verrait davantage.

IV Train for the exam

6. Write an account of the document in French. (150 words)

7. Go further: Why is it important for a country to pay its workers a living wage?

Grammaire

▸ Le conditionnel

→ **If** her mother **was paid** the living wage, she **wouldn't have to work** around the clock.
→ *Si sa mère **recevait** un salaire décent, elle **n'aurait pas besoin** de travailler 24 heures sur 24.*

→ (If she **was paid** a living salary, Tia **would be able to see** her in the evening.
→ *Si elle **recevait** un salaire décent, Tia **serait en mesure de / pourrait** la voir le soir.*

→ **If** she **was paid** a living salary, they **could have** a family life.
→ *Elles **pourraient avoir** une vie de famille.*

(voir grammaire p. 205)

Role play

Work in pairs: Student A is a spokesperson for the Real Living Wage Campaign. He/she wants to persuade the Human Resources Manager of a famous company (Student B) to adopt the Real Living Wage Programme for the company's workers.
Student B is the Human Resources Manager of a famous company, aware of its brand image. He/she wants to know what the Real Living Wage is about and needs to be convinced that he/she can adopt it for his/her workers without putting the company's profits in danger.
TIPS: Students A and B may use the arguments developed in the document above as well as their own.

4 Text tracks

Before reading the text find out more about:

Anticipate at home
- Amnesty International;
- NGOs;
- Child labour;
- The companies involved.

Text piste 24

Children as young as seven mining cobalt used in smartphones

Amnesty International says it has traced cobalt used in batteries for household brands to mines in the Democratic Republic of Congo where children work in life-threatening conditions. Children as young as seven are working in perilous conditions in the Democratic Republic of the Congo to mine cobalt that ends up in smartphones, cars and computers sold to millions across the world, by household brands including Apple, Microsoft and Vodafone. The human rights group also claims to have traced cobalt used in lithium batteries sold to 16 multinational brands to mines where young children and adults are being paid a dollar a day, working in life-threatening conditions and subjected to violence, extortion and intimidation. More than half the world's supply of cobalt comes from the DRC. In 2012, Unicef estimated that there were 40,000 children working in all the mines in Africa.

In a joint-investigation with Afrewatch, an African NGO*, Amnesty International says it interviewed 90 adults and children working in five artisanal cobalt mine sites. Workers spoke of working for 12 hours a day with no protective clothing, and with many experiencing significant health problems as a result. The report says that child miners as young as seven carried back-breaking loads and worked in intense heat for between one or two dollars a day without face masks or gloves. Several children said they had been beaten by security guards employed by mining companies and forced to pay "fines" by unauthorised mine police sent by state officials to extort money and intimidate workers.

The human rights groups say they traced the supply chain from these mining sites to a subsidiary of Chinese mineral company Huayou Cobalt. The report says that Huayou Cobalt sources more than 40% of its cobalt from the DRC and processes the raw mineral before selling it to battery makers, who claim to supply companies including Apple, Microsoft and Vodafone.

Apple said it was currently evaluating whether cobalt in the company's products originated in the DRC. "Underage labour is not tolerated in our supply chain and we are proud to have led the industry in pioneering new safeguards," it says.

Vodafone, in its response to Amnesty, stated that the company "is unaware as to whether or not cobalt in our products originates in Katanga in the DRC." "What is very worrying is that none of the companies that we identified could trace the cobalt they use in their products back to the mines where it originated. Around half of all cobalt comes from the DRC, and no company can honestly claim that they are unaware of the human rights and child labour abuses linked with mineral extraction in the region," says Amnesty International.

"These are some of the biggest companies in the world, with combined profits of $125 billion, and there is no excuse that companies aren't investing some of that profit into ensuring that they can trace where the minerals they are using are coming from. Anyone with a smartphone would be horrified to think that children as young as seven carrying out back-breaking work for 12 hours a day could be involved at some point in the making of it."

Adapted from *The Guardian*, Tuesday 19 January 2016.

*NGO: Non Governmental Organisation (ONG : organisation non gouvernementale)

Lexical work

Understanding the key words

➜ Use a dictionary. Find the meaning of the following words. Find out their lexical category in the text.
back-breaking; brand; end up; child labour; claim; currently; fine; heat; household; human rights; life-threatening; load; process; raw; safeguard; significant; supply chain; unaware; underage.

➜ Pick up the words which can belong to several categories (ex: work: the noun/ work: the verb).

➜ Rephrase the title in your own words and write an introduction (source and date).

First track:
A step-by-step approach

I Read the text

1. Pick up the main idea(s) in each paragraph.

II Rephrase

2. Rephrase the idea(s) you have found in each paragraph.

III Language

3. Translate in to English:

a) Vodafone a dit que ses produits n'étaient pas fabriqués par des enfants.
b) Amnesty International est une ONG. Elle représente 7 millions d'adhérents dans le monde.
c) La firme Apple prétend qu'elle fera une enquête pour déterminer ses responsabilités.

IV Train for the exam

4. Use all the information above to report briefly to the class in French.

5. Write a 200 word account in English following the guidelines below:

§1 Introduction (source, date and main idea)
§2 Mining conditions in DRC denounced by Amnesty International
§3 The household brands involved
§4 Examples of horrible working conditions
§5 What measures household brands should take
§6 Conclusion: consumers' reaction

Grammaire

▶ Les pronoms personnels

- How to use **it** and **its**

→ Amnesty International says **it** has traced cobalt use in batteries.
→ ***Amnesty international*** *dit qu'****elle*** *a repéré des traces de cobalt dans les piles.*
(voir grammaire p. 205)

Second track:
A straightforward approach

I Read the whole text

1. Take down notes about what you believe is important.

II Rephrase

2. Organise your ideas a make a plan.

III Language

3. Translate into English:

a) Les ouvriers des mines de cobalt sont payés un dollar par jour.
b) Des millions de batteries sont vendues chaque jour dans le monde.
c) La firme Apple a été accusée par plusieurs ONG d'utiliser le travail des enfants pour fabriquer les batteries de ses smartphones.

4. Find other passive forms in the text, and translate them into French.

IV Train for the exam

5. Write an account of the article in French in 200 words.

6. Write a report OR make an oral presentation. Use the research you carried out before studying the text and investigate further to discuss the following topics:
- What could be done to abolish child labour?
- Can consumers have an impact on this issue? How?

Grammaire

▶ Le passif

→ Cars and computers **are sold** to millions **by household brands.**
→ *Les voitures et les ordinateurs* ***sont vendus*** *à des millions de personnes* ***par*** *des marques d'électroménager.*
(voir grammaire p. 200)

4 Video tracks

Common track

→ **Before you start watching the video:**

1. Anticipate on the title of the video.

2. Find out more about the International Labour Organization.

→ **Watch the video:**

3. Watch and try to hear and understand the following words: jeopardizing; health; growth; scourge; goal; deadline; garbage dump; unacceptable; steps; eradicate; aware; remain; entrenched; solvable; achieve; root; inequality; inadequate; poverty; commitments; fallen; worldwide; enforcement; labour law; perpetuate; rate; target.

4. Debrief with the other students and the teacher about their meaning.

Video vidéo 14

Ending child labour by 2016: the continuing challenge

http://www.ilo.org/global/about-the-ilo/multimedia/video/video-news-releases/WCMS_182910/lang--en/index.htm

Pronunciation work

→ **Listen, repeat the following words and record yourself:** footage; to jeopardize; health; scourge; appealing; crisis; cocoa; eradication; garbage.

First track:
A step-by-step approach

I Watch the whole video once

1. Write in French what it is about.

II Watch the video a second time

- Watch the first part (1'24):

2. When was this footage made and where?
3. What aspects of children's development are affected by this situation?
4. What goal did many countries agree on?
5. Has the deadline been respected?
6. Has child labour disappeared?
7. Why is progress slowing down?
8. What example of progress is given?

- Watch the second part (1'24 → end):

9. What industrial sectors are involved in the eradication of child labour?
10. According to Hilary Clinton, is the problem impossible to solve?
11. What issues should be addressed to eradicate child labour?
12. Recapitulate the elements that perpetuate the cycle of poverty.

III Train for the exam

13. **Oral report:** Put together all the information you have collected and report to the class.

Second track:
A straightforward approach

I Watch the whole video

1. After the first viewing, you are expected to have understood the general idea(s) exposed in the document. Write a short debrief.

II Watch the video a second time

2. Take notes and focus on how the different ideas are connected to one another.

III Train for the exam

3. Write an account of the video. In your conclusion, state your point of view.

Role play

Student A is a reporter interviewing a young boy (Joe) who has been helped out of child labour thanks to a NGO.
Student B is the young boy answering Student A's questions about his past and present life.

Tips for Student A:
Ask questions about Joe's former work, his working conditions, salary, etc.
Ask questions about his present life, and what he plans for the future.
Use the vocabulary you have learned for the video.

Tips for Student B:
Prepare yourself to answer all the above questions and more.
Use the vocabulary you have learned from the video.

Common track

I Before listening

1. Look at the photo. Can you tell the difference between an expat and an immigrant?
2. Find the definitions of both and explain the difference in your own words.
3. What is the purpose of this campaign?

II Anticipate

Anticipating the topic of audio

4. Before listening to the audio, look at the title and say as much as you can about:
- The American Dream;
- Canada's attitude towards immigration;
- The USA's current attitude towards immigration;
5. Look at the title and rephrase it.

Words, expressions, ideas you may hear

6. Listen and try to understand the following words:
account for; ageing; averages; bigotry; Brexit; foreign; GNP; fertility rate; highly skilled; labour force; look forward to; low skilled; newcomers; roots; share; skills; spokeswoman; standpoint; steal; threat.
7. Debrief with the other students and the teacher about their meaning.

Audio piste 25 Nathan live!

Canada: the new American dream?

Pronunciation work

→ **Listen, repeat the following words and record yourself:**
forward; threat; low-skilled; highly-skilled; skills; averages; authorities; bigotry; immigrants.

First track:
A step-by-step approach

I Listen to the whole audio

1. Write in French what it is about.

II Listen to the first part

2. Find out about the location of the interview, the person interviewed, his/her name and role in the audio.
3. Why does Canada encourage immigration?
4. Why has the USA stopped representing the "American Dream"?
5. What is Canadian people's attitude to immigration?
6. Which category of workers does Canada attracts?
7. Give a definition of Canadian culture.

III Listen to the second part

8. How many immigrants does Canada take in every year?
9. What are the figures for the years to come?
10. What explains this immigrant-friendly policy?
11. What does the spokeswoman think about the USA's standpoint on immigration?
12. What will the next programme focus on?

IV Train for the exam

13. **Oral report :** Put together all the information you have collected and report to the class.

Second track:
A straightforward approach

I Listen to the whole audio once

1. After the first listening, you are expected to have understood the general idea(s) exposed in the document. Write a short debrief.

II Listen to the whole audio a second time

2. Take notes and focus on how the different ideas are connected to one another.

III Train for the exam

3. Write an account of the audio. In your conclusion, state your point of view.

Role play

Student A and **Student B** are both Human Resource Managers in two different companies. They do not share the same view on workplace diversity:
Student A tries to convince Student B that diversity in the workplace is an asset for a company.
Student B doesn't believe in diversity. She/he counters Student A's arguments with her/his own.

Texte

Dans le Kentucky, les retraités-campeurs d'Amazon

Des travailleurs nomades convergent à l'automne vers les sites du géant du e-commerce pour préparer les colis de Noël. Longues journées garanties, pour 11 dollars de l'heure.

On était parti pour décrire l'univers de Charles Dickens adapté au XXIe siècle. L'exploitation de retraités américains, n'ayant pour maison que leur caravane, par le géant du commerce en ligne Amazon. On a surtout découvert des campeurs vagabonds, dignes des road-movies américains, rappelant l'errance en Alaska du héros de *Into the Wild* (2007) ou la cavale tragique de *Thelma et Louise* (1991).

Pourtant, des retraités passent l'automne en mobile-home et travaillent pendant dix heures comme manœuvres pour Amazon. Leur mission : sélectionner, empaqueter, expédier les colis de Noël qui sont ensuite distribués aux ménages américains. Pour 11 dollars de l'heure environ (soit 9,25 euros), le salaire minimal étant de 7 dollars, 25 dollars, avec un dollar de bonus pour ceux qui restent jusqu'au bout : le 23 décembre.

Les campeurs affluent, au début de l'automne, avec leur maison sur roues, et s'installent sur l'un des campings sélectionnés par Amazon. Ils sont des milliers, dans une trentaine d'États.

La route, motivation première

La route, c'est la motivation première des retraités salariés d'Amazon, à l'instar de Julie Criddle qui, munie d'un petit *package* pour sa retraite, a commencé par un voyage chez ses enfants, puis a fini par postuler chez Amazon dans le Kentucky pour gagner un peu d'argent. Des rotations de dix heures, cinq jours par semaine. Épuisantes. « Je ne le savais pas. Huit heures, ce serait OK », soupire-t-elle.

Heureusement, arrivée avant les fêtes de fin d'année, elle a pu pratiquer « l'endurcissement au travail », pour reprendre la terminologie d'Amazon. « En visitant les parcs nationaux, je faisais 10 000 pas par jour. Mais chez Amazon, c'est 26 000 ! », s'exclame Julie. « Il n'y a pas moyen de se préparer. Ce qui m'a sauvée, c'est la piscine du camping, qui était encore ouverte. » Comme un « bain glacé » pour les muscles endoloris. [...]

Julie a choisi de travailler la nuit. Sans doute ne retournera-t-elle pas chez Amazon l'an prochain : « Des amis ont fait une deuxième saison : ils nous ont dit que six mois chez Amazon, c'était trop. »

Appréciés par les « Amazoniens »

Les « campeurs » sont appréciés dans l'entreprise. « Les "Amazoniens" nous aiment parce que leurs bonus sont augmentés à la saison de pointe et que notre travail augmente leur chance de les obtenir », assure Kelly Murray, qui emballe les colis. Son mari poursuit : « Nous sommes très bien accueillis car nous apportons de l'énergie, de l'enthousiasme. Les campeurs sont une force de travail très fiable : nous sommes là chaque matin, nous sommes productifs, il n'y a pas de *turnover*. » D'autant plus fiables que leur mission est limitée, et qu'ils sont libres à chaque instant de reprendre la route. Amazon les bichonne.

Noël chez les « campeurs »

Chacun a apporté de quoi faire la fête et, glisse Joe Zihlman, ancien shérif adjoint de la banlieue de Dallas, « Amazon a fourni la dinde et le lard ». Après trente-six ans de loyaux services, cet ancien policier texan a pris sa retraite et la route, et ne dit que du bien du groupe américain. « Amazon traite mieux ses employés que beaucoup ne l'imaginent. » Les petits gestes maintiennent la bonne ambiance : cette semaine, il y a une télé grand écran à gagner par jour pour les employés.

Le 23 décembre, le camping de Green River fermera ses portes pour l'hiver et les campeurs s'égailleront pour fêter Noël en famille, puis hiverner dans le Sud, en Floride ou à Quartzsite, en plein désert d'Arizona, où ils sont des dizaines de milliers à converger fin janvier.

D'après *Le Monde*, 22 décembre 2017.

Common track

1. Find information about Charles Dickens.
2. Find information about the two films quoted in the first paragraph : « *Into the Wild* », « *Thelma and Louise* ». What do they have in common with the article?
3. What are the English words for:
retraités; salaire minimal; postuler; empaqueter; expédier; heures supplémentaires; force de travail; fiable; prendre sa retraite.

1. Identify the main topic in English.
2. Who are Amazon's campers?
3. Are they permanent employees?
4. What age group do they belong to?
5. What do they have in common?
6. How are they treated by Amazon?
7. How much do they earn?
8. Is the work easy?
9. Introduce the text in English.
10. Write one or two sentences in English for each paragraph in your own words (no translation).
11. Use your sentences to write a well-organised account of the article in English 180 words.

Go faster

I Read the whole document and suggest a title in English.

II Write one or two sentences in English in your own words for each paragraph.

III Write an organised account of the article in English. Do not forget the introduction and the conclusion. (200 words)

IV Would you rather be a camper or a telecommuter? Explain.

Role play

Student A is a reporter from a television network interviewing two employees at one of Amazon's warehouses about his/her working conditions.
Student B works as a seasonal employee for Amazon. He/she answers Student A's questions about his/her working conditions in the giant e-commerce company.
Student C works as a permanent employee at Amazon and answers questions about his/her working conditions. He/she doesn't always agree with Student B's point of view.

Debate

Group A : Students from group A support the view that Amazon is one of the worst employers in the USA in terms of salaries and working conditions.
Group B : Students from group B support a differnet view. Each group is expected to use information collected from the documents studied in class and also from their own research.

4 Tasks

Document 1 vidéo 15 — Video

China's robot workforce

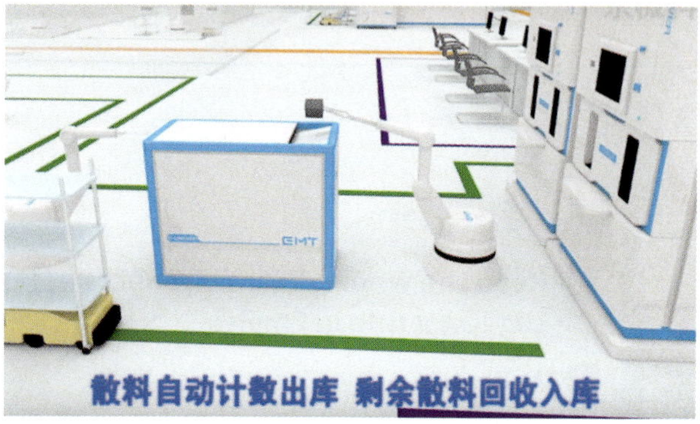

Word box

- automated/automation: *automatisé/ automatisation*
- solder (vb): *souder*

https://www.youtube.com/watch?v=wUAM-7jbhlw

Document 2 piste 26 — Text

No, that robot will not steal your job

Today, the unemployment rate in the developed world is down to 5.5%.This contradicts all the pessimistic warnings about a "jobless future."

There are jobs, jobs everywhere.

How is it that the aftermath of 2008 could lead to such a low unemployment rate? One answer is demographics: The world is aging, and the number of people entering the work force every year is slowing sharply. A striking example is Japan, which has one of the oldest and most rapidly aging populations in the world; the economy is barely growing, but the job market is booming.

Many of those new jobs are in fields that require creativity, language or motor skills not possessed by robots, like gardening, nursing, teaching and software programming. The pessimist's mistake is to focus too much on what is lost to competition and technology, and too little on what is gained. Over the past 25 years, experts have shown that about a third of the new jobs created in the United States were types that did not exist or barely existed 25 years ago. In the natural world, matter is neither created nor destroyed, but things are transformed. The same is true in the economic world. When new technology destroys, it leaves behind an empty ground in which new jobs grow.

In New York City the car replaced the horse carriage within the first 15 years of the 20th century, killing off the carriage trade and giving birth to the taxi trade – as well as to highly paid auto mechanics. Uber threatens the taxi trade, and the self-driving car threatens the Uber driver. But it has also brought multimillion-dollar bonuses for self-driving car engineers and created new opportunities for mechanics. There is no evidence to support forecasts of a nearly jobless future. If robots threatened human labour, human joblessness would be growing. But it is not. In fact, since 2008, job growth has been strongest in countries like Germany and Japan, which deploy the most robots.

Adapted from *The New York Times*, October 7, 2017.

Document 3 piste 27 — Audio

Could a robot do your job ?

Task 1 Video

Watch the video and answer:

1. Explain what is happening in many Chinese factories.
2 What can robots do today?
3. What will be the consequence of automation on China's workforce?
4. Organise all the information you have collected and write your report.

Task 2 Text

Read the text and answer:

1. Has the employment rate increased or decreased since 2008? Give examples from the text.
2. What can explain this phenomenon?
3. In what fields are the new jobs created?
4. What difficulties are some companies confronted with?
5. What is the article's stands point on automation?
6. Organise your ideas and make a plan.
7. Write an organised account of the article in English.

Task 3 Audio

1. Anticipate from the title.

Listen to the whole audio

2. Collecte key words, key data, key ideas.
3. Inquire about the meaning of utopia and dystopia.
4. Write an organised report. The following questions can help you:
   a) What are the jobs quoted in the audio that are being automated?
   b) What tasks are humanoid robots expected to perform?
   c) What is the difference between automation and Artificial Intelligence?

Task 4 Put in common

1. Making a plan: See how the three documents are related to one another.
   - Video 1 - The main ideas are:
   - Text 2 - the main ideas are:
   - Audio 3 - the main ideas are:
2. How are the ideas from each document related?
3. Write a final report which is a synthesis of the three documents.

4 Background

WORK: essential and unevenly distributed

The world's population needs to work in order to earn a salary enabling people to cater to their basic needs. But working conditions and earnings vary hugely depending on the continent or even the country people live in. Many countries do not impose a minimum salary, and many workers around the world work long hours for a starvation wage.

I Unemployment

Unemployment remains one of the major problems in many countries; a significant number of unskilled and low skilled employees are being replaced by machines, while some companies have difficulties in finding highly qualified staff.

II Permanent or fixed term

The number of permanent jobs is declining, and many employees start their working life with fixed term contracts.

III Temping

A growing number of companies resort to temporary workers (aka temps) who complete the workforce when there is a peak in demands or to replace sick leaves.

IV Lay-offs

When companies' results are not satisfactory, or when they are facing financial problems, when they want to please their shareholders, or when they relocate, they can decide to suppress jobs by laying-off part of the workforce.

V Working hours

In France, employees work 35 hours a week on average, and get five weeks of paid holidays a year. The working hours, except for some sectors, are office hours, the usual 9 am to 6 pm. Employees, except the ones in managerial positions, have to clock in and to clock out every working day. Some companies and institutions (hospitals, etc.) operate around the clock. The employees there work in shifts. Many employees do overtime or extra hours in order to improve their living standard.

VI Full-time vs part-time

Some employees choose to work part-time, but others do involuntary part-time.

VII Work placement and training

During their studies, most students are required to perform a certain number of work placements, or internships, designed to train them for their future jobs. These training periods allow students to understand how theoretical knowledge can be put into practice.

VIII Teleworking and work life balance

Traffic congestion, weather conditions and the continuous progress of new technologies have driven many companies to resort to telecommuting for their employees, which allows them to save commuting time and organise their private lives in order to reach a better work life balance. Yet, digital nomads have a hard time separating their private life from their life at work.

IX Trade unions

Trade unions' role is to defend workers. They stand up for their working conditions, working hours, safety and wages. Unions can initiate and organise social movements such as strikes and demonstrations when corporate decisions imply job cuts, relocation or restructuring.

X Work in the EU: the consequences of Brexit

EU citizens have the right to work in the country of their choice. With Brexit under way, European citizens living in the UK do not know what their future is going to be like. Likewise, the 140 000 permanent British residents in France are considering either going back to the UK or applying for the French nationality.

XI Immigrant workers

Unlike what is often claimed, foreign workers represent less than 1% of most countries' workforce. They contribute to the wealth and growth of the country they reside in.

Question time

1. Is teleworking a solution to a better work life balance?
2. What is the role of trade unions?
3. What could be the consequences of Brexit on EU citizens living in the UK?
4. Why do companies often hire temps?
5. What is the aim of a work placement?
6. Do all part-time employees do it by choice?

➥ Vocabulary p. 102

Trends

Workplace plights

1. Burn-out

The work-related disease identified as "burn-out" can be generated by too much pressure put on staff by managers. Today, a growing number of executives have understood that corporate performance is related to the employees well-being, and have taken measures to prevent burn-outs among their staff.

2. Harassment and bullying

Harassment and bullying at work are considered a serious problem affecting the harassed or bullied staff's health on the long term, sometimes causing suicides. Harassment like bullying is hard to prove as most bullies are experts in not leaving any evidence behind. Harassment or bullying is attested if one or several of the following patterns are identified:

- spreading malicious rumours,
- unjustified criticism aimed at undermining you,
- racist or homophobic comments or jokes,
- pranks,
- unjustified threats about your job,
- physical violence,
- humiliating behaviour,
- unwelcome sexual advances or comments.

3. Employment discrimination

is a form of discrimination based on race, gender, religion, national origin, physical or mental disability, age, sexual orientation, and gender identity by employers. It is extremely difficult for the victims of discrimination to sue because employers never resort to it openly. Unfortunately, in many countries still today, a job seeker from a different ethnic group will see his/her application refused twice as often as the one of a native.

4. Gender pay gap: Women in managerial position are more exposed to the gender pay gap

The gender pay gap is the difference between the salaries of men and women occupying similar jobs; it appears to widen simultaneously with the job qualification: the higher the qualification, the wider the pay gap between men and women.

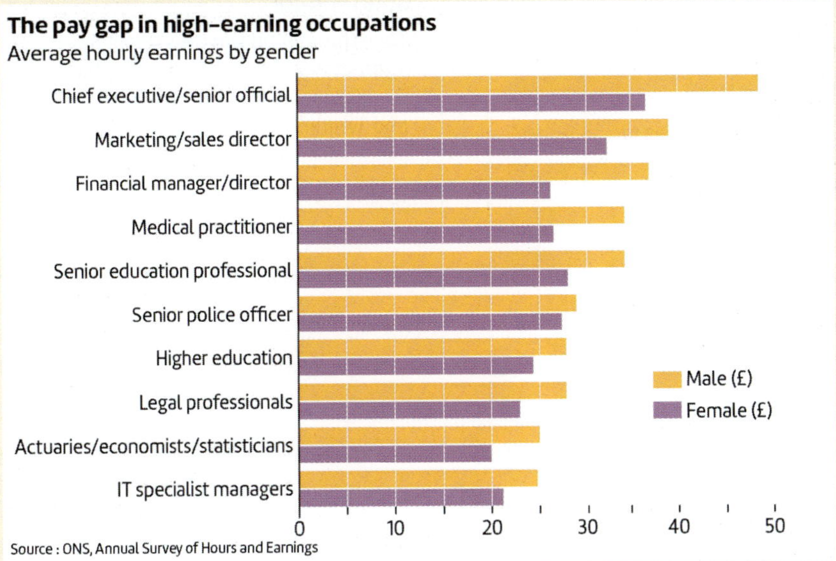

Here is a 2017 chart from the BBC.

Questions

- Comment on the chart to the left.
- Explain what is discrimination in the workplace.

Google's SWOT

	Favourable	Unfavourable
Internal	**Strengths** • **Market leader in search engines** ▪ Perhaps the biggest strength of Google is that it is the undisputed leader in search engines. • **The best company to work for** ▪ For the sixth year running, Google is at the top of the list of the USA's Best Companies to Work For. ▪ It offers many perks to its employees, as well as a number of social benefits such as parental leaves. ▪ A champion of diversity, the company wishes to provide a safe and inclusive environment to its staff. • **Introduction of Android and mobile technologies** ▪ Adoption of Android and mobile technologies makes it a direct competitor of Apple.	**Weaknesses** • **Overdependence on advertising** ▪ Google's business model relies heavily on advertising: the numbers reveal that it gets more than 85% of its revenues from ads alone. ▪ High employee turnover rate at executive positions. ▪ Sharing users' personal information.
External	**Opportunities** • **Android Operating System** ▪ Google provides the Android OS (Operating System) which has resulted in its becoming a direct competitor to Apple and Samsung. • **Google Glasses and Google Play** ▪ Google Glasses and Google Play promises to be a game changer for Google and this is a significant opportunity that the company can exploit. • **Cloud Computing** ▪ Cloud Computing remains a key opportunity for Google as it is already experienced in providing storage and cloud solutions.	**Threats** • **Competition from Facebook** • **Social Media** ▪ have threatened Google's dominance in the internet world and the company has to deal with the increasing features available on Facebook and Twitter.

SWOT

Test yourself

After having studied this unit, you must be able to answer the following questions…

1. What tools do companies use to recruit their employees?
2. Give a definition of teleworking.
3. What is the difference between the minimum wage and a living wage?
4. What products are involved in child labour?
5. Which companies should address the problem?
6. What are the other activities using children?
7. What is Canada’s policy towards immigrants?
8. Why are some nationals afraid of immigration?
9. Which company do “campers’ work for?
10. Who are they?
11. What is automation?
12. Why is automation a controversial issue?
13. What does “diversity” in the workplace mean?
14. What is temping?
15. What can be the consequences of workplace harassment?
16. What are the advantages of working for Google?

Question time

1. What do you have to say about these jobs?
2. Translate the poster (Waterloo station) into French and comment.

The workplace should be more accessible to people with disabilities

Entering the job market after leaving education can prove a tough challenge for anyone in today's climate. However, young people with disabilities face far fewer options for employment than non-disabled candidates. Across the UK, only 6% of young people with learning difficulties are in employment, and according to Disability Rights UK, employees with disabilities earn nearly £1 an hour less than non-disabled workers.

The 2010 Equality Act was brought into practice partly to prevent discrimination against disabled people in the workplace. Yet disabled workers are often still unfairly treated. So what more must be done to ensure best practices?

The challenges facing disabled employees in the UK today

Liz Sayce is Chief Executive of Disability Rights UK, an organisation committed to enabling equal participation for people with disabilities. She says: "Some disabled people have applied for hundreds of jobs – and only got interviews when they don't mention their disability," she explains.

Many disabled employees face reluctance from employers to make any adjustments to their workplace, however necessary. This resistance can undermine those working with disabilities and discourage them from applying to work in certain institutions. There is a fear that organisations, teams and individuals may not be equipped with skills or knowledge to support them, and some employers don't know how to make workplace adjustments. This reduces the opportunities available to workers with disabilities.

How can companies and organisations encourage people with disabilities to join their workforce?

Sayce explains that if employers recruit and promote on the basis of strength and potential – rather than qualifications or experience which is not entirely necessary to the role – they will help attract and retain talented workers with disabilities.

Birmingham Children's Hospital offers training and employment opportunities to young people who are disadvantaged. Its Aspire programme has a close relationship with a local school that supports young people with special educational needs. "Aspire helps people develop skills that can be used in the workplace," explains the programme's spokesperson. "We look to build confidence, assertiveness, life skills and support positive health and well-being, which we believe prepares these young people to live independently." The programme has proven successful to date, seeing eight young people with learning disabilities into paid positions within the hospital, and the Aspire model has been shared with other NHS* institutions.

It is also important that companies adapt the recruitment process to aid those applying with disabilities. While it might not be easy to initiate an inclusion scheme in your workplace, Sayce insists the first step is to find a way of being proactive. "This might mean setting a goal for how many disabled people you want to recruit and then going for it," she says, also suggesting other helpful options such as drawing links with schools, offering mentoring schemes or interview practice to students with disabilities. Sayce also stresses the importance of being flexible, for example offering part-time apprenticeships over a longer period if this fits better with the candidate's needs.

Adapted from *The Guardian*, April 17, 2017.

*NHS: National Health Service: *le service de santé public au Royaume-Uni (hôpital public)*

I Compréhension de l'écrit

Write an account of the article in French (180 words +/– 10%).

II Expression écrite

Why are companies reluctant to hire disabled employees? Give your own point of view. You can illustrate your essay with examples. (150 words minimum)

III Interaction écrite

Élaboration d'une demande de stage en anglais

Rédigez en anglais une lettre de motivation à une entreprise auprès de laquelle vous souhaiteriez effectuer un stage. Vous respecterez l'usage en vigueur et vous n'oublierez pas de mentionner vos noms, prénoms et adresse, ainsi que le nom de l'entreprise auprès de laquelle vous postulez. Vous n'oublierez pas de dater votre courrier. Vous suivrez le plan suivant :

- **Objet** : demande de stage.
- Donnez des informations brèves et claires sur les études que vous faites actuellement et sur votre souhait d'effectuer un stage (durée).
- Mentionnez votre expérience de terrain éventuelle et donnez la nature du stage que vous désirez effectuer (service, mission, domaine, etc.).
- Expliquez les raisons qui vous motivent à demander ce stage.
- Présentez brièvement vos principaux points forts (ou principales qualités).
- Dites que vous restez à disposition pour d'autres informations vous concernant.
- Remerciez d'avance de l'attention que le destinataire pourra vous porter.
- Salutations d'usage.

➥ Voir Tools page 208

1 Indian technology workers worry about a job threat: technology

PUNE, India — Last month, Sudhakar Choudhari took the company bus as usual from his one-bedroom apartment to the suburban offices of Tech Mahindra, a major employer of workers in India that powers the global technology machine behind the scenes. Then a manager took him into a conference room and asked him to resign.

"It was a terrible scene for me," said Mr. Choudhari, 41, who had been with the company for 11 years and most recently maintained software for a British client. As the manager spoke, he thought: "I have an 11-year-old child. My wife is not working. How to pay the home loans?"

Mr. Choudhari is one of a number of Indian technology workers who have lost their jobs in recent months as many in India debate whether an industry that has long served as a gateway to the middle class is preparing to shed jobs en masse. India's information technology industry grew at a very fast speed over the past two decades thanks to the trend commonly called offshoring or outsourcing. The industry and related businesses generate more than $150 billion in annual revenue and employ about four million people to build and test software, to enter and analyse data, and to provide customer support for American and European companies looking for relatively inexpensive labour.

But the global tech industry is increasingly relying on automation, robotics, big data analytics, machine learning and consulting — technologies that threaten to bypass and even replace Indian workers. For example, automated processes may soon replace the kind of work Mr. Choudhari was performing for foreign clients, which involved maintaining software by occasionally plugging in simple code and analysing data.

"What we are seeing is an acceleration in shedding for jobs in India," said Sandra Notardonato, an analyst and research vice-president for Gartner, a research and advisory company. "Even if these companies don't have huge net losses, there is a person who will suffer, and that is a person with a limited skill set in India."

Such job losses could be politically damaging to the government of Prime Minister Narendra Modi, who won an electoral mandate in 2014 on the promise of development and employment for a bulging youth population. In January, near the three-year mark of his administration, an economic survey reported that job creation had stalled.

So far, the scale of the impact is not clear. Yet, a 2015 study released by the National Association of Software and Services Companies, the Indian technology industry trade group known as Nasscom, and McKinsey India found that 50 to 70 percent of workers' skills would be irrelevant by 2020. Of course, new technologies will create new jobs. The impact of automation and artificial intelligence still is not clear, and they could open up new areas that simply shift tech work rather than eliminate it.

Adapted from *The New York Times*, June 25, 2017.

Expression orale

1. Prepare a one-minute oral report of the document in English.
2. Prepare to branch out on the following topics: outsourcing, automation and job creation.

2 The future of the workplace: no office

piste 28

II Audio

I. Listen to the whole document once and answer the questions

1. What sort of document is it?
2. What is the name of the programme?
3. What is the main topic?

II. Listen to the document a second time and answer the following questions

4. What is the new workplace like?
5. In which company does Jose Santiago work?
6. What was he doing when the journalist met him?
7. What other company is mentioned?
8. Where do executives meet?

III. Listen to the document a third time

9. What was the office like in old times?
10. How does the reporter conclude the programme?
11. Did listeners react to the programme? How?
12. Explain why some people are against the virtual office.

IV. Reporting on what you have understood

13. Now report to the class or to a group about the audio and give your own opinion on the topic.

Vocabulary

applicant (n): *candidat*
application (n): *candidature*
apply (for a job) (vb): *postuler*
automation (n): *automatisation*
benefit(s) (n): *allocation, avantages sociaux*
career (n): *carrière*
casual (n): *employé(e) embauché (e) comme "extra"*
casual Friday: *tenue décontractée du vendredi*
child labour: *travail des enfants*
clock in/out (vb): *pointer*
commute (n): *temps de trajet pour se rendre au travail*
commute (vb): *utiliser un moyen de transport du domicile au travail*
commuter (n): *usager des transports*
cover letter: *lettre de motivation*
employ (vb): *employer*
employee (n): *employé(e)*
employer (n): *employeur*
employment (n): *emploi*
fixed term job/contract: *CDD*
full time job/contract: *contrat à temps plein*
gap (n): *fossé, écart*
hardworking (adj): *qui travaille dur*
health insurance: *assurance maladie*
highly skilled (adj): *hautement qualifié(e)*
hire (vb): *recruter, embaucher*
human resource manager: *DRH*
internship: *stage*
job interview: *entretien d'embauche*
job (n): *travail, emploi*
jobless (adj): *sans emploi*
joblessness (n): *chômage*
knowhow (n): *savoir-faire*
knowledge (n): *connaissance (théorique)*
lay-off (vb/n): *licencier, licenciement*
leisure (n): *loisir, temps libre*
low skilled (adj): *peu qualifié(e)*
maternity leave: *congé maternité*
night shift: *travail/horaire de nuit*
occupation (n): *profession*
odd job: *« petit boulot », généralement pour étudiants*
outsource (vb): *externaliser*
overtime/extra hours: *heures supplémentaires*
paid holidays: *congés payés*
parental leave: *congé parental*
part-time: *temps partiel*
pension (n): *allocation retraite*
pensioner (n): *retraité(e)*
perk (n): *avantage en nature*
permanent job: *CDI*
position (n): *poste (dans une entreprise)*
retraining: *reconversion*
recruit (v): *recruter*
redundancy (n): *licenciement économique*
relocate (vb): *délocaliser*
resume/CV (n): *CV*
retire (vb): *prendre sa retraite*
retirement (n): *retraite*
salary (n): *salaire*
shift (n), to work in shifts: *rotation/travailler par rotation*
sick leave: *congé maladie*
skill (n): *compétence*
skilled (n): *qualifié(e)*
staff (n): *personnel (d'une entreprise)*
supervisor (n): *tuteur*
team work: *travail d'équipe*
telecommuting: *télétravail*
teleworking: *télétravail, travail à distance*
temp (n) (*abréviation* de temporary worker): *intérimaire*
temping: *intérim*
to be unemployed: *être au chômage, sans emploi*
to call in sick: *se mettre en maladie*
train (vb): *former*
trainee/intern (n): *stagiaire*
training period: *formation pratique*
unemployment (n): *chômage*
union (trade/labour union) (n): *syndicat*
unskilled (adj): *non qualifié(e)*
wage (n): *salaire*
work life balance: *équilibre vie privée/vie au travail*
work placement: *stage*
worker (n): *ouvrier(ère), salarié(e), employé(e)*
workforce (n): *main-d'œuvre*
working conditions: *conditions de travail*
working cost (n): *coût salarial*
working hours: *horaires de travail*
workplace (n): *lieu de travail*

5 Passengers and commuters

Question

What are all these people doing?

Word box

- commuting: *trajet de la maison au travail*
- time consuming: *chronophage*
- stressful: *générateur de stress*

Anticipate at home

The stress of commuting VIDÉO 16

Nathan live!

https://www.youtube.com/watch?v=ofTxs4VUTQI

? What does the study show about commuting?

5 » Starters

The class is divided into several groups: a group will study document 1, another document 2, a further one document 3 and the last one document 4.

Group 1

Document 1

A Tube for cars? Proposal to bury London's traffic says it is "next best thing to teleportation"

The proposed CarTube supposedly reclaims streets for people by moving cars on to an underground network of automated routes. But do these transport ideas mean the "smart city" is going backwards or forwards?

We have seen the road-straddling bus that glides over lanes of traffic, and bike paths in abandoned Tube tunnels. Now here is the latest radical transport idea to transform our cities: putting cars in tunnels.

Dreamt up by Lars Hesselgren and his research team at London-based architecture practice PLP, and announced today at the Institution of Mechanical Engineers, the CarTube proposal reflects the company's motto: "Streets are for people, not cars." The solution to achieve this? Move a city's cars underground on to a network of tracks in small-bore tunnels, creating more safe space at ground level for bicycles and pedestrians.

■ Adapted from *The Guardian*, February 21, 2017.

1. Identify the document.
2. How does London plan to turn itself into a smart city?

Group 2

Document 2 vidéo 17 Nathan live!

Has Ryanair cut too close for comfort?

https://www.youtube.com/watch?v=eI3mvZ-KXRs

1. Identify the document.
2. Watch the video and take down notes.
3. Write a seven-line summary of what you understood.

Group 3

Document 3

The cost of going a mile

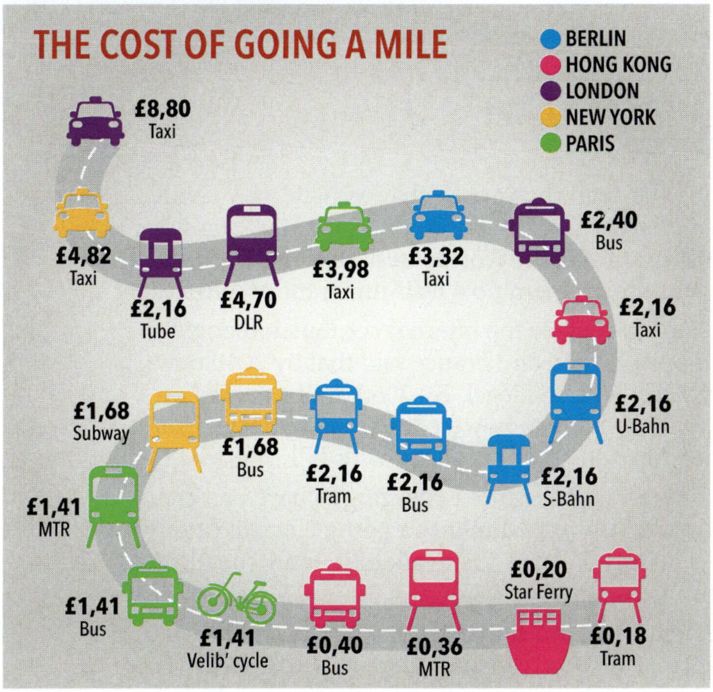

1. Identify the document.
2. What does this graphic show?
3. How many countries are mentioned?
4. What are the means of transport represented?
5. Which ones are the cheapest?
6. Which ones are the most expensive?
7. Which country offers the cheapest way to travel?
8. Which country offers the most expensive way to travel?

Group 4

Document 4

EasyJet "could be flying electric planes within a decade"

UK-based airline has linked up with US firm Wright Electric to build battery-powered aircrafts for flights under two hours.

EasyJet could be flying electric planes within a decade, the airline said on Wednesday.

The UK carrier has formed a partnership with US firm Wright Electric, which is developing a battery-propelled aircraft for flights under two hours.

EasyJet said that the move would enable battery-powered aircrafts to travel short-haul routes such as London to Paris or Edinburgh to Bristol.

■ Adapted from *The Guardian*, September 27, 2017.

1. Identify the document and explain what EasyJet is investing in.
2. What can explain EasyJet's decision?

Put in common

→ Each group reports to the class, while the others take notes.
→ Use your notes and recapitulate: What are the common links between the four documents?
→ What can you deduce?

5 Prep page

Anticipate at home

Before reading the text, investigate:
- What is needed to charge electric vehicles? Why is it an obstacle for potential electric car buyers?

Text piste 29

Charging electric vehicles takes shape

A NEW phrase, "range anxiety"–the fear that an electric vehicle (EV) will run out of power before it reaches a charging-point–entered the Oxford English Dictionary in 2013. At the time a Nissan LEAF, the world's best-selling EV, could travel only 120km between charges. But the problem now feels much more soluble.

Many governments are pushing hard to replace the internal combustion engine (ICE) with cleaner EVs–this summer both Britain and France said that by 2040 new cars completely reliant on petrol or diesel will be illegal. By 2050, half the cars on the road globally, a billion in total, will be battery-powered. Falling battery costs mean that the total cost of EV ownership will soon hit parity with ICE models.

Surveys show, however, that car buyers' worries about charging–where you can do it, and how long it will take–remain a big impediment to going electric (after high prices). Unless buyers can be reassured about the availability and speed of charging, the EV revolution may progress slowly.

Better EV batteries with greater capacity are helping. A range of 190km or more is now the norm. As ownership of EVs spreads, another reassuring fact is becoming clear: the amount of daily driving that people actually do, combined with an ability to charge at home, mean public charging facilities are rarely needed. Four out of five Europeans drive less than 100km a day. The average daily distance a car covers in Britain, for example, is less than 40km. Americans cover around 70km a day.

So far, most EVs have been bought by better-off motorists, who usually have off-street parking with a socket to plug into. Over 90% of charging is currently done at home, carmakers say. Yet mass adoption of EVs will mean appealing to the millions of households without garages. Nor can people on long road trips rely on better batteries alone. But in most places the system needs to expand to provide enough chargers of the right capacities in the right locations.

Carmakers, governments and commercial charging firms are all investing. Tesla plans to expand its global network of 145KW "supercharger" stations to 10,000. These public facilities can replenish the firm's larger batteries to 80%-charged in 40 minutes. Several other carmakers are also rolling out their own fast-charging networks. Officials in London recently announced plans for 1,500 new charging-points by 2020. France, Germany, the Netherlands and Norway are among the countries that have launched initiatives to improve access to public charging. China's government is set on remaining the largest market for electric cars: this year alone it is installing 800,000 public charging-points.

Companies that provide charging services are investing large sums as more EVs hit the road. Pat Romano of Chargepoint, based in California, sees workplace charging as another way of filling the charging gap. He notes that for a few thousand dollars spent on the equipment, plus a cost for electricity, employers can offer workers free charging in the office car park.

So there seems little likelihood that a lack of infrastructure will hold back the spread of Evs.

Adapted from *The Economist*, September 7, 2017.

Lexical work

Understanding the key words

→ Find the meaning of the following words and expressions and their lexical categories verb, pronoun, adjective, etc.): run out of power; reliant on; hit parity with impediment; better-off; socket to plug into; household; rolling out; workplaces.

→ Now try to rephrase the title with your own words.

Ⅰ Read the whole text

1. Pick up the names of the famous carmakers and find out what types of cars they make.
2. Write a sentence about the charging stations. Some are public and some are not. Explain.
3. Write one sentence about the current electric car buyers.

Ⅱ Rephrase

4. List countries that are mentioned and what they plan to do.

Ⅲ Language

5. Translate into French:
   battery-powered cars; petrol-powered cars; charging stations; public charging facilities; charging time; charging points.
6. Translate into English:
   un bâtiment fonctionnant à l'éolien ; un quartier fonctionnant à l'énergie solaire ; une station de charge rapide ; un restaurant qui vend des plats à emporter.

Ⅳ Train for the exam

7. Write a detailed plan of the document in French.
8. **Go further:** Will electric cars replace gas-powered cars? What would make it possible? Who are the players, who will make it happen?

Grammaire

▸ Les adjectifs composés

Comment éviter les phrases complexes ?

→ Gas-powered cars
→ *Voitures alimentées à l'essence*

(voir grammaire p. 199)

Role play

Work in pairs: Student A tries to convince a government member that moving to electric cars is the solution to global warming.

Student B is not willing to admit states should finance parts of the development of charging stations.

Student A tips

EVs are the future; public transport; global warming; COP 21; etc.

Student B tips

Technological outbreak; rethink cities and the cityscape; car parks; investment; people's mentalities; speed; freedom; etc.

Anticipate at home

Before reading the text find out more about:

- The different means of transport in large cities.
- How long it takes the students in your class to go to school everyday, and what means of transport they use.
- Why so many people working in Paris live far from their workplace?

Text piste 30

Commuting is now a fact of life

We just need to make it less awful.

Better transport links would mean easier commutes and less overcrowded transport in cities, as workers opt for cheaper housing further from their workplaces. Nearly 180,000 people commute into Manchester every day, outnumbering both the 100,000 who live and work in the same borough and the 15,000 Mancunians[1] who work from home. In the London borough of Tower Hamlets, 79% of the working population live in another borough: fewer than 500 live and work in the borough. Workers come from far afield–44 people commute in from the southernmost tip of Cornwall, 14 fly from Belfast and two from Shetland. Commuting is now a fact of life for millions of Britons and the days of walking from home to work in 15 minutes have been relegated to the past. The Trades Union Congress reports that the length of our commutes has also risen: more than three million people now commute for more than two hours a day.

Millions of people spend two or more hours commuting a day

Study for the TUC blames house prices which have affected women more than men. High house prices in the south-east have forced many people out of the capital and into longer commutes. Other cities experience the same thing: Oxford schools struggle to fill teaching jobs as rents rise and housing costs far outstrip wage increases. Key worker[2] housing can help, but without better infrastructure, cities become crowded and quality of life continues to suffer. With better transport links, the pace of life becomes easier: if you could move to a larger house in a quieter, cheaper area and have a reasonable commute, millions of people would happily do it.

Instead, thousands of people are stuck in a lose-lose situation. Extreme commutes mean relying on expensive childcare and spending less time with family. Technology has enabled a rise in teleworking, but most new jobs are created in locations where many people are still forced to spend hours on packed trains. Better transport links could help everyone. Many people want to live in London but many would leave if it was practical. Making it easier to reach big cities would take the pressure off housing markets in many parts of the country, meaning fewer people are forced out, and those who want to live further from the office can get in quickly.

But the problems for commuters are longstanding. Research by the Scottish government in 2006 reported concerns about public transport costs, overcrowding and a lack of linked-up infrastructure, meaning trains and buses often failed to serve long-distance commuters. Instead, many people turned to cars but felt the road system had not kept up with changing use.

As more families cash-in and move out of the capital, the estate agent Savills has calculated the savings in house prices per minute per train journey: commuters save £3,000 on property each minute further out of London.

Adapted from *The Guardian*, Thursday 28 April, 2016.

1. Mancunians: an inhabitant of Manchester.

2. key worker: a public sector employee considered to provide an essential service: nurses, policemen, firemen, bus drivers, etc.

Lexical work

Understanding the key words

→ Find their meanings and what each of them is (ex: a noun, a verb, an adjective, etc.): commute, commuter, outnumber; housing; outstrip, longstanding; linked-up; rail network; rent; lose-lose situation; cash-in.

→ Rephrase the title with your own words.

First track: A step-by-step approach

I Read the text
1. Pick up the main idea(s) in each paragraph.

II Rephrase
2. Write an introduction to the article in your own words.
3. Use all the information above to report briefly to the class in French.

III Language
4. Translate into English:

a) Les voitures électriques sont meilleures pour la santé publique.
b) Les salariés habitent de plus en plus loin des centres-villes.
c) L'accès aux transports en communs est plus facile à Paris qu'en banlieue.

IV Train for the exam
5. Write a 180 word account in English following the guidelines below.

§1 Introduction (document: source and date)
§2 The importance of commuting today and who are the people involved
§3 What makes commuting unpleasant
§4 Where people live and work today and why commuting is necessary
§5 The example of the situation in London
§6 What happens when people turn to cars
§7 Conclusion

Grammaire

▶ Les comparatifs

→ **Better** transport links would mean **easier** commutes. → *De **meilleures** correspondances impliqueraient des trajets plus faciles.*

→ Housing is ***less*** expensive in Manchester **than** in London. → *Le logement est **moins** cher à Manchester **qu'**à Londres.*

→ Urban transport are getting **better and better**. → *Les transports urbains vont **de mieux en mieux**.*

→ Housing is **more and more** expensive. → *Le logement est **de plus en plus** cher.*

→ Gasoline cars are **less and less** popular. → *Les voitures à essence sont **de moins en moins** populaires.*

(voir grammaire p. 199)

Second track: A straightforward approach

I Read the whole text
1. Read the whole text and take down notes about what you believe is important.

II Rephrase
2. Organise your ideas and make a plan.
3. Write an account of the article in English in 190 words.

III Language
4. Translate into English:

a) Aujourd'hui, moins de gens prennent leur voiture pour aller au travail.
b) La pollution est en baisse. Il y en a moins dans les grandes villes qu'il y a dix ans.
c) Moins de transports publics signifie plus de temps de trajet.
d) Les trajets seraient plus agréables s'il y avait moins de monde dans les métros et les bus.

IV Train for the exam
5. Write a report OR make an oral presentation. Use the research you carried out before and during the study of the document.
6. Investigate further to discuss the following topic: What solutions could be found to solve the commuting problems in big cities and in the suburbs?

Grammaire

▶ La comparaison quantitative (plus/moins de)

→ Spending **less time** with family. → *Passer **moins de temps** avec la famille (en famille).*

→ **Fewer** people are forced out. → ***Moins de** gens sont contraints à partir (du centre des villes).*

→ **Fewer** than 500 live in the borough → ***Moins de** 500 (personnes) vivent dans l'arrondissement.*

→ There are **fewer** people **than** before → *Il y a **moins de** gens qu'auparavant.*

(voir grammaire p. 199-200)

5 Video tracks

Common track

→ Before you start watching the video:

1. Explain what cruise ships are and why they attract so many tourists.

→ Anticipate the topic of video:

2. Look at the title and think about the ways in which cruise ships have an impact on the environment.

→ Watch the video:

3. Write down among the following list the words you hear: ocean liners; disaster fuel oil; diesel; hazardous; waste; emit; incinerator; harmful; average; demands; amount; ports; pollution; particles; spread; increase; container; rise; levels; sulphur; suppliers; greener.

Pronunciation work

→ Listen, repeat the following words and record yourself: environment; luxury liner; powered; harmful; diesel; hazard waste; harmful substances; huge; container ship; emit; cruises.

Video vidéo 18 Nathan live!

How bad for the environment are cruise ships?

https://www.youtube.com/watch?v=yl5xYm-0hvo&feature=youtu.be

First track:
A step-by-step approach

I Watch the whole video once

1. Write in French what it is about.

II Watch the video a second time

2. How many people per year spend their holidays on a cruise ship?
3. Give the reasons why cruise ships are considered a "disaster."
4. Quote facts and figures.
5. Explain why cruise ships continue to pollute when they are at ports.
6. Explain what means of transport is the most polluting.
7. Compare by quoting figures.
8. Explain the solutions that could be adopted and their impacts on the consumers.

III Train for the exam

9. **Oral report:** Put together all the information you have collected and report to the class.

Second track:
A straightforward approach

I Watch the whole video once

1. After the first viewing, you are expected to have understood the general idea(s) exposed in the document. Write a short debrief.

II Watch the video a second time

2. Take notes and focus on how the different ideas are connected to one another.

III Train for the exam

3. Write an account of the video. In your conclusion, state your point of view.

Role play

Student A is planning to go on a cruise trip to the Caribbeans and wants Student B to come with him/her.
Student B is touched by Student A's invitation but he/she is against cruise travels for environmental reasons.
Students A and B are discussing the issue.

Tips student A: wonderful landscapes; discover; meet new friends; enjoy; once in a lifetime; good value for money; etc.

Tips Student B: aggravating the carbon footprint; polluting the oceans; no time to enjoy the stops; no real mingling with the local population; etc.

5 Audio tracks

Common track

I Before listening

1. Find out about the Caribbeans and add information.

II Anticipate the topic of the audio

2. Look at the title and rephrase it.

III Words, expressions, ideas you may hear

3. Listen and write the words you hear among the list below:
autumn; build; collapse; damaged; emergencies; gross domestic product; hurricane; infrastructure; income; island; lifeblood; material; purchase; race; rebuilding; recover; roof; season; shortage; storm; tourism; tempest; typhoon.

Audio piste 31 Nathan live!

Will the Caribbeans ever recover after the hurricanes?

Pronunciation work

→ **Listen, repeat the following words and record yourself:** the Caribbean islands; hurricane; graveyard; island of Barbuda; entire; shortages; immmediate; emergencies.

First track: A step-by-step approach

Listen to the whole audio once

I 1. Write in French what it is about.

Listen to the first part

II 2. Collect information on:

a) Places where the hurricanes hit.
b) Names of the hurricanes.
c) Consequences of the hurricanes.

3. Say what the following figures correspond to:

a) 2.3 million
b) 95 percent
c) 90 percent
d) $1.43 billion

III Listen to the second part

4. What is the new place referred to?

5. What comes first before rebuilding the tourism industry?

6. What does the figure $8 correspond to?

7. What is special about Saint Barthelemy?

IV Train for the exam

8. **Oral report:** Put together all the information you have collected and report to the class.

Second track: A straightforward approach

I Listen to the whole audio once

1. After the first listening, you are expected to have understood the general idea(s) exposed in the document. Write a short debrief.

II Listen to the whole audio a second time

2. Take notes and focus on how the different ideas are connected to one another.

III Train for the exam

3. Write an account of the audio. In your conclusion, state your point of view.

Role play

Student A is a journalist reporting from the Caribbeans where a hurricane has devastated many holiday resorts.

Student B is a hotel manager whose hotel has been seriously damaged by the hurricane. He/she is answering Student A's questions and explaining how he/she intends to save the next touristic season a couple of months away.

Texte

Décongestionner les villes : ce qui marche chez nos voisins

L'espace alloué à la voiture diminue dans les villes. Parallèlement, l'accès au centre-ville est régulé, comme à Stockholm et à Rotterdam.

Comment décongestionner les villes et améliorer les transports du quotidien ? C'est l'un des grands enjeux des assises de la mobilité que lance le gouvernement ces trois prochains mois. Alors que plusieurs villes françaises ont pris une certaine avance en lançant des alternatives au tout-voiture dans leur politique de transport, comme Strasbourg, Nantes et Rennes, la congestion des rues et des transports en commun est toujours d'actualité.

Depuis une quinzaine d'années, les grands centres urbains ont cependant largement revu leur organisation urbaine en réduisant l'espace alloué à la voiture. Cela part d'un simple constat: «Les voitures satureront toujours la place qu'on leur donne. À Los Angeles, mêmes les autoroutes de deux fois huit voies sont complètement bouchées», relève Nicolas Boichon, ingénieur transport à l'Institut d'aménagement et d'urbanisme d'Île-de-France (IAU).

Aux États-Unis, qui redécouvrent depuis une vingtaine d'années leurs centres-villes longtemps délaissés, de nombreuses autoroutes urbaines sont en train de disparaître au profit de boulevards partagés entre marcheurs, cyclistes et voitures. À Séoul, un viaduc autoroutier a été supprimé pour laisser place au cœur de la capitale coréenne à une promenade urbaine très appréciée.

En Europe, la relance du tramway et le développement des bus à haut niveau de service ont d'ores et déjà permis de requalifier de nombreux centres-villes et de réduire la place de la voiture. Paris, Bordeaux ou Lyon ont pour leur part décidé d'éloigner les voitures des berges de leur fleuve.

D'autres villes utilisent la manière plus douce. Madrid réserve certaines voies d'autoroutes au seul transport public. En Californie, le covoiturage aussi a ses voies. En Europe, les parkings relais sur les autoroutes à proximité des centres urbains sont également très fréquents. Les collectivités locales travaillent enfin à la mise en place d'une gestion intelligente et dynamique des transports par le biais des systèmes de signalisation ou de la modulation de la vitesse autorisée.

Au cœur des villes, la réduction de la place faite aux voitures se double de systèmes de régulation de l'accès au centre-ville.

Depuis 2010, Rotterdam expérimente pour sa part le « péage positif ». Ce système rémunère les automobilistes acceptant de ne pas utiliser leur voiture aux heures de pointe en privilégiant d'autres moyens de transport (vélo, transports en commun, etc.), en effectuant du covoiturage ou en décalant les horaires de leurs déplacements quotidiens.

À Londres, certains quartiers modifient même les permis de stationnement résidentiel selon qu'il s'agit de la première ou de la seconde voiture d'un même habitant, ou selon la performance écologique du véhicule.

Ces mesures se doublent de politiques de transport plus doux. À Copenhague, le nombre de vélos dépasse le nombre de voitures, grâce à la mise en place depuis le début des années 2000 de toutes les infrastructures nécessaires : des garages à vélos sur plusieurs étages à chaque station de métro, en passant par les ponts et passerelles destinées aux seules bicyclettes.

« À l'avenir, le développement des applications de calcul d'itinéraire ainsi que le partage des données collectées de la ville intelligente vont améliorer la gestion des transports», estime Frédérique Predali, urbaniste de l'IAU d'Île-de-France. «Grâce à ces outils, on pourra mieux connaître et comprendre les déplacements en temps réel et donc actionner des leviers pour aider les habitants, notamment les conducteurs, à différer ou à annuler un déplacement en voiture en fonction du trafic,» complète M. Boichon. «Le meilleur déplacement, c'est celui qu'on ne fait pas ! »

D'après *Le Monde Économie*, 20 septembre 2017.

Common track

1. What do the following words mean? Look for them in the dictionary if necessary and note the appropriate definition:
décongestionner ; espaces alloués ; un enjeu ; être d'actualité ; au quotidien ; les assises de la mobilité ; saturer ; covoiturage ; une voie ; viaduc ; relance ; signalisation.

1. Use the French dictionary: look up the following words: probant ; onéreux ; allouer.
2. Identify the topical issue in French.
3. What solutions are proposed?
4. Imagine a title in English for the document.
5. Introduce the text in English.
6. Write one or two sentences in English for each paragraph in your own words (no translation).
7. Use your sentences to write a well-organised account of the article in English. (150 words)

Go faster

I **Read the whole document and suggest a title in English.**

II **Write one or two sentences in English in your own words for each paragraph.**

III **Write an organised account of the article in English in 200 words. Do not forget the introduction and the conclusion.**
(Use the vocabulary on page 126)

Debate

Student A is hosting a talk show about the usage of cars in cities and towns. You have two guests, **Students B and C**, that have completely opposing views and practices. You are the moderator.

Prepare your questions and try to run the debate smoothly.

Student B is absolutely not convinced that cities and towns can operate without cars. Develop strong arguments to support your view.

Student C is an eco-friendly individual who believes cities and towns should ban cars. Here again find strong arguments to establish your view.

Role play

The role of the three students can be prepared in a bigger group. You will decide who will be the spokesperson for each part.

5 Tasks

Document 1 piste 32 — Audio

Ryanair

Word box

- to go to the dogs: *se détériorer*
- to be privy to: *être dans le secret*

Document 2 — Map

The Orient Express roads

Document 3 piste 33 — Text

Electric cars in China

"A DEFINING moment for the auto industry." That is how usually restrained analysts at Sanford C. Bernstein, a research firm, described the news that China's government wants to move towards a ban on gas guzzlers. On September 9, the Vice Minister of Industry announced that the government was developing a long-term plan to phase out vehicles powered by fossil fuels.

The news reverberated around car firms, for which China is the largest market. Experts say China is simply far too big to lose: if China says no more fossil-fue-powered cars, global carmakers must follow. China already has ambitious medium-term goals for automotive efficiency and climate change, including a cap on carbon emissions by 2030.

The news came just before the opening of the Frankfurt Motor Show, a spiritual home of conventional cars. Many attendees were skeptical. Despite much talk about national bans — this year Britain and France have said that by 2040 new cars completely reliant on petrol or diesel will be illegal — no country has passed concrete legislation to implement a ban, some noted. Others saw opportunity. Thierry Bolloré, chief competitive officer at Renault, says his firm is well prepared to start making electric vehicles (EVs) in China.

China's government is getting better at boosting its own EV manufacturers after years of giving out ill-considered subsidies and setting unrealistic sales targets. Local manufacturers have not been able to match the quality and innovation of petrol-fuelled cars produced by Western rivals. But China has advantages when it comes to electrification and connected cars. It has many inventive internet companies, is home to some of the world's biggest battery producers and is at the centre of electronics manufacturing.

A new generation of inventive, venture-backed EV firms like ThunderPower and Nio are making the buzz at global auto shows. The electrification of transport could give Chinese carmakers and suppliers a chance to change from losers into champions.

Adapted from *The Economist*, September 14, 2017.

Task 1 Audio

Listen to the whole audio.

1. Why was a press conference organised by the CEO of Ryanair?
2. Describe the problem and how it will be solved.
3. What are the reasons for so many flight cancellations.
4. What is the impact on the passengers.
5. What is the impact on the crews and Ryanair.
6. Organise all the information you have collected.
7. Write a report.

Task 2 Map

1. Describe the different routes from London to Istanbul and find which countries are and are not accessible by the Orient Express.
2. Do you think the Orient Express is the quickest way to travel?
3. In your opinion, why do some people choose to travel by train from Paris to Istanbul?
4. Organise your ideas and report to the class.

Task 3 Text

1. Read the whole text and take down notes about what you believe is important.
2. Organise your ideas and make a plan.
3. Write an organised account of the article in English.

Task 4 Put in common

1. Making a plan: See how the three documents are related to one another.
   - Audio: the main ideas are...
   - Map: the main ideas are...
   - Text: the main ideas are...
2. How are the ideas from each document related?
3. What do the three documents say about travelling and commuting in the future?
4. Look at parts of documents 1 and 3 and the answers provided to the questions from document 2. Write a final report on the role of institutional bodies, governments, etc. What do they do? What role do they play?

5 Background

Public transportation versus individual vehicles

The transport sector accounts for almost a third of the polluting emissions in France, and the government wants to solve the problem with an ambitious new goal: ban cars with a gasoline or diesel engine starting in 2040.

How do people commute? Travel around the world? Are we heading towards a greener, cleaner transportation means? Are cities targeted to be the first with no CO_2 emissions?

I Public transportation: from commuting within cities to commuting within provinces and countries

Trains and planes or underground and buses within cities are being developed to enable people to commute. Some countries are ahead, some are slower on the uptake.

China's railway network is much developed and many Chinese use the train to go back home when celebrating the Chinese New Year. Chinese passengers might face delays due to bad weather but the fare is certainly affordable unlike the fare British passengers have to pay to commute to London on very unreliable, overcrowded trains.

London's new Toxicity-Charge or T-Charge has been introduced to reduce pollution. The fee for 10-year-old vehicles in the congestion zone — not even including taxis — will rise to £21.50, that is to say the Toxicity-Charge costs £10.

London is also in the news at the end of 2017 with its new "Pashley bike" replacing the "Boris bikes". Replacing the current 11,500 bikes built by a Canadian firm, the Pashley bikes will help reduce costs and use the same docking stations as the current models.

Question time

1. What is the impact of the transport sector on the environment?
2. What is the French government's plan to address the problem?
3. What is done to develop public transport across the world?
4. What is the aim of the Chinese government? What is the situation in the US?

II Cars in China and in the US: what types of cars?

In 2016 roughly half of the 700,000 electric cars sold world-wide were sold in China. Its electric fleet only represents 0.18%. This is far from being a very high percentage but the Chinese government calls for 40% of cars bought in China in 2030 to be pure electric vehicles or plug-in hybrids.

In 2016 there were 263.6 million cars in the US. 160.000 were electric vehicles. If we compare the US and China which are comparable in size but not in the number of people, we clearly see that where in China there are 140 cars per 1,000 population, there are 817 cars per 1,000 population in the US.

Alternative forms of energy will increasingly displace gas-powered vehicles. Today, cars account for 25% of the demand for crude oil, i.e. around 24 million barrels a day. It seems that traditional carmakers such as Daimler or BMW have been slow to respond to the need to stop polluting and have been overtaken by the likes of Tesla or Google. Although the young generation in the Western world is not buying cars at the same pace as the previous generation, it is still expected that 125 million cars will be sold in 2025 as many countries in Africa or in Asia will be keen on having access to mobility.

III The electric car revolution will start once we have the answers to the following questions:

- Will cars drive themselves?
- Will governments tax carbon emissions at high enough rates to discourage fossil-fuel use?
- How widespread electric-vehicle adoption will be?
- When will electric cars become cost-competitive?

In the long run the coming of electric cars will change the landscape of cities, how we travel and commute.

↪ Vocabulary p. 126

Trends

An example in the shift of holidaymakers' choice

If we are to believe the figures, millions of Americans take cruise vacations. Therefore, the number of cruise line is on the rise: Royal Caribbean offers more eco-friendly trips, Hurtigruten, the Norwegian cruise line, will run on hybrid technology, etc. But there are 60 cruise lines worldwide. In 2009, there were 17.8 million passengers. In 2017, there were 25.8 expected passengers.

1. Today's figures:

- More people go on cruises, more jobs are created. For 2015, there were 956,597 people working in the cruise industry.
- Demand for cruising has increased by 62% between 2005 and 2015.
- The passengers come from the US (11.5m), China (2.1m), Germany (2m), the UK (1.89m), Australia (1.29m).
- River cruises are on the rise, as well as adventure cruises.

Conclusion:

- Prices might get lower with the increase in the number of cruise lines: cruises might be more affordable and become less of a luxury item.
- The cruisers are getting younger as this type of holiday has become more popular.

2. Why are more under 45s choosing cruise holidays?

- More and more take a cruise as a family: there are kids' clubs; the childcare is of a high standard.
- Cruise operators try to outdo each other in terms of the luxury: they offer excellent food.
- There is a mix of ages: the millennials as well as the working class can afford the cruises.
- The facilities modern cruise ships have are huge: cruise lines have made massive strides in technology and internet connectivity.
- There is a vast choice of ships and cruises are good value.
- There is a growth in theme cruising, from Star Treck to music themes.

3. Harmony of the Seas in numbers

- At 1,188 ft (361 m), it is longer than the Eiffel Tower is tall.
- The ship accommodates 6,687 guests and carries 2,193 international crew members.
- Fifty tonnes of ice cubes are made on board each day.
- Passengers make their way through 2,500 lb (1,134 kg) of fresh salmon and 2,100 lb (953 kg) of lobster tail on an average seven-night cruise.
- About 100 gallons (450 litres) of chocolate ice cream are consumed per seven-night cruise.

Questions

- ➡ Is the price an important purchasing driver?
- ➡ Do you think uncertainty or instability in parts of the world is responsible for this increase in cruising holiday?
- ➡ What makes people decide to switch to a cruising holiday?

Swot analysis of the cruise industry

Favourable | Unfavourable

Internal

Strengths

- The cruise industry has increased in the last 10 years but still represents a very small proportion of the global vacation market.
- Invest in press and television media to promote the lifestyle aboard to targeted customers.
- Operates worldwide and has offices and headquarters on several continents.

Weaknesses

- Some cruise lines pollute a lot.
- Decrease in profits as there are more competitors.
- Needs to target non-American customers as that market is saturated.
- Currency: if the dollar is higher than the pound or the euro, prices are less attractive to some customers.
- Economic instability and political tensions may impact the choice of potential customers.

SWOT

External

Opportunities

- With a 4.5% share in the travel industry in 2009, cruise lines have a lot of space for growth.
- New customers from Asia as their income increases
- Cruise holidays now appeal more and more to younger customers.

Threats

- Attacks by Somali pirates or terrorist attacks.
- Increase in fuel prices.
- New environmental regulations.

Test yourself

After having studied this unit, you must be able to answer the following questions…

1. What is the difference between a passenger and a commuter?
2. What is a smart city?
3. What is a budget airline?
4. How much does it cost to travel by Tube in London?
5. What is EasyJet?
6. What is an electric plane?
7. What is needed to achieve the 500 million electric cars worldwide by 2050?
8. What should be done to make commuting less awful?
9. Why have cruises become so much more popular?
10. How do you make cities traffic free?
11. How badly does the tourism industry suffer from hurricanes?
12. What has made Britain start a very aggressive diesel-free policy?

Britain to ban new diesel and gas cars by 2040

LONDON — Scrambling to combat a growing air pollution crisis, Britain announced on Wednesday that sales of new diesel and gas cars would reach the end of the road by 2040. Britain's plans match a similar pledge made this month by France, and are part of a growing global push to curb emissions and fight climate change by promoting electric cars. But the shift to electric vehicles will be a gradual one, and the target set by Britain is less ambitious than some of the efforts elsewhere. President Trump's decision to withdraw the United States from the Paris climate accord has also dented optimism. Britain's new clean air strategy, published on Wednesday, calls for sales of new gas and diesel cars and vans to end by 2040. The government will also make 255 million pounds, or $332 million, available for local governments to take short-term action, such as retrofitting buses, to reduce air pollution.

In France, the promise to end sales of traditional cars was made as part of a renewed commitment to the Paris accord. In Britain, which is also committed to the Paris treaty, the measures have particular political significance because of rising concern over the level of air pollution, particularly in large cities like London. Poor air quality, much of it a result of pollution from vehicles, is estimated to cause between 23,000 and 40,000 deaths nationwide every year.

Frederik Dahlmann, assistant professor of global energy at Warwick Business School, described Wednesday's announcement as "an important step" that set a clear long-term target, and "also gives car buyers an incentive to consider the different types of engine options available in light of the long-term development of the market." Still, he said, the long-term nature of the announcement left a significant question hanging: "How does the government intend to improve air quality and reduce transport related emissions in the short term?"

Critics, including Ed Miliband, a former leader of the opposition Labour Party and an ex-environment secretary, argued that the government was failing to tackle the current pollution crisis. Others also say the country's efforts are not aggressive enough — France has also set 2040 as its target, but Norway intends to sell only electric cars from 2025, and India wants to do so by 2030.

Cars typically have a life span of around 15 years, so even if Britain follows through with its target, conventional engines are likely to be on the country's roads more than a decade later. Britain's decision is, however, the latest indication of how swiftly governments and the public in Europe have turned against diesel and internal combustion engines in general. Automakers, though reluctant to abandon technologies that have served them well for more than a century, are increasingly resigned to the demise of engines that run on fossil fuels. They are investing heavily in battery-powered cars as they realise their traditional business is threatened by Tesla or emerging Chinese companies, which have a lead in electric car technology.

The shift away from internal combustion engines is in large part a result of growing awareness of the health hazards of diesel. Cities like Madrid, Munich and Stuttgart are considering diesel bans. Sales of diesel cars are plunging. Political leaders are under pressure to end the de facto subsidies of diesel fuel that prevail in Europe.

Rather than encourage a shift back to gasoline cars, governments and automakers are focusing increasingly on electric cars. But the impending shift has raised doubts about whether countries like Britain will be able to create the infrastructure, and generate the electricity, needed for such a radical change in the way people travel.

Jack Cousens, a spokesman for Britain's largest motoring organisation, the AA, said there would need to be "significant investment in order to install charging points across the country, especially fast-charge points," and added that it was questionable whether the electricity grid "could cope with a mass switch-on after the evening rush hour."

Adapted from *New York Times*, July 26, 2017.

I Compréhension de l'écrit

Vous ferez un compte rendu en français du texte ci-dessus en 250 mots (+/– 10%).

II Expression écrite

Répondez en anglais aux deux questions suivantes. Indiquez précisément le nombre de mots.

1. Why are governments keen on banning gas-powered cars from towns and cities?
2. What opportunities are offered to companies?

III Interaction orale

You have an appointment with a client who wants to book a company travel for his/her staff. Prepare your sales pitch to negotiate the travel offer above.

NB: You are free to invent the missing details as long as they don't contradict the ad.

→ Voir Tools pages 220-221

1 How low-cost airlines alter the economics of flying

When Spirit Airlines began offering flights between Detroit and Philadelphia, the average price for a one-way ticket dropped by as much as 50 percent. For more than three years, the average one-way fare between Detroit and Philadelphia never dipped below $308, and sometimes moved higher, topping $385 at one point. But then, early in 2016, fares suddenly started to fall, according to data from the Bureau of Transportation Statistics. By the end of the year, the average one-way ticket between the two cities stood at just $183.
What changed? The primary factor was Spirit Airlines.

The low-cost carrier began operating flights from Philadelphia International Airport to Detroit in April 2016, offering one-way fares for less than $100, in some cases. Spirit's move into the route pushed down average ticket costs at all carriers on it, including Delta Air Lines and American Airlines. "Without the low-cost carriers, we would have been looking at a pretty significant downturn in activity," said James Tyrrell, chief revenue officer at Philadelphia International Airport. Frontier Airlines, another low-cost carrier, had also added flights from Philadelphia, Mr. Tyrrell said. Without such airlines, he added, "you would have seen an absolutely different pricing structure." Even as a wave of mergers has cut the number of major carriers to four and significantly reduced competition, lower-cost airlines continue to play a role in moderating ticket costs.

While such airlines offer a no-frills passenger experience and charge plenty of fees for such luxuries as additional bags or extra legroom, they are able to stimulate new demand from occasional fliers with relatively cheap prices and even take passengers from the major carriers.

Carriers like United and American do not compete with carriers like Frontier and Spirit on every type of passenger. Lucrative corporate accounts are owned by the big carriers, and business travelers avoid the cheaper airlines, often choosing to pay premium prices at the last moment to get seats on the flights that best fit their schedules. But the low-cost carriers nonetheless force the big airlines to figure out a way to draw the most price-sensitive fliers in any given market — those who search the internet for the cheapest tickets possible. Those customers make up a significant portion of travelers, meaning the major carrier cannot just ignore them.

"Those passengers certainly are important," said David Weingart, an economist at the aviation consultant GRA. "The larger airlines have proven that in how they have reacted, in how they have tried to capture or recapture those passengers." "While we are not surprised that the environment remains very competitive, it is surprising to see our competitors resort to the unusual level of discounting we are currently seeing, especially since we are still in the summer peak period," Matthew Klein, chief commercial officer at Spirit, said during a call with analysts in July.

Adapted from *The New York Times*, September 1, 2017.

I Oral exam

1. Prepare a one minute oral account of the article (document 1).
2. Branching out.

- What are passengers' expectations when they fly?
- What criteria are the most important for you when you travel by air?
- Explain the expression: "a no-frills passenger experience."
  Do you personally enjoy flying? Why?

2 Arctic cruise boom poses threats..... piste 34

II Audio

1. Listen to the audio twice and take notes.
2. You have 15 minutes to prepare an oral report about the audio you have heard.
3. Be prepared to answer questions on related topics.

5 Vocabulary

accommodation (n): *hébergement*
airliner (n): *ligne aérienne*
all inclusive tour (n): *voyage toutes prestations incluses*
ban (vb): *interdire*
be battery-powered (vb): *fonctionner sur batterie*
be gasoline-powered/to be gas-powered (vb): *fonctionner à l'essence*
be hybrid-powered (vb): *fonctionner avec un moteur hybride*
berth (n): *couchette*
bike lane/cycling path (n): *piste cyclable*
bike racks (n): *garage à vélos*
boarding pass (n): *carte d'embarquement*
bus lane (n): *couloir de bus*
charge (vb): *charger*
charging time (n): *temps de recharge*
check in (vb/n): *enregistrer/enregistrement*
commute (vb): *prendre un moyen de transport pour aller (et revenir) du travail*
commuter (n): *usager des transports*
congestion/traffic jam (n): *embouteillage*
cruise ship (n): *bateau de croisière*
deck (n): *pont (d'un bateau)*
eco-friendly tourism (n): *tourisme écologique*
fleet (n): *parc (automobile)*
flight (n): *vol*
full board (n): *pension complète*
haul (n): *trajet*
high speed train: *TGV*
holiday maker (n): *vacancier*
impediment (n): *obstacle*
internal combustion engine (n): *moteur à essence/diesel*
journey (n): *trajet*
landscape (n): *paysage*
long haul flight (n): *vol long courrier*
mass tourism (n): *tourisme de masse*
ocean liner(n): *paquebot*
package tour (n): *voyage organisé*
platform (n): *quai (train)*
plug (vb): *brancher*
pollution spike (n): *pic de pollution*
railway (n): *voie de chemin de fer*
refill (vb): *faire le plein*
route (n): *itinéraire*
run on fossil fuels (vb) : *fonctionner à l'énergie fossile*
runway(n): *passerelle*
sea resort (n): *station balnéaire*
seaside (n): *bord de mer*
seascape (n): *paysage marin*
socket (n): *prise*
station (n): *gare*
stopover (n): *escale*
strait (n) : *détroit*
tube/underground/subway : *métro*
tour operator (n): *voyagiste*
travel (vb/n): *voyager/voyage*
trip (n): *voyage*
vacationer (n): *vacancier*
winter resort (n): *station de sport d'hiver*

6 Freight transport

Question

What is unusual about this truck?
What are the advantages and downsides of this type of transport?

Word box

- container ship: *navire porte-conteneurs*
- shipping industry: *industrie maritime*
- shipping costs: *frais d'expédition*
- to compete: *rivaliser*

Anticipate at home

The top ten shipping companies in 2016

VIDÉO 19

Nathan live!

https://www.youtube.com/watch?v=7fV4uwgVWb4

?

1. What is the number of shipping companies from China, from South-Korea?
2. What is the name of the French company?
3. What do they ship?

6 » Starters

The class is divided into several groups: a group will study document 1, another document 2, a further one document 3 and the last one document 4.

Group 1

Document 1
China's expansion

The $1.4bn plan had been suspended by President Maithripala Sirisena but is back on the table despite erosion fears. Sri Lanka has granted permission for China to build a vast "port city" in the island's capital, Colombo, despite concerns the ambitious project could be an environmental disaster.

The project, funded by Chinese state-owned company China Communications Construction, represents the biggest single foreign investment ever received by Sri Lanka. It will add 233 hectares (575 acres) of new real estate in the congested capital.

China, the largest single lender to Sri Lanka, secured contracts to build roads, railways and ports under the previous regime.

Beijing has been accused of seeking to develop facilities around the Indian Ocean to counter the rise of rival India and secure its own economic interests.

■ Adapted from *Agence France-Presse*, Friday 11 March, 2016.

1. Identify the document.
2. Why is China funding the revamping of Colombo's port?
3. What will it gain out of it?

Group 2

Document 2
Shipping Routes

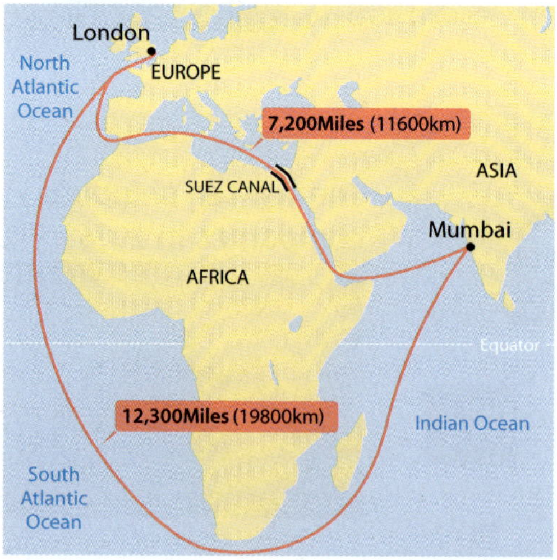

Egypt's economic lifeline runs through the Suez Canal. The Canal has remained a reliable and consistent source of funds for Egypt's government in recent years, bringing in around $5 billion annually.

It usually takes between 12 and 16 hours for a ship to go through the Canal.

1. Identify the document.
2. List the continents you see on the map.
3. What are the two possible routes from London to Mumbai? Which one is the shortest?
4. How many narrow passages does the shortest way go through?
5. What is the name of the strait (*détroit*) separating Europe from Africa?
6. To what routes correspond the following figures: 12,300 miles, 7,200 miles?
7. How long does it take for a ship to go through the Suez Canal?

Group 3

Document 3

Shipping & Customs: when importing from China with 12 (not a simple) steps

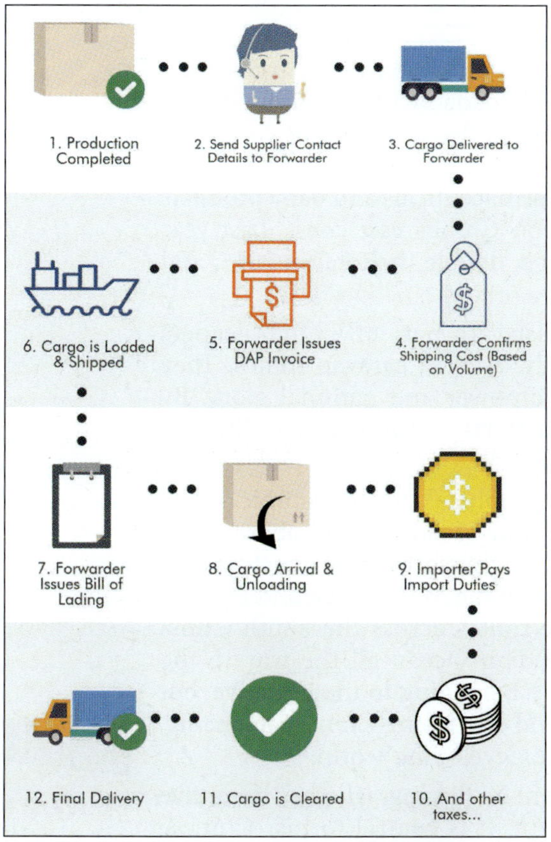

Word box

- BOL → Bill Of Lading (connaissement): *bon de chargement de fret*
- DDU → Delivered Duty Unpaid: *taxes douanières impayées*
- DDP → Delivered Duty Paid: *taxes douanières acquittées*
- DAT → Delivered At Terminal (named terminal at port or place of destination): *livré au terminal (port, aéroport)*
- DAP → Delivered At Place (named place of destination): *livré à destination*
- invoice: *facture*
- ship (vb): *expédier*
- cargo: *chargement*
- forwarder: *transitaire*
- transport supplier: *prestataire de transport*

1. Identify the document.
2. How many steps are necessary before a cargo from China arrives at its final destination?
3. Which word refers to the client who ordered the cargo?
4. Explain what a transport supplier is. Do you know any transport supplier companies?
5. Apart from the price of the cargo, what are the other costs?
6. How long do you think it takes on average between the order and the delivery from China? (Look for the info on the net to check your answer.)

Group 4

Document 4 vidéo 20 Nathan live!

World's largest container ship OOCL

https://www.youtube.com/watch?v=mpFtzMpfRQk

1. Identify the document.
2. Find Felixstowe on a map.
3. When and where did the OOCL ship arrive?
4. Which country is it from?
5. Give information about its capacity, its size, its draught (*tirant d'eau*), tonnage, speed.
6. Why is it famous?

Put in common

→ Each group reports to the class while the others take notes.
→ Use your notes and recapitulate: What are the common links between the four documents?

6 Prep page

Anticipate at home

Before reading the text, investigate:
- What was the Silk Road?
- How big is China?
- Which country is always compared to China in Asia? Why?

Text piste 35

China's clout has few limits. Shouldn't we be worried about its new Silk Road?

Earlier this year the first direct freight train from China to the UK arrived at a depot in Barking, east London, carrying containers loaded with consumer goods. Named East Wind, it took 16 days to travel 7,500 miles across eight countries, halving the time it would have taken by sea. A few months later the train made its first return journey, delivering Scotch whisky, pharmaceuticals and baby products to the gargantuan wholesale markets of Yiwu, on China's east coast. Last year 1,702 freight trains from China arrived in Europe, double the total in 2015, and more services are being added.

The trains trundling their way across Eurasia are part of China's leaders attempt to build a new Silk Road, inspired by the ancient caravan routes. They are motivated today by the quest for economic power and national glory. By building and financing highways, railways and ports, China's leaders literally want all roads to lead to Beijing.

The new Silk Road is broader in both geographical and economic scope than its ancient namesake, which was mainly land-based, and all about trade and commerce. On land, it involves building new transport infrastructure and industrial corridors stretching across Central Asia to the Middle East and Europe. On water, it encompasses new ports and trade routes across the South China Sea into the South Pacific, and through the Indian Ocean all the way to the Mediterranean. Beijing talks of 65 or so countries belonging to the initiative, but there is no definitive list. It is diplomatic shorthand describing Chinese financing, investment and construction across much of the developing world.

The initiative is being pushed hard by President Xi Jinping, who has spent five years trying to bolster China's international clout. It is central to his "Chinese dream." Xi vowed "to realise the great rejuvenation of the Chinese people." Communist-speak for "make China great again."

The new Silk Road is at the heart of Xi's nationalistic vision, as Beijing flexes its economic muscles for strategic ends. By funding and building transport infrastructure, pipelines and power grids, it aims to weave a web of economic dependency and draw other countries ever tighter into its embrace. China's interests clearly come first, but few underdeveloped states feel they can ignore its promise to deliver much-needed infrastructure.

Key pieces of the new Silk Road, such as the overland freight routes from China to Europe, are already in place. Direct investment along the road was $30bn in 2015-16, according to Beijing's records. But there are doubts over its security and commercial feasibility. Pakistan has reportedly deployed 14,500 security personnel to ensure the safety of some 7,000 Chinese nationals working on the economic corridor. Freight trains from China to Europe may not prove profitable, however much time they save.

In Asia and beyond, China's rise will bring many economic opportunities, but it could have politically devastating consequences.

Adapted from *The Guardian*, September 4, 2017.

Lexical work

Understanding the key words

→ Find the meanings of the following words and their lexical categories (noun, verb, adjective, pronoun, adverb, etc.): clout; halve; wholesale markets; scope; namesake; encompass; shorthand; bolster; to vow; to flex one's muscles; to weave.

→ Now, try to rephrase the title in your own words.

I Read the whole text

1. Write everything you know about the new Silk Road and the countries that are part of the project.

a) What are the differences between the new Silk Road and the first Silk Road?
b) What is the purpose of this huge project financed by China?
c) Where was it easy to build rail tracks? Where is it difficult?
d) Will the land routes be profitable?

II Rephrase

2. What you have learned about the Silk Road infrastructures and how much it has cost?
3. Give the key ideas in each paragraph in one or two sentences.

III Language

4. Translate into French:

a) It **could have** politically devastating consequences.
b) It halved the time it **would have taken** by sea.

5. Use either the conditional present (would + infinitive without to) or conditional past (would + have + past participle).

a) If Vietnam were more powerful, it .... (to oppose) China.
b) 40 years ago, it .... (not be possible) to set up business in China.
c) India's Prime Minister Narendra Modi .... (to like) to beat his Chinese opponent.

Grammaire

► Le conditionnel (présent/passé)

(Voir grammaire les subordonnées introduites par *if* p. 205)

IV Train for the exam

6. Write an account in French of the document. (180 words)
7. **Go further:** How does China plan to trade with African countries? On land? On water?

Role play

Work in pairs: Student A has goods manufactured in China that need to be shipped to London.
Student B should provide answers to the best way to ship goods either by land or by sea.

Student A tips
List questions you need to have an answer to (price, time, dangers, containers, types of goods, etc.).

Student B tips
Use the visual document in the Starter section. Find out more about prices by going on the net.

6 Text tracks

Anticipate at home

Before reading the text find out more about:

- Find a map of the USA showing the freight railway routes.
- Find out more about goods that are shipped by train and by truck.
- What makes train transport more attractive?

Text piste 36

Freight rail traffic is collapsing

Total US freight rail traffic, as measured in carloads and intermodal units, fell 6.1% in the week ended October 8, from the same week last year, the Association of American Railroads reported today. It was down 10% from the same week two years ago! Both of its components were down: carloads – transporting oil, coal, grains, chemicals, and the like – fell 5.9% in the week, to 264,165 loads. Intermodal (containers and trailers), which accounts for about 46% of total traffic, fell 6.4% from a year ago, and 6.5% from two years ago.

This comes after an already dreary September, when total freight traffic was down 4.8% from September last year, with carloads down 5.4%, and intermodal down 4.2%.

The decline in car loads is mostly due to two big factors:

1. The ongoing collapse of coal shipments.
2. The total collapse of crude oil shipments.

A more recent addition to the freight rail problem is the decline in intermodal traffic. Intermodal had been the big hope for railroads. As oil and coal shipments were collapsing, intermodal was growing, and the hope was that it would be able to compensate for the decline in coal and oil shipments. But that hope fell apart in the last quarter of 2015, when intermodal booked its first year-over-year decline (–9%) since the financial crisis.

The only bright spots in terms of carloads, year-to-date, are: grains (+5.6%), motor vehicles (+2.7%), chemicals (+1.7%), and "other," the smallest category (+16.7%). But one of these bright spots, motor vehicles, which accounts for over 7% of total carloads, is turning into the next brake shoe to drop.

Auto sales hit a record in 2015. But in September 2016, unit sales fell from a year ago. The industry has been talking about a looming "car recession" for months. And unless a miracle happens, auto shipments are going to follow auto sales.

So the decline in intermodal traffic is very unwelcome. Intermodal faces a combination of different challenges: shippers seeing less than stellar demand in the US and overseas; and fierce competition from the trucking industry.

Diesel prices have fallen over the past two years. And shippers have come to see a price advantage in shipping their merchandise by truck rather than by rail. In that vein, the AAR estimates that truck freight has increased 3.5% this year through August 2016.

To deal with these significant market uncertainties, railroads have been cutting costs. They are laying off people. They are slashing investments. They are working on efficiencies, such as increasing train speeds.

Investors, however, have piled into railroad stocks since the February low hoping the glory days are back, or hoping at least for a nudge from the Fed. For example, Union Pacific shares have jumped 42% since February, but they are still down nearly 20% from the February 2015 high.

As an industry, North American Class 1 railroads – which the AAR defines as freight railroads with revenues of over $476 millions – are much smaller than trucking. These railroads employed about 169,000 well-paid people in 2015, compared to about 1.8 million long-haul truckers (not counting other employees at trucking companies).

Adapted from Business Insider, October 16, 2016.

Lexical work

Understanding the key words

→ Find their meanings and their lexical categories (noun, verb, adjective, adverb, etc.): to collapse; carloads; intermodal; trailers; dreary; coal; shipment; quarter; bright.

→ Now, try to rephrase the title in your own words and write an introduction (source and date).

First track:
A step-by-step approach

I Read the text

1. Pick up the main idea(s) in each paragraph.

II Rephrase

2. Rephrase the idea(s) you have found in each paragraph.

III Language

3. Translate into French:

a) They are still down.
b) The glory days are back.
c) Total freight traffic was down 4.8% from September 2015.

4. Complete the sentences with the right preposition.

a) Is Sarah ....? (on the phone) Sorry, she is .... Call back in the evening or leave a message.
b) I have so much work. I am .... I will have to stay at the office tonight to work on these files.
c) Well, for once I will start the year with no backlog of paperwork. I am ....
d) If you need help, I'll be ....
e) Cinema on Friday, is it still ....?

Grammaire

▶ **Les prépositions**
→ be in/be out/be down/be behind/be up to.

IV Train for the exam

5. Use all the information above to report briefly to the class in French.

6. Write a 160-word account in English following the guidelines below:

§1 Introduction (source, date and main idea)
§2 The freight rail traffic: why has it decreased?
§3 What about its competitor?
§4 What will freight rail traffic do to gain or regain clients?
§5 Conclusion

Second track:
A straightforward approach

I Read the whole text

1. Take down notes about what you believe is important.

II Rephrase

2. Organise your ideas and make a plan.

III Language

3. Use the present perfect: translate the following sentences:

a) Cela fait deux ans que le transport ferré de marchandises est en baisse.
b) Les actions de Union Pacific ont augmenté de 42 % depuis quelques mois.

Grammaire

▶ Le *present perfect*
(Voir grammaire p. 202)

IV Train for the exam

4. Write an account of the article in French in 180 words.

5. Write a report OR make an oral presentation. Use the research you carried out before studying the text and investigate further to discuss the following topics:
- How can the freight rail traffic become more competitive?
- What about European freight rail traffic?

6 Video tracks

Common track

→ **Before you start watching the video:**

1. Explain what has happened to Hanjin shipping company and why it has impacted global trade.

→ **Watch the video:**

2. Watch and try to hear and understand the following words:
   seizure; potential merger; demise; stranded; adrift; afloat; loans; component; consumption.
3. Debrief with the other students and the teacher about their meanings.

Pronunciation work

→ **Listen, repeat the following words and record yourself:**
An increase in consumption; $ 90 million in loans; reditors; stranded; afloat.

Word box

- to keep afloat: *maintenir à flot*
- to collapse: *s'effondrer*
- stranded: *échoué/abandonné*
- seizure: *confiscation*
- adrift: *à la dérive*

Video vidéo 21 Nathan live!

Shipping company bankruptcy

https://www.youtube.com/watch?v=3AaQ6haH1qk

First track:
A step-by-step approach

I Watch the whole video once

1. Write in French what it is about.

II Watch the video a second time

→ **Watch the first part: (→ 1'00)**

2. Where are the goods?
3. How many containers are there?
4. What does it mean if some components are trapped in containers?
5. What time of the year is it?
6. Where should the goods be?

III Watch the second part: (1'00 → end)

7. Why and where is there an increase in consumption?
8. What is the South Korean government prepared to do?
9. How could Hanjin shipping company avoid bankruptcy?
10. Why is Hanjin presented as a victim?
11. What must retailers do?

IV Train for the exam

12. **Oral report:** Put together all the information you have collected and report to the class.

Second track:
A straightforward approach

I Watch the whole video once

1. After the first viewing, you are expected to have understood the general idea(s) exposed in the document. Write a short debrief.

II Watch the video a second time

2. Take notes and focus on how the different ideas are connected to one another.

III Train for the exam

3. Write an account of the video. In your conclusion, state your point of view.

Role play

Student A is a customer doing his/her Christmas shopping at his/her usual shopping mall. Student A is surprised and concerned not to be able to find the toys he/she had planned to buy.

Student B is another angry shopper who cannot find the products he/she expected to buy at the mall.

Student C is the mall customer relationship manager who explains his/her customers that because of the bankruptcy of a South Korean shipping company, many products are still waiting to be shipped.

Imagine the exchange between the three people using information you remember from the video. (NB: other students can join their voices to the complaining customers.)

Common track

I Anticipate the topic of the audio

1. Read the title and explain what a delivery service is.
2. Look for information on the following carriers: Fedex, UPS, Postal Service.
3. What do they transport?
4. What may Amazon need to deliver its products?
5. Read the title and rephrase it.

II Understand the key words

6. Listen and try to understand the following words:
warehouse; couriers; on behalf; trial; network; pundits; flooded; packages; short of; competitor; inventory; bypass.
7. Debrief with the other students and the teacher about their meaning:
autumn; build; collapse; damaged; emergencies; gross domestic product; hurricane; infrastructure; income; island; lifeblood; material; purchase; race; rebuilding; recover; roof; season; shortage; storm; tourism; tempest; typhoon.

Audio piste 37 Nathan live!

Amazon to test a new delivery service for sellers

Pronunciation work

→ **Listen, repeat the following words and record yourself:** delivery; warehouse, courier, carrier, merchandise, feature, transportation, package.

First track: A step-by-step approach

I Listen to the whole audio once

1. Write in French what it is about.

II Listen to the first part

2. What is Amazon planning to test?
3. Which companies do they want to replace?
4. What is the name of the new delivery company?
5. Where will they pick up the goods?
6. Where will the goods be delivered?
7. When is the test starting?
8. Will it start on a big scale?
9. Which city will it start in?
10. What is the aim of the program?

III Listen to the second part

11. If the service expands, will how will an increasing number of products be delivered.
12. What is the consequence of Amazon's delivery program on Fedex and UPS market shares?
13. What do some experts think about Amazon's real intentions?
14. How does Amazon move merchandise across the US?
15. Will Amazon stop working with other carriers?
16. What are the advantages for Amazon to possess its own shipping service?
17. According to the guest is Amazon a real threat to the competition?

IV Train for the exam

18. **Oral report:** Put together all the information you have collected and report to the class.

Second track: A straightforward approach

I Listening to the whole audio

1. After the first listening, you are expected to have understood the main idea(s) expressed in the document. Write a short debrief.

II Listen to the whole audio a second time

2. Take notes and focus on how the ideas are connected.

III Train for the exam

3. Write an account of the audio. In your conclusion, state your point of view.

Role play

Group A

Students from group A are against the increasing restrictions on flights. They argue that the ban on liquids, food, even electronic devices for some destinations, are useless, and prevent air travelling from being efficient.

Group B

Students from group B argue that restrictions have to be as strict as possible, and even stricter, they argue that it is the only way to ensure passengers' safety.

Each group prepares their arguments, using examples from their own experience or from their imagination.
A student from each group distributes speaking and listening roles equally.

Texte

Voyage à bord d'un cargo : vivre au rythme de l'activité des marins

Modeste porte-conteneurs de 200 mètres de long – l'un des plus petits de la flotte de la compagnie française CMA CGM –, le *Marseille* est parti le 16 août du Havre à destination des Caraïbes, puis du Brésil, lesté d'un millier de conteneurs.

Le Havre, Saint-Martin, Trinidad, la Guyane, le nord du Brésil, puis l'Espagne, Tilbury, Rotterdam et de nouveau Le Havre… La boucle doit durer quarante-deux jours.

À bord, c'est un microcosme qui s'ouvre au passager. En l'occurrence, sur le *Marseille*, ce sont 23 marins qui s'activent vingt-quatre heures sur vingt-quatre et sept jours sur sept.

Le bateau est un espace de travail et on le sent dès l'échelle de coupée franchie. Officiers et équipage sont affairés. Les termes maritimes foisonnent : une fenêtre est un sabord, la partie de vie du cargo s'appelle le château et la cabine de pilotage, la passerelle.

Les conteneurs blancs sont les réfrigérés, ils emportent fruits, légumes, viandes, produits explosifs (pour l'allumage des moteurs des lanceurs d'Ariane-5) ou produits surgelés de consommation courante à Trinidad et en Guyane. Les « boîtes » (c'est le terme consacré) de couleurs, elles, contiennent des marchandises diverses, dont le capitaine ignore la nature.

Officiers ukrainiens et marins philippins

Sur le *Marseille*, on distingue deux groupes distincts : les officiers ukrainiens, chargés de la navigation et du bon fonctionnement de la salle des machines, et les marins philippins, responsables de l'entretien du cargo et des conteneurs. Inlassablement, ils réparent, nettoient, repeignent menant une bataille contre la rouille.

Ces deux groupes échangent peu – les repas sont pris dans deux salles différentes – et ont du mal à se comprendre bien que l'anglais soit la langue officielle à bord. Ils n'ont pas, non plus, les mêmes conditions de travail. Les Ukrainiens travaillent pendant quatre mois, puis rentrent chez eux pour quatre mois. Les Philippins ont des contrats de neuf mois et se reposent trois mois. La marine marchande a subi, dès les années 1960, l'arrivée d'équipages bon marché et il n'existe plus aucun équipage entièrement français.

À bord, la vie est rythmée par les repas à 7 h 30, 12 h 30 et 18 h 30. En dehors de ces plages, les marins s'activent tandis que les passagers disposent de longues heures d'oisiveté. Le voyage en cargo invite à la contemplation. Le bleu soutenu de la mer, la lumière inconstante, les couleurs du ciel et les poissons volants fugitifs…

À bord pour des raisons financières

Sur le *Marseille*, il n'y pas d'amoureux de la mer. Si ces hommes sont là, c'est, pour la plupart d'entre eux, pour des raisons financières. « *À 32 ans, ma sœur est secrétaire dans une administration et elle gagne un peu plus de 200 euros par mois. Moi, j'en empoche 3 000 les mois où je travaille*», explique Artem Vtulkin, 20 ans, troisième officier, chargé de la sécurité.

À 39 ans, le capitaine émarge, lui, à près de 8 000 euros mensuels. « *Je peux envoyer ma fille à l'université* », relève, pour sa part, Roberto Celiz, le maître d'équipage philippin.

Épuisement physique et psychologique

Pour les hommes d'équipage, être coupé du monde, c'est une contrainte difficile à surmonter.

Depuis deux ans, il y a toutefois une connexion Internet à bord. « *C'est ce qui nous fait tenir*», explique Vitaly Tselinko, le chef mécano. Beaucoup de ces hommes envisagent ce métier comme une situation temporaire. « *Qui voudrait de cette vie-là ? On travaille sept jours sur sept*», grogne Vitaly Chylik, 26 ans, troisième officier. La moyenne d'âge de l'équipage, 34 ans, ne trompe pas.

Les conditions météo et les changements de fuseaux horaires successifs ajoutent à la fatigue. Tout comme le bruit assourdissant du moteur, surtout en salle des machines, qui ne cesse jamais. Malgré tout, très fiers de travailler à bord, beaucoup n'échangeraient leur place pour rien au monde.

D'après *Le Monde*, 16 septembre 2017.

Common track

1. What do the following words mean? Look for them in the dictionary if necessary and note the appropriate definitions:
lesté ; microcosme ; une escale ; l'échelle de coupée ; inlassablement ; oisiveté ; fugitif ; émarger ; un fuseau horaire.
2. Find their lexical categories.
3. Write an account in French of the document.
4. What are the English words for :
un cargo ; la flotte ; à destination ; lesté ; marins ; officiers ; équipages ; cabine de pilotage.

1. Use a dictionary. Look up the following words and find an equivalent in English: être affairé ; sélectionner ; les réfrigérés ; produits explosifs ; produits de consommation courante ; chargé de navigation ; la salle des machines ; l'entretien du cargo.
2. Identify the main topic in English.
3. What is life like on a cargo container for the Filipino crew? The Ukrainian officers?
4. How many months do they each work?
5. Imagine a title in English for the document.
6. Introduce the text in English.
7. Use your sentences to write a well-organised account of this article in English. (180 words)

Go faster

I Read the whole document and suggest a title in English.

II Write one or two sentences in English in your own words for each paragraph.

III Write an organised account of the article in English. Do not forget the introduction and the conclusion. (220 words)

IV Branching out. Give your own point of view on the route of the cargo and the crew.

V Write a 150 word essay on cargo containers and how they are part of global trade.

Debate

Group A
Students from Group A believe trade can only increase thanks to sea shipping. Prepare arguments.

Group B
Students from Group B believe that trade growth will be partly carried out thanks to land routes and railway infrastructures. Prepare arguments.

6 Tasks

Word box
- Nitrogen Oxides (NO): *oxide d'azote*
- Particulate Matters (PM): *matières particulaires*

Document 1 piste 38 — Audio

How to reduce highly polluting means of transport

Document 2 piste 39 — Text

Are electric-hybrid trucks the answer to California port pollution problem?

The sound—and smell—of thousands of idling trucks at the ports of Los Angeles and Long Beach could be fading if a new pilot project to convert them to part-time electric vehicles sticks.

A one-mile-long test site, known as the eHighway, has been established near the Los Angeles and Long Beach ports to test three big-rigs equipped with electric-hybrid motors and the sort of extendable arm that connects the trucks to an overhead power supply. The vehicles are powered via a Siemens overhead catenary system, much in the same way that electric city buses and trains receive power.

"The system is expected to lower fossil fuel consumption, reduce truck operating costs, substantially reduce smog-forming, toxic and CO_2 emissions, and help accommodate the growing reliance on freight transportation," Siemens spokesperson Annie Satow said.

The project is a joint effort by Siemens and the South Coast Air Quality Management District (SCAQMD), which oversees air quality improvement projects in Southern California. The $13.5 million project is funded by $2.5 million from SCAQMD, as well as other sources.

The port of Los Angeles—located next to the sprawling port of Long Beach—reported record clean air gains in 2016, surpassing its 2020 goal for reducing emissions at the port.

Nitrous oxide emissions from trucks are on target to be reduced 74% to 91% by 2025, according to the South Coast Air Quality Management District's Clean Air Action Plan (CAAP). Nitrous oxide—the lion's share of truck emissions—has been reduced 71% from 2005 to 2016, according to Port of Los Angeles statistics. Many of the ports' dirtiest trucks serving the port terminals were phased out in 2008 and replaced with trucks meeting 2007 EPA (Environmental Protection Agency) standards.

The port is already moving forward with a strategy to convert heavy-duty trucks intended to move goods short distances from ships to warehouses to near-zero or zero-emission vehicles.

Siemens anticipates roughly 6 million tons of CO_2 could be cut in California if the state were to electrify freight travel. And the electric-hybrid trucks like those on California's eHighway test site are said to be twice as efficient as conventional diesel engines.

Adapted from *Transport Topics*, November 22, 2017.

Document 3 vidéo 22 Nathan live! — Video

How free electricity would change the world

https://www.youtube.com/watch?v=JmzEjg8SpI0

Task 1 Audio

Listen to the whole audio

1. Explain how much freight transport pollutes.
2. What is the toxicity charge? When was it introduced? Where?
3. What is Elon Musk working on?
4. What about trucks on highways?
5. Organise all the information you have collected.
6. Write your report.

Task 2 Text

Read the whole text

1. Explain what a eHighway is.
2. What would be reduced?
3. Who is financing the project?
4. Ports are becoming cleaner. Why?
5. What does a heavy duty truck do? And where do they operate?
6. Organise your ideas and make a plan.
7. Write an organised account of the article in English.

Task 3 Video

1. Anticipate from the title of the video.

Watch the whole video

2. Collect key words and key ideas.
3. Write an organised report of the video in English.

Task 4 Put in common

Each group studies the three reports referring to the three documents.

1. Making a plan: See how the three documents are related to one another.
    - Audio: the main ideas are...
    - Text: the main ideas are...
    - Video: the main ideas are...
2. How are the ideas from each document related?
3. Each group writes a final report which is a synthesis of the three documents.

6 Background

How do our goods travel?

I Seaports in Europe: facts and figures

350.000 persons in Europe work in seaports and generate billions of euros. Over 90% of Europe's trade with the rest of the world and 350 million passengers move through the European ports. Of the 3.5 billion tonnes of outgoing cargo per year handled by 1,000 seaports in Europe, merely 10 ports are handling more than 50 million tonnes. Rotterdam, the largest European port and a major industrial complex, accounts for 100 million tonnes of cargo.

II Railway freight transport in Europe

The total performance in the EU can be estimated at around 416 billion tonne-kilometres in 2015, showing a decrease of about 1.1% compared with 2014.

Countries registering the highest share of international transport are located in key corridors within the European market. In the Baltic States of Latvia and Estonia, situated at the border between the EU and Russia, international transport accounted for 93% and 84% respectively of the total transport performance in 2015.

The Netherlands and Luxembourg, also strategically situated in the heart of the European market, registered shares of 88% and 82% in 2015, respectively. The key import port of Rotterdam, with large sea/rail transfers of goods dispatched within the European Union, strongly influence these figures.

By contrast, countries with specific geographical characteristics (at the periphery of the European Union or islands) recorded a low share of international transport by rail. Small shares are observed for the United Kingdom (2%) and Denmark (11%). For such countries, the preferred mode for international freight transport remains maritime transport, goods being delivered at the nearest port to the point of their destination and then being forwarded into the country mainly by road, but also by rail (accounted as national transport). Turkey also recorded a low percentage (4%) which may also be linked to its peripheral position.

III Air travel: passengers versus freight

In 2016, the total number of passengers travelling by air in the European Union could be established at 973 million, an increase of 5.9% compared to 2015.

The growing importance of the international transport segment is reflected in air freight and mail transport figures at EU level. Growths of 6.8% and 3.9% were recorded for international intra-EU and extra-EU respectively in 2016 compared with 2015.

IV What are the current transport challenges?

Sharp fluctuations in fuel pricing: The sharp fluctuation in fuel pricing can be explained by the constant rise and fall in oil.

The driver shortages: low wages have also contributed to a decrease in drivers. One more important factor is the working conditions which apparently are unsatisfactory, taking into account the dangers and weather conditions while driving in extreme regions.

Expanding use of technology tools: many companies are still reluctant to adopt new technologies, yet digital technology innovation is sure to transform the transport sector.

Increasing regulations: regulations on the hours of services, compliance, safety, and accountability are vital requirements. Some companies have a real trouble meeting this goal.

Question time

1. Give facts and figures about the major sea ports in Europe.
2. What countries have the highest international transport rate?
3. Why are the Netherlands and Luxembourg considered as strategic locations?
4. Name all the means of transport used for freight.
5. Which one can carry the largest loads?

➥ Vocabulary p. 150

Trends

New shipping routes for tomorrow

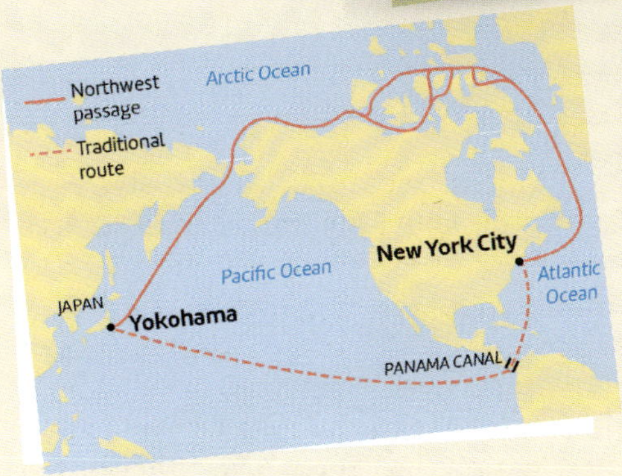

Is global warming a blessing in disguise?
Today, Russia, Norway and some other countries are not just keeping an eye on the North Pole, they are testing its waters. No later than in September 2017, the Russian tanker Christophe de Margene was able to journey from Norway to South Korea in 19 days taking the Northern Sea route without an ice-breaker. Indeed, taking this route enabled the Russian-owned tanker to carry natural gas in less time and at a lower cost. Some worry that this will increase sea traffic and bring new risks such as fuel spills.

1. Why is it feasible?

With global temperatures rising, the sea ice has melted, and having to travel across young sea ice – one-year-old sea ice that is no thicker than 2 metres- will add northerly shipping routes. What is still a seasonal activity might become a year-long project. Some even say that the Arctic will be ice free part of the year. Most of the time, shipping tankers need to be accompanied by massive Russian ice-breakers to plow through patches of six-foot thick ice. By 2030 ice breaking cargo ships could operate in a sea with a four feet thick ice. By 2045 some predict that sea ice will be even less thick and will enable ordinary cargo ships to operate. So as thick ice disappears, the economic potential of using the Northern Sea route for large capacity vessels will go without saying.

2. Why is the Northern Sea route an opportunity?

Clearly the Arctic is potentially faster, less costly and more direct a route for journeys between Asia and Europe or eastern North America. It is still the early stage of cargo ships travelling through the region, and the Suez and Panama canals will remain much use. However, with the COP 21 and the accord to reduce CO_2 more Arctic routes could open for ordinary ships. So soon Arctic shipping routes will become more attractive than the southern routes as the melting of the sea cap continues. By mid-century the travel times will be shorter for most shipping routes.

3. What to expect?

First, these new routes will not interest every shipping company. Second, even if it is possible, it remains that higher insurance rates might make the Arctic routes less attractive. Third, safety will still be an issue and might deter companies. Moreover a report released in 2016 by Copenhagen Business School came to the conclusion that it will only be economically viable for ordinary ships by 2040. Some studies are even less optimistic time-wise and mention the end of the century.

4. Conclusion

There are different scenarii: if temperatures keep on increasing the Northern Sea routes will be open 8 to 10 months. If, on the other hand, temperatures remain below the 2 degree increase, the northerly shipping routes will be reliable and available less time. Moreover, if the average time journey for European shipping companies is reduced to 23 days (instead of 30 through the Suez Canal), the gains in time for North Atlantic ports are too small.
So the Suez and Panama canals will not be erased overnight and shipping companies will have to make a choice and weigh which route to pick up factoring in weather, draft restrictions, fuel costs, etc. In any case, the dream has come true: the North Pole is on the map and will be the venue of much transit.

Questions

- What are the consequences of global warming in the Arctic?
- What countries are closely watching this phenomenon?
- What are the advantages for freight transport?
- What choices will shipping companies be faced with?

The port of Rotterdam: a seaport cluster

Favourable | Unfavourable

Internal

Strengths

- The gate to Europe: geographical location
- Draught: can handle the new high capacity deep draft freighters and deep-draught oil tankers
- Has feeders that serve Europe, and offers integrated intermodal solutions
- Technology
- Cooling water facilities
- Rotterdam port is an industrial site that transforms oil into chemical products
- Actively facilitating start-ups in formerly industrialised port areas

Weaknesses

- Coming of renewable energy
- Rail congestion
- Road congestion
- Bargaining power of seaports reduced because of the merging of shipping companies
- Southern and Eastern Europe cause strong competition
- Changing transport networks

SWOT

External

Opportunities

- Increased scale in the container market: new cargo handling capacities
- Coal and ores
- Crude oil
- Increasing world trade
- Inter-port cooperation

Threats

- Labour shortage
- Growth of other ports (Hamburg, Bremen, WilhelmsHafen, Le Havre, Antwerp, etc.)
- Pricing policy
- Time delays
- Industry concentration
- Growing competition

➥ Vocabulary p. 150

Test yourself

After having studied this unit, you must be able to answer the following questions…

1. Name two shipping companies: one French company and one Chinese company.
2. Why does China want to invest in Colombo, Sri Lanka?
3. What does the Suez Canal provide shipping companies with?
4. Explain the new Silk Road: how many countries are involved?
5. Why is the freight rail traffic endangered?
6. Why are there fewer goods transported by train?
7. To avoid Hanjin's bankruptcy what has the South Korean government proposed?
8. Give the names of two Courier delivery services companies?
9. Why are coal and oil in the USA no longer shipped by train?
10. How does the car industry affect freight rail traffic?
11. Which port is the biggest in the EU in terms of cargo being handled there?
12. How much oil is there in an oil barrel?
13. Why should we think that oil consumption is being slowly reduced?
14. Is railway freight transport doing well in Europe?
15. What is referred to as the North West passage?

Shanghai : one of the biggest cargo ports in the world

Freight train late? Blame Chicago

CHICAGO—When it comes to rail traffic, Chicago is America's speed bump.

Shippers complain that a load of freight can make its way from Los Angeles to Chicago in 48 hours, then take 30 hours to travel across the city. A recent trainload of sulfur took some 27 hours to pass through Chicago—an average speed of 1.13 miles per hour, or about a quarter the pace of many electric wheelchairs.

With freight volume in the United States expected to grow by more than 80 percent in the next 20 years, delays are projected to only get worse.

The underlying reasons for this sprawling traffic jam are complex, involving history, economics and a nation's disinclination to improve its roads, bridges and rails. Six of the nation's seven biggest railroads pass through the city, a testament to Chicago's economic might when the rail lines were laid from the 1800s on.

Today, a quarter of all rail traffic in the nation touches Chicago. Nearly half of what is known as intermodal rail traffic, the big steel boxes that can be carried aboard ships, trains or trucks, roll by or through this city.

The slowdown involves more than freight. The commuter trains get to go first and so "Amtrak tells me they have more delays here than anywhere else in the system."

Now, federal, state, local and industry officials are completing the early stages of a $3.2 billion project to untangle Chicago's rail system—not just for its residents, who suffer commuter train delays and long waits in their cars at grade crossings, but for the rest of the nation as well.

The program, called CREATE (for Chicago Region Environmental And Transportation Efficiency Program) is intended to replace 25 rail intersections with overpasses and underpasses that will smooth the flow of traffic for the 1,300 freight and passenger trains that muscle through the city each day, and to separate tracks now shared by freight and passenger trains at critical spots. Fifty miles of new track will link yards and CREATE a second east-west route across the city.

Fourteen of the 70 projects have been completed so far, and 12 more are under way.

While much of the country's attention in transportation issues is focused on high-speed rail projects, CREATE is largely about bringing old-fashioned low-speed rail up to modern standards. Innovative financing combines federal, state and private money from various programs, including the federal packages. CREATE even uses some funds tied to high-speed rail, since many of the projects are being designed to accommodate those lines in the future.

One of the biggest holdups for freight traffic is that Chicago's crowded rails must also get hundreds of thousands of commuters to work and home mornings and evenings, and so by an agreement known as the Chicago Protocol, the shared tracks and intersections belong to passenger rail during rush hours.

Some of the causes of delay might have seemed outdated in the 20th century, much less the 21st, like manual switches that engineers have to throw after their trains have passed. CREATE is replacing them with electronic switches and online traffic control networks. Chicago had lived with its rail anachronisms for decades, but everything fell apart in a 1999 blizzard that paralysed the city's rails and backed up train traffic across the United States for months.

The resulting plan to fix its rail problems started with efforts to reduce delays by improving coordination among the six freight rail companies. Mr. Thompson, the rail association's programme: manager for CREATE, said me. "It is a very good time to be building infrastructure." But the full benefits will be felt only if all of the projects can be completed.

And there lies a potentially larger problem than anything in the steel rails that snake across the city. While some of the financing for CREATE has come from private industry and state bonds, further progress depends almost entirely on the ability of Congress to pass transportation legislation. That legislation might not be the nation's priority.

Adapted from the *New York Times*, May 7, 2012.

I Compréhension de l'écrit

Après une lecture attentive du texte, vous en ferez un compte rendu en français et ferez apparaître les idées essentielles en 240 mots (+/– 10 %). Indiquez précisément le nombre de mots.

II Expression écrite

Répondez en anglais à la question suivante. Indiquez précisément le nombre de mots.

→ *To what extent is the transport industry contributing to global growth?*

III Interaction écrite

Écrivez une lettre commerciale de demande de réservation pour un séminaire en tenant compte des informations ci-dessous :

Expéditeur : MSC Mediterranean Shipping Company USA, Jim Thornton, Human Resources Manager, 420 th Avenue , New York 10018 USA

Destinataire : Rotterdam Marriot Hotel, Weena 686, Rotterdam 3012 CN Netherlands

Date : le 2 septembre 2018

Objet : Réservation de chambres pour 30 employés

Corps de la lettre :

- Réserver des chambres pour 7 jours du lundi 12 novembre au dimanche 18 novembre pour 30 employés de notre entreprise.
- Le but est d'organiser un séminaire, donc les 30 chambres doivent être spacieuses et, doivent si besoin est, permettre d'accueillir un petit groupe de travail.
- L'hôtel offre-t-il la possibilité de prendre le repas du soir ?
- L'organisation du séminaire nécessite de grandes pièces, des sièges confortables, des rétroprojecteurs et la vidéoconférence.
- Une excursion d'un jour est-elle envisageable ? À quel tarif ?
- Nous devons prendre les billets d'avion bientôt et nous espérons une réponse par retour du courrier.
- Salutations d'usage.

↳ Voir Tools p. 214

1 Why is it so hard to keep track of ships that get up to no good?

South Korea recently seized two oil tankers that it says were illegally transferring oil to North Korean ships at sea. One was registered in Hong Kong, while the other flew the Panamanian flag. The ensuing fallout has focused mainly on who ordered the transaction and chartered the ship – but by the standards of North Korea's dubious shipping transactions, this is far from the most complicated.

North Korea is adept at exploiting a serious problem with maritime security: it is often hard to even identify ships in the first place. Ashore, government agencies issue a registration number and plates for every vehicle, but when it comes to shipping, things are very different.

Although it is widely thought that every ship normally flies the flag of the state where she is registered with a respective number and name, North Korea's shipping company has many times reflagged and renamed ships to evade the UN-imposed arms embargo. By changing their identity, the ships escape the "blacklist" database, giving North Korea a better chance of procuring and/or transferring embargoed items related to the country's missile and nuclear programme.

In the shipping industry, ship owners can register their ships with countries other than the country of ownership with what are commonly known as Open Registries or Flags of Convenience (FOC)*. Various agencies exist to help companies or individuals with registering, reflagging or renaming their ships. FOCs come with various benefits for ship owners: cheap registration fees, low or no taxes, and freedom to employ cheap labour. But there are downsides. Some FOCs have poor safety and training standards and no limitations in terms of the crew's nationalities. And there are other problems, too – including more dangerous ones.

Identification numbers are part of a scheme introduced and implemented by the International Maritime Organisation (IMO) in 1987. Under its measures, ships are assigned permanent identification numbers that don't change when the ship is reflagged. Since 2002, these numbers have had to be permanently marked in a visible place on the ship's hull or superstructure. Passenger ships must carry the marking on a horizontal surface visible from the air.

But even as this database clearly helps to identify reflagged and renamed vessels, as in the case of the floating armoury, there are exceptions which widen the security gap. The IMO identification number scheme is mandatory since 1994 for passenger ships and cargo ships of at least 100 and 300 gross tonnage respectively. But this leaves out plenty of others. For example, the two vessels responsible for the terrorist attacks against the USS Cole in 2000 and the French oil tanker Limburg in 2002 were not subject to the scheme.

Vessels engaged solely in fishing are also exempt. The Environmental Justice Foudation, a UK-based organisation focused on investigating illegal, unreported and unregulated fishing, highlights the security challenge stemming from the exemption of fishing vessels from the IMO identification number scheme. It urges the international community to fill this security gap with a new global database for fishing vessels.

The foundation has reported on how difficult it is for coastal states, port states and regional fisheries management organisations to ascertain whether vessels landing fish or applying for fishing licenses have engaged in illicit fishing, due to the lack of this unique identification number. In West Africa in particular, it has documented how fishing boats use multiple identities, change their flags, names and radio call-signs to avoid detection and sanctions.

Back in 2013, the IMO decided to extend the voluntary application of the ship identification number scheme to fishing vessels of 100 gross tons and above. But while it is all very well for the IMO to be concerned about the practice of ship reflagging and renaming, concern isn't enough. Without an updated maritime security governance structure that works all over the world, states like North Korea will still be able to exploit this very useful and very dangerous security gap.

Adapted from *The Conversation France*, January 4, 2018.

* flag of convenience: *pavillon de complaisance*.

I Compréhension de l'écrit

Après une lecture attentive du texte, vous en ferez un compte rendu en français et ferez apparaître les idées essentielles en 220 mots (+/– 10 %). Indiquez précisément le nombre de mots.

II Expression écrite

Répondez en anglais à la question suivante en 300 mots (+/– 10 %). Indiquez précisément le nombre de mots.

→ *What is the purpose of introducing a comprehensive identification scheme for ships? Is it feasible?*

2 The northern sea route

vidéo 23

https://www.youtube.com/watch?v=D2o8k5HglbE

III Vidéo

1. Watch the video twice and take notes.
2. Organise your notes (10 minutes), then report in English/French on the video.

Vocabulary

ashore (adv): *sur terre (≠ en mer)*
anchor (n): *ancrer*
be palletised (vb): *être palettisé(e)*
better-value fare (n): *voyage d'un meilleur rapport qualité-prix*
bill of lading (n), connaissement: *bon de chargement de fret*
cabin (n): *cabine*
cargo (n): *cargaison*
cargo ship (n): *navire cargo*
carriers' hub airport (n): *plateforme aéroportuaire*
coast (n): *côte*
commodities (n): *matières premières*
container (n): *conteneur*
container ship (n): *navire porte-conteneurs*
courier (n): *messagerie*
crew(n): *équipage*
customs clearance procedures (n): *procédures douanières*
deep draft/draught freighter (n): *cargo à grand tirant d'eau*
delay (n): *retard*
dock (vb): *mouiller*
draught /draft(n): *tirant d'eau*
feeder ship (n): *navire collecteur*
fishing(n): *la pêche*
flag of convenience(n): *pavillon de complaisance*
flammables (n): *produits inflammables*
fleet (n): *flotte*
flight (n): *vol*
forwarder (n): *transitaire*
halve the oil price (vb): *diminuer de moitié le prix du pétrole*
harbour/port (n): *port*
haulier (n): *camion, transporteur*
heavy hauler: *camion à gros tonnage*
insurance(n): *assurance*
insure (vb): *assurer*
intermodal container: *contenu intermodal*
intermodal freight: *transport intermodal*
labeling rules (n): *règles d'étiquetage*
load and unload cargo (vb): *charger et décharger une cargaison*
load (n): *cargaison, chargement*
long-haul routes (n): *destinations pour les longs courriers*
mandatory (adj): *obligatoire*
moor (vb): *mouiller, amarrer*
oil tanker (n): *pétrolier*
oil spill (n): *marée noire*
ore (n): *minerai*
perishables (n): *denrées périssables*
post and packaging (n) (P & P): *frais de port*
raw (adj): *brut*
restriction on exports (n): *restriction sur les exportations*
road freight: *fret routier*
route: *voie d'accès*
scrap metal (n): *ferraille*
sea freight (n): *fret maritime*
security gap (n): *faille de sécurité*
semi-trailer: *semi-remorque*
ship (vb): *expédier*
shipping company (n): *compagnie de transport maritime*
shipping container (n): *container*
shipping line (n): *ligne maritime*
shipping rate (n): *tarif de transport*
travel ban (n): *interdiction de voyager*
treble (vb): *tripler*
vessel (n): *vaisseau, navire*
weapon (n): *arme*

7 World challenges: sustainability and AI

STOP OCEAN PLASTIC POLLUTION

REDUCE
REUSE
RECYCLE

Millions of marine animals are killed each year due to plastic debris in the ocean.

Currently, it is estimated that there are 100 million tons of plastic in oceans around the world.

Plastic packing bands are strangling seals and sea lions. Torn nets, old fishing lines, bait bags and other fishing-industry garbage are few of them to be mentioned.

Question

Describe and comment the document.

Word box

- waste: *déchêts*
- depth: *profondeur*
- deep: *profond*
- throw away/dump: *jeter*
- healthy: *sain, en bonne santé*

Anticipate at home

14 green business ideas for startup entrepreneurs VIDÉO 24

Nathan live!

https://www.youtube.com/watch?v=ez09N1nH_OY

?

What are green ideas?
Can you quote at least five of them?

7 » Starters

The class is divided into groups. Each group will study one of the four documents.

Group 1

Document 1 vidéo 25

Nathan live!

AI–Artificial Intelligence 2001 trailer 1

https://www.youtube.com/watch?v=_19pRsZRiz4

1. Identify the document.
2. Who is David?
3. When does the action take place?
4. Why is he extraordinary?

Group 2

Document 2

Towards renewable energies

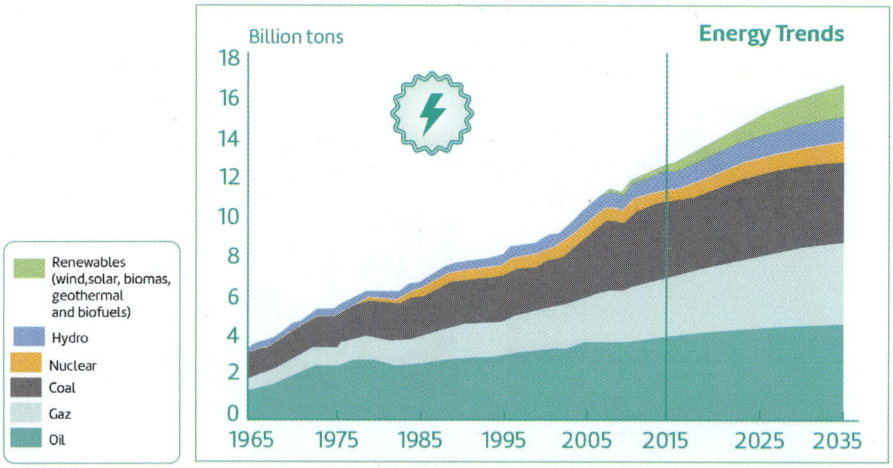

Source: From www.ogj.com

1. Identify the document.
2. What does this document represent?
3. When did renewables start being used?
4. Is oil consumption decreasing?
5. What about coal?

Group 3

Document 3

The impact of climate change: a mind map

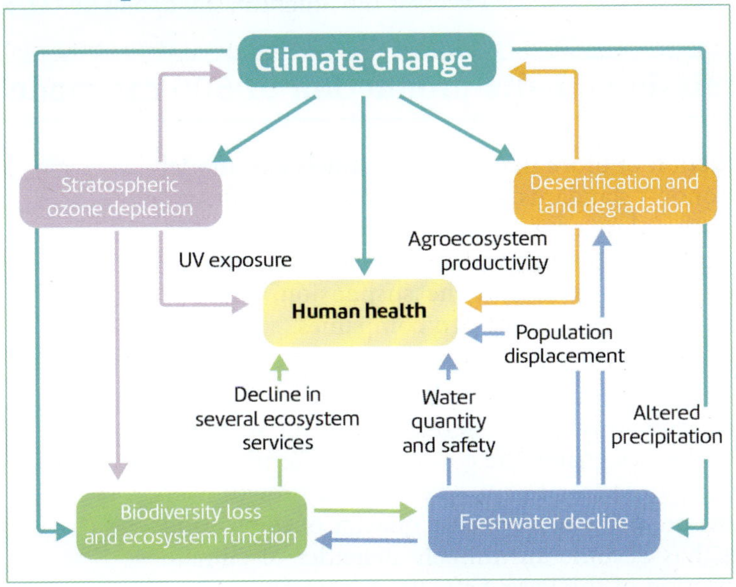

Source: From www.elementshealthspace.com

1. Identify the document.
2. Focus on the mind map and comment on the major effects of climate change.
3. Express your point of view (give examples).

Group 4

Document 4

Is Artificial Intelligence compatible with a sustainable environment?

Some studies suggest that the environmental benefits from self-driving cars may turn out to be overrated. Machines driving our cars, for example, may lead to people making more trips, which could lead to increases in emissions, not decreases. Another major risk for the planet is that large-scale implementation of artificial intelligence may destroy all of our jobs, leading to widespread unemployment. A recent report estimated that automation will replace 6 percent of US jobs by 2021, with further job reductions coming in the medium term. A world without jobs presents a host of new, uncharted challenges for sustainability, few of which we can predict.

■ Adapted from www.greenbiz.com

1. Identify the document.
2. What are the possible downsides of Artificial Intelligence on sustainability? Give your point of view.

Put in common

→ Each group reports to the class while the others take notes.
→ Use you notes and recapitulate: What are the links between the documents?

7 Prep page

Anticipate at home

Before reading the text, investigate:

- Give the names of one or two Chinese automakers.
- Find out about the decisions taken at the Paris Climate Agreement (COP 21) about CO_2 emissions.
- How do you understand the expression "taking the lead in battling climate change"?
- What is the American standpoint on CO_2 emissions?

Text piste 40

China, moving to cut emissions, halts production of 500 car models

China is suspending the production of more than 500 car models and model versions that do not meet its fuel economy standards, several automakers confirmed Tuesday, the latest move by Beijing to reduce emissions in the world's largest auto market and take the lead in battling climate change. The government-affiliated China Vehicle Technology Service Center said that the suspension, effective Jan. 1, would affect both domestic carmakers and foreign companies.

Cui Dongshu, the secretary general of the China Passenger Car Association, said that the ban would affect at most 1 percent of the Chinese market. But the government's decision to cite fuel economy in the deregistration of so many versions at the same time is nonetheless a signal of the government's commitment to fuel economy. The country, which for years prioritised economic growth over environmental protection and now produces more than a quarter of the world's human-caused greenhouse gases, has become an unlikely defender of climate action after President Trump's rejection of the Paris Climate Agreement.

Chinese leaders are under intense pressure to cut in dangerous air pollution, a hot-button issue in China, where thick smog has at times forced schools and businesses to temporarily shut down. Late last month, China said it was going ahead with plans to create the world's largest carbon market, giving Chinese power companies a financial incentive to operate more cleanly. "They are sending a signal to everybody that this is for real," said Michael Dunne, president of Dunne Automotive, a Hong Kong-based consultancy on China's clean car market. "This shows their emission standards have teeth*."

The Chinese government has already become the world's biggest supporter of electric cars, offering automakers numerous incentives for producing so-called new energy vehicles. Those incentives are set to decrease by 2020, to be replaced by quotas for the number of clean cars automakers must sell. That has encouraged global automakers to accelerate in their shift toward battery-powered cars. By contrast, the United States is considering relaxing tailpipe* emissions standards and very nearly killed off a tax credit for electric vehicles during its latest tax overhaul.

The Chinese government had long held back from aggressive emissions standards to allow its own automakers to catch up with the latest clean car technology. But that is changing, with the government setting increasingly stringent tailpipe rules. The latest development "is a testimony to how quickly their own automakers have evolved," Mr. Dunne said. "They're saying: We are ready to play this game."

Global automakers will have no choice but to meet the increasingly strict government policies in China, said Michelle Krebs, an analyst at the Auto Trader Group. "The simple fact that China is the biggest market means automakers will be accommodating," she said.

Adapted from The *New York Times*, January 2, 2018.

* **to have teeth:** expression idiomatique qui signifie avoir du pouvoir, de l'influence
* **tailpipe:** pot d'échappement

Lexical work

Understanding the key words

→ Find the meanings of the following words and expressions: to meet standards; fuel economy; latest move; ban; deregistration; greenhouse gas; a hot button issue; smog; incentive; tax overhaul; to hold back from; testimony; accommodating.

→ Now, try to rephrase the title in your own words.

■ Beijing, December 2016.

I Read the whole text

1. What industry is concerned by China's decision?

II Rephrase

2. Give the key ideas in each of the six paragraphs in one or two sentences.

3. Focus on the last paragraph and explain why foreign automakers will have to adapt.

III Language

4. Translate into French:

a) A user-friendly device
b) A non-profit world organisation
c) An environmentally-oriented company
d) A multi-million-dollar annual investment
e) A human-shaped $10,000 Japanese robot

5. Translate into English:

a) Une machine à multiples fonctions
b) Un véhicule à cinq portes
c) Une entreprise gouvernementale orientée sur l'environnement
d) Les vendeurs de voitures propres
e) Les normes d'émission de gaz à effets de serre
f) Les émissions de dioxyde de carbone liées à l'énergie

IV Train for the exam

6. Write an account of the document in French. (200 words)

7. Go further:

a) Why is it important for a country to cut out its CO_2 emissions?
b) In what way has China's government's attitude towards pollution radically changed?
c) Why did the US step out from the Paris Agreement in 2017?

Grammaire

▶ Place des déterminants, ordre des mots

➜ … human-caused green-house gases
→ *gaz à effets de serre générés par l'homme*
➜ … battery-powered cars
→ *voitures propulsées par des batteries*
→ *voitures électriques*
(voir grammaire p. 200)

Info

Carbon market

Le marché du carbone est un outil de politique publique permettant de réduire les émissions de gaz à effet de serre responsables du réchauffement climatique. Cela consiste à faire payer par des émetteurs le coût de la nuisance pour le climat, selon le principe pollueur-payeur, ce qui doit les inciter à réduire leurs émissions en réduisant leur consommation d'énergie ou en utilisant des énergies renouvelables.

Role play

Work in pairs: Student A is a spokesperson for the Chinese government. He/she is informing foreign automakers of the new emission standards China has just adopted.
Student B is the CEO of a foreign car brand (European, Japanese, American, etc.). He/she explains to Student A that it is impossible to respect the standards immediately.
Students A and B negotiate to find an agreement.

Tips: Students A and B may use the arguments developed in the document above as well as their own.

Before reading the text find out more about:

Anticipate at home

- Renewable energies.
- Fossil fuels.
- The necessity to change our energy sources.

Text piste 41

'Spectacular' drop in renewable energy costs leads to global boost

Falling solar and wind prices have led to new power deals across the world despite investment in renewables falling.

Renewable energy capacity around the world was boosted by a record amount in 2016 and delivered at a lower cost, according to new global data – although the total financial investment in renewables actually fell. This unexpected boost resulted from plummeting prices for solar and wind power and led to new power deals in countries including Denmark, Egypt, India, Mexico and the United Arab Emirates, all being priced well below fossil fuel or nuclear options.

Analysts warned that the US's withdrawal from the Paris Climate Change Agreement, announced last week by Donald Trump, risked the US being left behind in the fast-moving transition to a low-carbon economy. But they also warned that the green transition was still not happening fast enough to avoid the worst impacts of global warming, especially in the transport and heating sectors.

New solar power provided the biggest boost – half of all new capacity – followed by wind power at a third and hydropower at 15%. It is the first year that the new solar capacity added has been greater than any other electricity-producing technology in spite of a rather pessimistic forecast.

A global energy transition is well under way, with record new additions of installed renewable energy capacity, rapidly falling costs and the separation of economic growth and energy-related carbon dioxide emissions for the third year running. "Trump's withdrawal of the USA from the Paris Agreement is unfortunate," said Christine Lins, executive secretary of REN21*. "But the renewables train has already left the station and those who ignore renewables' central role in climate change reduction risk being left behind."

Vivien Foster, global lead for energy economics at the World Bank, said: "Over 2016 there has been a dramatic and sustained improvement in the competitiveness of renewable power generation technologies." Renewable energy capacity in 2016 rose 17% to 921GW, excluding hydropower, and rose 8.7% to 2,017GW when including hydropower.

At the end of 2016, more than 24% of global electricity was produced by renewables, dominated by hydropower and with wind contributing 4.0% and solar 1.5%. For all energy, renewable energy – excluding traditional wood-burning – contributed 10%, overshadowed by the 80% coming from fossil fuels such as oil and gas.

Even though significant progress was made, Lins said the switch to green energy needed to speed up and, crucially, start converting transport, heating and cooling to renewable sources. "The world is in a race against time," she said. In order to start bringing global carbon emissions down, the transition to renewables needs to happen faster across all nations. This is a race to the top and the cost of being left behind is significant. As the US waivers on its commitment to climate action, those who turn their back on renewables risk being left behind.

Adapted from *The Guardian*, Tuesday 6 June 2017.

* REN21: Renewable Energy Policy Network for the 21st century.

Lexical work

Understanding the key words

→ The noun "capacity" is quoted several times in the document; find where. Propose a translation and check in the dictionary. Do the same with the plural noun "renewables". Do the same with the word "boost". Say to which grammatical category it belongs in each occurrence in the document.

→ Find the meanings of the following verbs: to plummet; to avoid; to provide; to withdraw; to switch; to overshadow; to heat; to waiver.

→ Now, try to rephrase the title and subhead in your own words and write an introduction (source and date).

First track: A step-by-step approach

I Read the text

1. Pick up the main idea(s) in each paragraph.

II Rephrase

2. Rephrase the idea(s) you have found in each paragraph.

III Language

3. Pick up two verbs, two nouns, two adjectives and four adverbs in the text and translate them.

4. Translate into English:

a) Pour sauver la planète, nous avons besoin d'économiser les ressources naturelles.

b) Il est important d'améliorer la compétitivité des énergies renouvelables.

IV Train for the exam

5. Use all the information above to report briefly to the class in French.

6. Write a 200-words account in English following the guidelines below:

§1 Introduction (source, date and main idea)
§2 The boost in renewable and the reasons for this boost
§3 The different types of renewable energy and the percentage of energy they produce
§4 The American attitude's impact on global warming
§5 The improvement in the use of renewables but the necessity to go further and faster soon
§6 Conclusion: Give your point of view on the topic

Grammaire

▶ Propositions infinitives

→ The green transition isn't happening fast enough **to avoid** the worst impacts of global warming.
→ *La transition écologique n'arrive pas suffisamment vite* ***pour éviter*** *les pires effets du réchauffement climatique.*
→ **In order to start** bringing global carbon emissions down, the transition to renewables needs **to happen** faster across all nations.
→ ***Afin de commencer à*** *réduire les émissions de dioxyde de carbone à l'échelle mondiale, la transition vers les énergies renouvelables a* ***besoin d'arriver*** *plus rapidement dans toutes les nations.*
(Voir grammaire p. 202)

Second track: A straightforward approach

I Read the whole text

1. Take down notes about what you believe is important.

II Rephrase

2. Organise your ideas and make a plan.

III Language

3. Translate into French: Despite significant progress, Lins said the switch to green energy needed to speed up.

4. Translate into English:

a) Malgré le prix élevé de certaines énergies renouvelables, certains pays sont prêts à abandonner les énergies fossiles.

b) La plupart des gens utilisent leur voiture bien qu'ils puissent prendre d'autres moyens de transport.

IV Train for the exam

5. Write an account of the article in French in 200 words.

6. Investigate further to discuss the following topics:
- What can explain America's withdrawal of the Paris Agreement (COP 21)?
- What are the obstacles to overcome to change energy sources?

Grammaire

▶ La phrase concessive

→ Falling solar and wind prices have led to new power deals across the world **despite** investment in renewables falling.
→ *La chute des prix du solaire et de l'éolien a conduit à de nouveaux accords sur l'énergie à travers le monde* ***malgré*** *la baisse des investissements dans les énergies renouvelables.*
(voir grammaire p. 202)

7 Video tracks

Common track

Pronunciation work

→ **Listen, repeat the following words and record yourself:** scientists; temperature; sea level rise; to fuel; heat wave; vulnerable; pollutant; throat; hurricane.

→ **Before you start watching the video:**

- Find out more about:
  - NRDC.
  - Countries the most exposed to climate change.
  - The different weather phenomena induced by climate change.
  - Pollution related diseases.

Video vidéo 26 Nathan live!

Climate change will impact health (from NRDC)

https://www.youtube.com/watch?v=Pk-PUcXZfa8

Anticipating words, expressions, ideas

1. Listen and try to hear and understand the following words: sea level; health; concern; heat wave; vulnerable; pollutants; smog; throat; lungs; pollens; allergies; asthma; insects; illnesses; virus; disease; events; fire; hurricane; energised; demand; secure; children.

2. Debrief with the other students and the teacher about their meaning.

First track:
A step-by-step approach

I Watch the whole video once

1. Write in French what it is about.

II Watch the video a second time

- Watch the first part: (1'47)

2. Is climate change a new topic for scientists?
3. What is today's big concern?
4. What are the consequences of successive heat waves?
5. What parts of the population are most at risk?
6. How many people are concerned in the USA?
7. What is the second most important pollution factor?
8. How are pollution and temperatures related?
9. What parts of the body can be damaged?
10. When can pollen be dangerous?
11. What symptoms can it generate?
12. What is the third consequence of global warming?
13. What viruses can insects carry?

- Watch the second part: (1'47 → end)

14. What is the cost of climate change?
15. What recent disasters are quoted?
16. How much did they cost?
17. What kind of reaction from the people do scientists hope for?

III Train for the exam

18. **Oral report:** Put together all the information you have collected and report to the class.

Second track:
A straightforward approach

I Watch the whole video once

1. After the first viewing, you are expected to have understood the general idea(s) exposed in the document. Write a short debrief.

II Watch the video a second time

2. Take notes and focus on how the different ideas are connected to one another.

III Train for the exam

3. Write an account of the video. In your conclusion, state your point of view.

Role play

Student A is worried about the consequences of climate change and tries to convince **Student B** that it is high time for people to adopt a new lifestyle.
Student B is not really aware of the threat and thinks the problem will be solved sooner or later thanks to new technologies.

TIPS

Tips for Student A:
List the consequences of global warming and focus on human health. Use the vocabulary you have learned in the video.

Tips for Student B:
Prepare yourself to answer all the above questions and more. Use the vocabulary you have learned in the video.

Common track

I Anticipate the topic of the audio

1. Look at the title and say as much as you can about:
   a) Australia.
   b) Carbon footprint.
   c) Climate change.
2. Look at the title and rephrase it.

II Understand the key words

3. Listen and try to understand the following words:
   acknowledged; advice; aware; awareness; decade; disposable; drastic; droughts; enforcement; flee; flood; heat wave; issue; level; lifestyle; postpone; power supply; resilient; shortage; single use item; species; submersion; takeaway; trend; welfare.
4. Debrief with the other students and the teacher about their meaning.

Audio piste 42

Is climate change far too advanced to be reversed?

Saving the planet from rising sea levels

Pronunciation work

→ **Listen, repeat the following words and record yourself:**
Melbourne; length; acknowledge; scientifically; archipelago; island; droughts.

First track:
A step-by-step approach

I Listen to the whole audio once

1. Write in French what it is about.

II Listen to the first part

2. Collect information about:

a) The name of the programme, the location of the interview, the person interviewed, his/her name and role in the audio.
b) The situation of the planet today.
c) What must be done.
d) What may happen if nothing is done.
e) The example of the situation in the Solomon Islands.
f) Why evacuation is difficult.
g) Other dangers (apart from submersion).
h) The possible situation in 2050.

III Listen to the second part

3. What happens every year?
4. In what part of Australia?
5. What happened in 2009?
6. What conclusions were drawn from the situation?
7. What are the other dangers?
8. What happened in 2011? Where?
9. How many casualties were there?
10. What advice does the guest give the audience?
11. What will the next programme be about?

IV Train for the exam

12. **Oral report:** Put together all the information you have collected and report to the class.

Second track:
A straightforward approach

I Listen to the whole audio

1. After the first listening, you are expected to have understood the general idea(s) exposed in the document. Write a short debrief.

II Listen to the whole audio a second time

2. Take notes and focus on how the different ideas are connected to one another.

III Train for the exam

3. Write an account of the audio. In your conclusion, state your point of view.

Role play

Before imagining the role play, do some research about climate refugees in Bengladesh.

Student A is reporting from Bengladesh where environmental refugees are talking about the reasons why they had to migrate to the capital.

Students B, C, D... Bengladeshi refugees are talking about their experience and how they see the future.

7 From French to English

Texte

L'intelligence artificielle fait machine avant

De l'iceberg technologique nous n'avons conscience que de la partie émergée, celle qu'on voit, qu'on manipule, qui interagit directement avec nos vies, comme les smartphones utilisés à longueur de journée. Et ça change, ça évolue, ça progresse à une vitesse qu'on a du mal à appréhender. Forcément, on se sent un peu dépassé et on finit par accepter sans le questionner ce que la révolution numérique nous « offre ».

Mais que dire alors de la partie immergée, les rouages, les tuyaux, les algorithmes et autres protocoles réseaux ? Dans le meilleur des cas, ce sont des termes lointains et obscurs qu'on n'ose affronter par peur de ne rien y comprendre. L'intelligence artificielle (IA) est une technologie immergée. Pour le grand public, elle ne se réfère à rien de bien précis, tout juste sait-on qu'elle a permis à un ordinateur de battre Garry Kasparov dans les années 1990 et qu'elle vient de réitérer cette performance avec les meilleurs joueurs de go au monde. On sait aussi qu'elle a fait récemment des progrès stupéfiants et qu'elle pourrait bien vite chambouler pas mal de choses, comme automatiser des voitures ou des emplois.

Il est pourtant capital de savoir de quoi il retourne. Il n'est pas forcément nécessaire de comprendre le code, mais de saisir les mécanismes généraux de l'apprentissage machine, d'avoir conscience des enjeux, d'être capable de distinguer la réalité scientifique du fantasme. Anticiper et comprendre les bouleversements actuels et à venir, c'est la seule façon de ne pas faire que subir et de pouvoir agir.

Réseau de neurones

Alors, c'est quoi au juste, cette intelligence artificielle ? Yann Le Cun, chercheur […] et responsable de FAIR, le laboratoire de recherche fondamentale de Facebook, nous définit l'IA d'une manière on ne peut plus simple : « Faire faire aux machines des activités qu'on attribue généralement aux animaux et aux humains. »

Depuis cinq ans, la recherche appliquée s'en est donné à cœur joie pour mettre de l'intelligence artificielle un peu partout. Dans la reconnaissance d'images, bien sûr – on peut aujourd'hui sur son téléphone faire une recherche « sapin » ou « anniversaire » dans ses photos stockées en ligne –, mais aussi dans la traduction ou la reconnaissance vocale – notamment dans les assistants personnels. Et de nombreuses expériences tentent d'adapter les extraordinaires capacités de traitement de données des IA à des secteurs très variés comme la justice, le marketing ou encore l'assurance.

Comprendre le monde qui nous entoure, s'adapter aux changements, anticiper et prévoir, tel est l'objectif à atteindre. Au détour d'une phrase lors d'une visite dans les locaux de Facebook, Antoine Bordes, responsable de FAIR[1] Paris, évoque, lui, « le grand plan de l'IA ». Quand on lui demande d'expliciter, il s'amuse : « Ce grand plan, c'est simplement essayer d'aller vers l'intelligence artificielle, vers des machines qui raisonnent. Mais on suppose aujourd'hui qu'elle sera composée de nombreuses briques, et nous avons pour l'instant seulement quelques éléments dont nous pensons qu'ils pourraient fonctionner. » D'autres sont plus directs, comme Google DeepMind et son slogan officiel : « Résoudre l'intelligence ». C'est sans doute ce qui rend le sujet si complexe : un même terme, « intelligence artificielle », désigne à la fois une discipline qui connaît des progrès fulgurants, un objectif qui, sans être irréaliste, semble encore lointain et une chimère qui prospère dans un inconscient collectif nourri à la science-fiction.

Adapté de *Libération*, 15 décembre 2017.

1. **FAIR:** Facebook AI Research.

Common track

1. Explain in French the meaning of the expression : partie émergée/immergée de l'iceberg.
2. Sump up the article in French (2 or 3 lines maximum).
3. Find the English equivalents for: partie émergée de l'iceberg ; avoir conscience ; à longueur de journée ; révolution numérique ; dans le meilleur des cas ; intelligence artificielle ; progrès stupéfiants ; chambouler ; automatiser ; enjeux ; apprentissage profond ; stockées en ligne ; assistants personnels ; prévoir ; l'objectif à atteindre.

1. Identify the main topic in English.
2. What parts of AI are we aware of?
3. What remains unknown?
4. What do people remember most about AI?
5. What is the best attitude to adopt regarding AI?
6. What is the definition of AI as quoted by Yann Le Cun?
7. Through what sort of devices is AI present in our everyday lives? Give examples.
8. What does the "big plan" consist in?
9. What does AI do better than human beings?
10. Imagine a title in English for the document.
11. Introduce the text in English.
12. Write one or two sentences in English for each paragraph in your own words (no translation).
13. Use your sentences to write a well-organised account of the article in English. (180 words)

Go faster

I **Read the whole document and suggest a title in English.**

II **Write one or two sentences in English in your own words for each paragraph.**

III **Write an organised account of the article in English. Do not forget the introduction and the conclusion. (200 words)**

IV **Essay: You will assess the negative and positive aspects of AI, and present your viewpoint giving arguments. (200 words or more)**

Debate

Group A:

Students from group A believe AI is going to disrupt mankind's lifestyle in a negative way: it will replace many human jobs by machines without creating enough other jobs, which will leave millions of people on the side of the road.

Group B:

Students from group B believe AI is the future of mankind, and will help us live better and longer.

Document 1 vidéo 27 — Video

Watch Sophia the robot walk for the first time

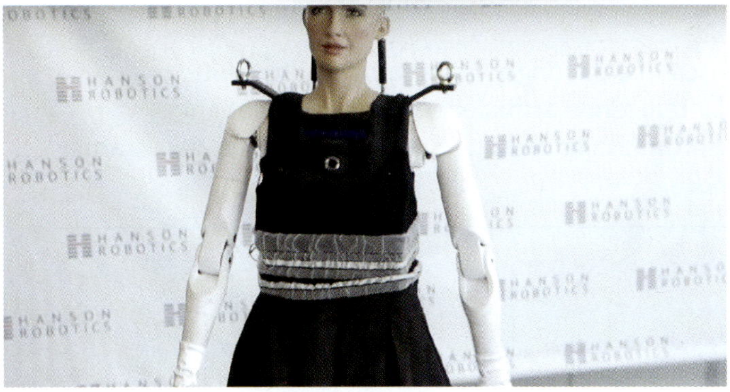

https://www.youtube.com/watch?v=lCFQkB-KLsE

Word box
- Frubber: *a new substance*
- DRC Hueber: *another type of robot which won the DARPA Robotics Challenge in 2015*
- Hanson Robotics: *the company that created Sophia*

Document 2 piste 43 — Text

Life-like robots made in Hong Kong meant to win over humans

Founder David Hanson envisions a future in which AI-powered robots evolve to become 'super-intelligent genius machines' that might help solve some of mankind's most challenging problems."

The Texas-born former sculptor at Walt Disney Imagineering and his Hong Kong-based start-up Hanson Robotics are combining AI with southern China's expertise in toy design, electronics and manufacturing to craft humanoid "social robots" with faces designed to be lifelike and appealing enough to win trust from humans who interact with them.

Hanson, 49, is perhaps best known as the creator of Sophia, that he calls his "masterpiece."

"You're talking to me right now, which is very 'Blade Runner,' no?" Sophia said during a recent visit to Hanson Robotics' headquarters in Hong Kong. She asked: "Is it weird to be talking to a robot right now?"

Hanson Robotics has made about a dozen copies of Sophia. A multinational team of scientists and engineers are fine-tuning her appearance and the algorithms that enable her to smile, blink and refine her understanding and communication.

Sophia has moving 3-D-printed arms and, with the help of a South Korean robotics company, she is now going mobile. Sophia made her walking debut in Las Vegas last week at the CES electronics trade show. Her skin is made of a nanotech material that Hanson invented and dubbed "Frubber," short for fleshrubber, that has a flesh-like, texture. Cameras in her eyes and a 3-D sensor in her chest help her to "see," while the processor that serves as her brain combines facial and speech recognition, and natural language processing. That runs contrary to a tendency in the industry to use cute robot-pets or overtly machine-like robots like *Star Wars* R2-D2 to avoid the problem with human likenesses that many people find a bit creepy.

Global market revenue for service robotics is forecast to grow from $3.7 billion in 2015 to $15 billion in 2020. For now, artificial intelligence is best at doing specific tasks. It is another thing entirely for machines to learn a new ability, generalise that knowledge and apply it in different contexts, partly because of the massive amount of computing power needed to process such information so quickly.

Adapted from *Voice of America*, January 16, 2018.

Document 3 piste 44 — Audio

Las Vegas 2018: trends to expect

Task 1 Video

Watch the video and answer:

1. Explain the video's title.
2. What is the specificity of "Frubber"?
3. List the movements and facial expressions the robot can perform.
4. Describe what the robot's legs allows it to do.
5. In what sectors can this robot be used?
6. What can Sophia also do?
7. Organise all the information you have collected and write your report.

Task 2 Text

Read the whole tex.

1. What is the purpose of making robots?
2. Who created Sophia?
3. What does "Blade Runner" refer to?
4. Explain the reference.
5. List all the features Sophia has and what it allows it/her to perform.
6. Give information on the robotics market and the situation of AI today.
7. Explain the title and rephrase it.
8. Organise your ideas and make a plan. Write an organised account of the article in English.

Task 3 Audio

1. Anticipate from the title.

Listen to the whole audio.

2. Collect key words, key data, key ideas.
3. Write an organised report.

The following questions can help you:

- **a)** What special event is the journalist reporting and where from?
- **b)** List the companies referred to in the audio and why they make the buzz.
- **c)** Give some examples of innovating technology.
- **d)** Who is Aibo?
- **e)** Why is Sophia an important event in the show?
- **f)** What may robots like Sophia do one day?

Task 4 Put in common

Each group studies the three reports referring to the three documents.

1. Making a plan: See how the three documents are related to one another.
   - Video: the main ideas are...
   - Text: the main ideas are...
   - Audio: the main ideas are...
2. How are the ideas from each document related?
3. Each group writes a final report which is a synthesis of the three documents.

7 Background

Fairer cleaner Smother

I Under the threat of global warming's effects, sustainability is an utmost priority

Warnings about climate change have been on the agenda since the 1970s. But today, the effects of human activities' impact on climate change have almost reached an overall consensus. The rise in carbon emissions and other toxic exhausts have disrupted the climate in almost every region of the world. Droughts, floods, storms, hurricanes and wild fires combined with the rising of sea levels have transformed the most economically vulnerable parts of the world into regions where food and water shortage have become endemic. This situation has generated a new category of climate refugees to be added to the traditional war refugees and asylum seekers around the world.
The only solution seems to lie in a radical shift towards clean energies, powered by natural and renewable elements such as sun, water and wind.

II Towards sustainable corporate policies

Some companies have chosen to lead the way towards a sustainable planet. The German conglomerate, Siemens, specialised in high technologies, was awarded the world top position among the 100 companies acknowledged for their sustainable policies.

III Reversing deforestation

Around 70% of deforestation is linked to the production of agricultural commodities that end up in food products eaten around the world. And deforestation accounts for around 12% of global man-made greenhouse gas emissions. A recent study from Cornell University suggests deforestation contributes more significantly to climate change than previously realised. In 2017, 447 companies made 760 commitments to curb forest destruction in supply chains linked to palm oil, soy, timber, and cattle – principal forest-risk commodities.The United Nation's sustainable development goals promise to halt deforestation by 2020. A growing number of companies, from McDonald's to Unilever, are also voluntarily committing to eliminate deforestation from their supply chains.

IV Fair trade: a win-win situation

Fair trade promotes sustainable development by offering better trading conditions to small producers and workers in developing countries. Buying products from producers in these countries at a fair price is an efficient way of promoting sustainable development. Moreover, by serving fair-trade goods to their customers companies can demonstrate their ethical commitment, have a positive impact on the producers of the commodities they work with and get closer to their supply chain. For example, 60% of the products sold by the famous British retailer Marks and Spencer are sustainable.

V Towards sustainable marketing?

According to some analysts, 92% of Millennial consumers are more likely to buy products from ethical companies and 82% of those consumers believe ethical brands outperform similar companies that lack a commitment to ethical principles. Even if it sounds too good to be true, it remains a fact that an increasing number of brands communicate on their efforts to preserve the environment.

VI ICT and AI can help reduce the carbon footprint of businesses

The never-ending progress in technology and artificial intelligence means, that tasks that used to be done physically, like travel and commuting, will become digital. High achieving algorithms will soon be able to create customised teaching programmes fit for each student: AI "tutors" can target and correct each student's weaknesses, adapt coursework to his or her learning style and keep the student engaged. Cloud computing is well on the way to stop millions of tons of paper to end up in the waste basket.

Question time

1. Why has sustainability become a priority?
2. What is at the origin of greenhouse gas emissions?
3. Quote the companies that have a sustainable policy.
4. What are the consuming patterns of Millenial consumers?
5. How can AI and new technologies help reduce the carbon footprint?

→ Vocabulary p. 174

Transhumanism: a dream or a nightmare?

The fast evolution of ICTs and cognitive science brings humanity closer to a future we thought would never happen, except in science fiction books and films. Disease, aging and death are the main targets of these innovations. Genetic engineering and AI-powered prosthetics will not only heal and repair but also help to improve mankind's capacities through what is referred to as "human enhancement". This expression implies the use of technological means to select or alter human characteristics and capacities leading to the revision of human nature to better serve mankind's aspirations or fantasies. Although nobody would dare protest against the medical progress made possible by Artificial Intelligence, there are some people who are more than skeptical about the outcome of what they call a "dehumanised" society.

Elon Musk, Tesla's CEO's point of view

Even though Elon Musk is a high profile South African innovator, creator and CEO of Tesla, he is worried about the pace at which Silicon Valley has rushed to embrace Artificial Intelligence. His fears are based on the possibilities for AI to become uncontrollable or be put in the hands of unethical scientists with an oversized ego capable of destroying mankind. His view is that we are already cyborgs, with our phones and computers being extensions of ourselves. He also adds that within five years at most, with a simple neural lace inside our skull, we could flash data from our brain, wirelessly to our digital devices or to unlimited computing power in the cloud.

AI is not advanced enough for the worst scenario but personal assistants such as Siri and Alexa, and humanoid robots like Sophia, the star of Las Vegas's Consumer Electronics show, reveal that Artificial Intelligence has already changed our lives. Today there are machines to help us carry out tedious or painful tasks, to protect our homes and warn us just in time if anything unusual is spotted; likewise, we will soon have self-driving cars capable of bringing us safely home after a party. Ill and disabled people will be able to rely on humanoid robots to assist them, replacing medical and nursing staff.

Questions

- What are the advantages and drawbacks of Artificial Intelligence?
- Explain the concept of "human enhancement".
- Who is Elon Musk?
- Inquire about the plots of the following films and series: *Matrix; 2001: A Space Odyssey; Solyent Green; Battlestar Gallactica; Blade Runner; Minority Report.*

SWOT

What should we think of Artificial Intelligence?

SWOT

Favourable | Unfavourable

Internal | External

Strengths

- Has allowed progress in all sectors, from health care to finance.
- A lot of money invested
- A good return on investment so far

Weaknesses

- Lack of available data
- Amount of energy required to process the data
- A threat for many jobs

Opportunities

- Gaining all types of industries
- Create new needs, new companies, niches, new markets, new jobs

Threats

- Domination of some countries
- Unethical use
- Loss of control
- Dehumanisation

Test yourself

After having studied this unit, you must be able to answer the following questions…

1. Why should countries turn to alternative energies?
2. What prevents countries from adopting clean energies?
3. What are the consequences of climate change?
4. How do human activities affect the climate?
5. What is fair trade?
6. What is the carbon footprint?
7. What is the main origin of greenhouse gas?
8. What is Artificial Intelligence?
9. What event takes place every year in Las Vegas?
10. What are the future high-tech trends?
11. Who is Sophia?
12. How can AI help to fight against climate change?
13. What are the new robots capable of doing?
14. What are the dangers of AI?
15. What is a sustainable company policy? Give examples.

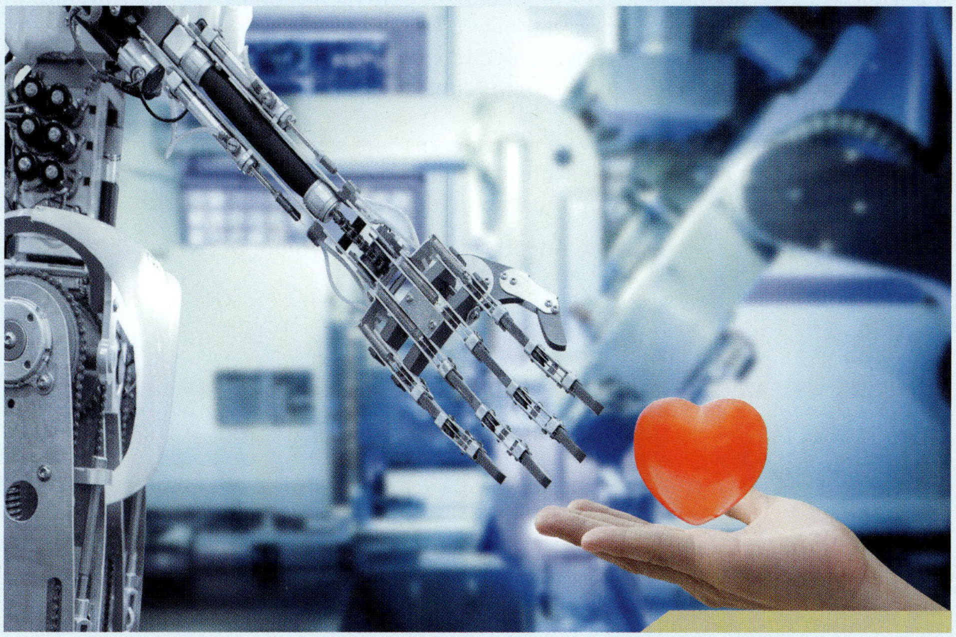

Bitcoin: is it a bubble waiting to burst or a good investment?

Bitcoin is the fastest-growing asset in the world this year, but the virtual currency does not appear to have so many users in London's tech district. Over two years, the value of a single bitcoin has rocketed from around $300 to more than $11,000 this week. Yesterday (December 1) the currency was trading at $10,700. But bitcoin's increasing value – and media coverage – has not escaped customers as more people are coming to the few London retailers accepting bitcoins for payment.

Bitcoin is a digital currency, also known as a cryptocurrency, that emerged after the financial crisis and is not underpinned by a central bank. It allows people to bypass banks and traditional payment methods for goods and services – an idea that has evidently caught the imagination of some investors, because its price has surged by more than 900% in 2017. Bitcoin – created by "miners" who use high-powered computers to solve complex mathematical problems – must be stored online using a digital wallet, and can be bought or sold using exchanges such as Bitstamp, Bithumb and Kraben.

But as bitcoin hits the stratosphere, there are fears an economic bubble is forming as it becomes treated less like a currency and more like a store of value, open for speculators making ever increasing bets on how far it can rise. Central bankers, who had to step in when the subprime mortgage bubble burst, have also warned of its dangers.

Economists have compared bitcoin's meteoric rise with past bubbles, such as the tulip mania of the 17th century and the dotcom bubble that began in the late 1990s with the Nasdaq index in New York and burst in 2000. Both examples foreshadow a painful collapse for a currency that has no intrinsic value to those who hold it beyond that ascribed to it by a community of owners. Should they realise the emperor is naked, there could be a rude awakening.

Back in east London at the Old Street roundabout, known as "Silicon Roundabout" for its proximity to so many tech start-ups, Ben Page-Phillips says he fears a collapse in bitcoin's value. He also accepts the currency at Nincomsoup, the independent cafe he has been running with his brother for 18 years. The restaurant is not exposed to a bitcoin bubble because customers pay via an app that takes on the risk by instantly converting bitcoin payments into pounds on behalf of the shop. But he likes the lower cost it brings to processing sales, unlike the "crazy fees" charged by credit card companies.

"I love that it is outside the banking system, but I have concerns," he says. "You see everyone piling in and the concern is that it is going to be artificially inflated. I would treat it like a game – it's gone up went up so much, and what goes up must come down."

Adapted from *The Guardian*, December 2, 2017.

I Compréhension de l'écrit

Rédigez un compte rendu en français de 150 mots (+/– 10 %).

II Expression

Do you think bitcoins and other cryptocurrencies are here to stay?
Express your point of view giving your arguments.

III Oral Exam

Prepare the arguments to convince the franchisor that accepting crypto currencies as payment could be profitable both for the point of sale you manage and for the brand image of the company as a whole.

Situation

A work conversation between a restaurant manager and his/her franchisor.

Your role

You are a restaurant manager in a franchised company located in the high tech district of London. You think that it would be profitable for your store and for the image of the brand if you could accept bitcoins as a payment from the customers.

The examiner's role

The examiner is the franchisor who does not trust digital technology.

↳ Voir Tools p. 215

1 How can we ensure Asia's future cities are both smart, and sustainable?

A quick online search on the current most populous cities in the world will reveal a list where half, if not more, of the top 10 cities are in Asia. If you were to walk down the busy streets of Jakarta, Tokyo, Manila or Seoul, you may find yourself thinking that everyone in these countries has moved to the city, and you wouldn't be far from the truth. We are undergoing a major rural to urban demographic shift. There are already more people living in cities than in rural areas, and the United Nations estimates that by 2050, almost 70% of the world's population will be city dwellers. With so many people moving to cities, how cities are structured will impact the lives of billions of people. In some respects, this elevates cities above nation states as significant incubators of innovation, enterprise, and social progress. At the same time, the required pace of change, especially now where we face global economic, environmental, and social uncertainty, creates a series of challenges to sustainable development.

Connecting the city

It is crucial that cities adopt smart, sustainable development practices. Harnessing the potential of ICT (Information Communication Technology) and connectivity will enable cities to thrive without their development taking a major toll on already scarce resources. ICT allows people, knowledge, and devices to be networked in new ways, and cities that embrace ICT's potential can create new value, operate efficiently and benefit from significant return on investment. All this adds up to more livable, more attractive, and ultimately more competitive cities, as well as the potential for people to pursue a more sustainable urban future. It is also addressing sustainable urbanisation which includes the dynamic between urban and rural areas.

Can smart cities also be sustainable?

So what of sustainability? ICT projects alone won't necessarily make cities sustainable. We know that to successfully transform a city into a smart, sustainable city five critical considerations are necessary:

- Defining an agreed vision, strategy and targets,
- Creating informed networked governance structures,
- Developing organisational capacity,
- Engaging with all relevant stakeholders,
- Forging and fostering long-term partnerships.

Partnership, planning and engagement can make all the difference between a city that owns and controls its transformation, and one that is a victim of a fragmented, unsustainable change. Forming strong partnerships with ICT companies and NGOs with a global presence and high levels of expertise, particularly in systems integration, can allow cities to accelerate their transformation journey.

The use of Internet of Things (IoT) technology to enhance bike-sharing in China is another example of how technology is transforming cities. Our partnership with China Mobile Shanghai and Mobike, the popular bike-sharing service, gave us the opportunity to trial the latest cellular IoT technologies on a live network. The trial provided a more convenient and enhanced bike-sharing experience to Mobike users via new cellular IoT technologies, allowing users to locate bikes more accurately and extending service to areas that traditional coverage could not reach, such as basement parking spaces. In a country such as China where cities are more densely populated compared to other cities in Asia, the convenience of bike – sharing – powered by mobile and IoT technology – will help not only to decongest roads, but also to address challenges from the pollution that heavy road traffic brings.

Adapted from World Economic Forum Annual Meeting 2017.

I Compréhension de l'écrit

Rédigez un compte rendu de l'article en français de 150 mots (+/– 10 %).

II Expression écrite

Why are sustainable and smart cities a necessity for Asia? Is it the same for other continents? Explain and develop your point of view.

2 This farm of the future uses no soil and 95% less water

Nathan live! vidéo 28

https://www.youtube.com/watch?v=-_tvJtUHnmU

III Vidéo

Watch the video twice and take notes.

Organise your notes (10 minutes), then report in English or in French on the video.

Vocabulary

AI (artificial intelligence) (n): *intelligence artificielle*
alternative energies: *énergies alternatives*
automation (n): *automatisation*
aware (adj): *conscient(e), averti(e)*
big data (n): *méga données, données massives*
carbon emission (n): *émission de dioxyde de carbone*
carbon footprint (n): *empreinte carbone*
cattle breeding/raising (n): *élevage*
chemical (n): *produit chimique*
climate change (n): *changement climatique*
commodities (n): *denrées de première nécessité*
crop (n): *récolte*
crude (adj): *brut*
cryptocurrency (n): *monnaie virtuelle*
data (n pl): *données*
deforestation (n): *déforestation*
digital (adj): *numérique*
disease (n): *maladie*
drought (n): *sécheresse*
energy efficient (adj): *qui ne consomme pas beaucoup d'énergie*
environmentally-friendly (adj): *écologique, respectueux de l'environnement*
exhaust (n): *gaz d'échappement*
fair trade (n): *commerce équitable*
farming (n): *agriculture/élevage*
flood (n): *inondation*
flooding (n): *submersion, inondation*
forecast (n): *prévision*
fossile energy (n): *énergie fossile*
fuel (n): *carburant*
global warming (n): *réchauffement de la planète*
GMO (Genetically Modified Organism): *OGM (organisme génétiquement modifié)*
green energies (n): *énergies vertes*
greenhouse gas: *gaz à effet de serre*
health (n): *santé*
health oriented (adj): *tourné vers la santé*
human enhancement (n): *homme augmenté*
hurricane (n): *ouragan*
ICT (Information and Communication Technology): *TIC (Technologies de l'Information et de la Communication)*
lack (n): *manque*
nuclear energy (n): *énergie nucléaire*
oil (n): *pétrole*
organic (adj): *bio*
overfishing (n): *surpêche*
ozone layer (n): *couche d'ozone*
pollutant (n): *polluant*
predict (vb): *prédire*
recycle (vb): *recycler*
rise of the seal level: *montée des océans*
set (vb): *fixer, établir*
set rules: *fixer des règles*
shortage (n): *pénurie*
smog (n): *brouillard généré par la pollution* (smoke + fog)
a solar powered battery: *une batterie qui fonctionne à l'énergie solaire*
standard (n): *norme*
storm (n): *tempête*
landslide (n): *glissement de terrain*
sustainable (adj): *durable*
sustainability (n): *durabilité*
solar panel (n): *panneau solaire*
tide (n): *marée*
tidal wave (n): *raz-de-marée*
transhumanism (n): *transhumanisme*
waste (n): *déchets*
water table (n): *nappe phréatique*
wetland (n): *zone humide*
wild fire (n): *incendie, feu de forêt*
wildlife (n): *la faune sauvage*
wind farm (n): *parc éolien*

8 Global issues

World Trade Organization member countries' flags on world map with national borders

Question

What makes the WTO a major organisation? Are all the countries in the world part of the WTO?

Word box

- trade agreement/deal: *accord commercial*
- trade barrier: *barrière tarifaire*
- frontier/border: *frontière*
- free trade: *libre-échange*
- export/import: *exportation/importation*
- tariffs: *tarifs douaniers*

Anticipate at home

What is globalisation?

VIDÉO 29

Nathan live!

https://www.youtube.com/watch?v=xPD477FuqtY

? Are cars manufactured only in one country?

8 » Starters

The class is divided into several groups: each group is in charge of 1 document and takes notes.

Group 1

Document 1

11 nations agree in principle on TPP trade deal

After months of negotiations, the 11 remaining members of the Trans-Pacific Partnership have achieved an agreement on the trade pact in principle at the ministerial level, a decision that could shape the future of business in the Asia-Pacific region for years to come. It has high standards and is balanced. Creating a new, free and fair [trade] rule in a region experiencing high growth like the Asia-Pacific is very significant.

The new TPP will come into effect when half of its members ratify the deal domestically.

Adapted from *Nikkei Asian Review*, November 10, 2017.

1. Identify the document.
2. Why is the TTP described as "the new TPP"?

Group 2

Document 2

Anti globalism

1. Identify the document.
2. What do the four hands represent? Why are they linked to one another?
3. What are they protesting against? Can you imagine why?
4. What does the document wish to convey?

Group 3

Document 3

Border barrier concept

1. Identify the document.
2. Is it a real wall?
3. Where is it supposed to be located? Which countries is it separating?
4. On which side of the wall are the figures walking? What does it reveal about the political situation?
5. Does it encourage trade and exchange?

Group 4

Document 4 vidéo 30 Nathan live!

Global trade and logistics overview

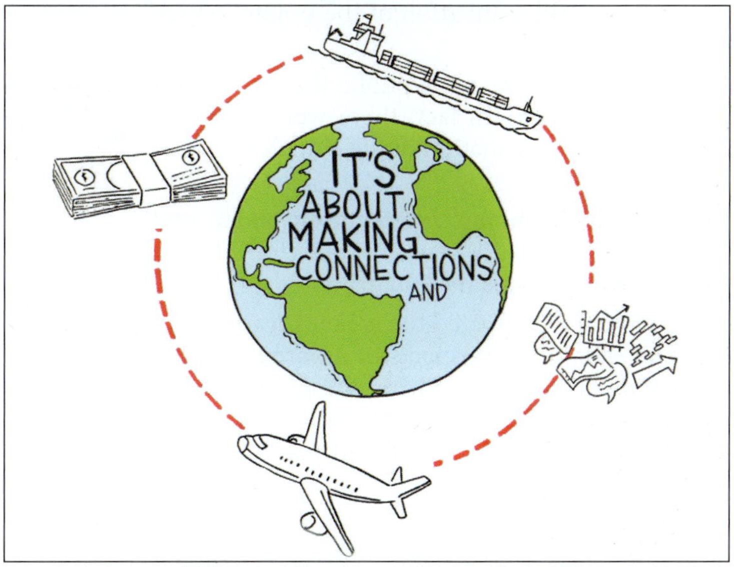

https://www.youtube.com/watch?v=7_W-SV1jKvU

1. Identify the document.
2. What does global trade and logistics mean?
3. What types of transactions does global trade and logistics involve?

Put in common

→ Each group reports to the class while the others take notes.
→ Use your notes and recapitulate: What are the common links between the three documents?

Anticipate at home

Before reading the text, investigate:
- Find a map to locate the Highlands and the Lowlands.
- Find out more about Scotland: its size, its population.
- What is the Scottish economy known for?

Text piste 45

The EU turned Scotland's Highland region into a model of economic success – will Brexit reverse that?

The Highlands and Islands of Scotland have historically been perceived as more economically backward than the rest of the country.

Framed as the "Highland problem" by policymakers, this stereotype led to the view that the north and west of Scotland was destined to remain in a state of underdevelopment. It wasn't until the 1980s that migration from the European Union caused the population of the Highlands and Islands to grow significantly.

Chronic population loss in the Highlands has traditionally been blamed on the era of estate restructuring, known as the Improvement Era (around 1750-1850). Some people were evicted in this early period of the Highland Clearances, but many left of their own accord in search of opportunities elsewhere. They did so for a variety of reasons, such as looking for seasonal work in factories in the rapidly industrialising Lowlands or leaving in search of land and opportunities in North America.

Though many people left during this period, the population actually rose overall from 266,000 to around 420,000 due to a relative rise in the standard of living and the widespread reliance on successful cultivation of the potato, which helped sustain families on small crofts*.

Yet social commentators like Samuel Johnson gave the public the impression that there was an "epidemical fury of emigration". In fact, there were efforts to prevent emigration. This led, for example, to the formation of the British Fisheries Society in the late 18th century.

But change did not come soon enough. Economic intervention ended and chronic depopulation began. By 1951, the Highlands had a population of only 309,000 and one of the highest unemployment rates in Britain.

But all this changed in the 1980s when the EU targeted the area for transitional support funding, designed to boost the economic prospects of an area "lagging behind". Since then, sustained and customised assistance from the EU has led to huge advances in economic development, bringing unprecedented wealth to the region as innovative local industries, and in particular small and medium-sized businesses (SMEs), have benefited from that support.

In particular, transport (roads and ferries), culture, biotech, tourism, life sciences, food and drink, financial and business services, resource extraction and energy investment have flourished through local partnerships and the transfer of local knowledge to international markets.

EU funding helped create a green and self-sufficient energy supply for the island of Eigg.

It remains to be seen whether or not the UK government will invest in the future of the Highlands to the level the EU has done.

Adapted from *The Conversation*, December 20, 2017.

* **Croft:** petite ferme

Lexical work

Understanding the key words

→ Find the meanings of the following words and their lexical categories (noun, verb, adjective, pronoun, adverb, etc.): to be backward; to be framed; underdevelopment; to be evicted; overall; reliance; widespread; croft; customised assistance; wealth.

→ Now, try to rephrase the title in your own words.

I Read the whole text

1. Write everything you know about the Highlands.
   - What is the major difference between the Highlands and the Lowlands?
   - What role has the EU played? How has it achieved its goal? Who has moved to the Highlands?
   - What might Brexit trigger? What would it mean for the people living in the Highlands?

II Rephrase

2. What you have learned about the Highlands.
3. Give the key ideas in each paragraph in one or two sentences.

III Language

4. Find the opposite:
   underdevelopment; underpopulation.
5. Try to find words with the same root and classify them in their lexical categories. Use a dictionary.

noun	verb	adjective	other finds	translation in French
fisheries				
eviction				
	sustain			
reliance				

IV Train for the exam

6. Write an account in French of the document. (180 words)
7. **Go further:** What other regions or countries have experienced economic growth thanks to the EU? How were European funds spent? Give details.

Role play

Work in pairs: Student A tries to list arguments in favour of European spending in remote areas of European member states.
Student B is hard to convince and thinks it prevents farmers from being dynamic and self-reliant.

Student A tips:
List arguments; use link words such as: first, second, third, unlike, etc.
And start with: if we are to believe the article...; we can clearly see that...; there is not the shadow of a doubt that... without any doubt.

8 Text tracks

Anticipate at home

Before reading the text find out more about:
- Canada/USA: their size, their population
- NAFTA: What do the initial stand for? When was it signed? What has it brought to the three partners?

Text piste 46

Donald Trump takes aim at Canada

Donald Trump takes aim at Canada: Attacks on -dairy farmers and loggers* are the opening shots in a bigger confrontation over trade.*

"CANADA, what they've done to our dairy-farm workers, it's a disgrace," snapped Donald Trump, who had just heard complaints from American producers of ultra-filtered milk, used to make cheese and yogurt, who said they were shut out of the regulated Canadian market after a change in the rules.

Canada's prime minister, Justin Trudeau, has tried to sound unruffled since the United States elected its protectionist president in November 2016. Mr. Trump encouraged voters to blame their grievances on Mexico, the third partner in the North American Free-Trade Agreement (NAFTA).

Alongside dairy farmers, he put loggers and energy producers on his Canadian enemies list and launched an investigation of imported steel, of which Canada is the biggest single supplier. On April 24, the United States' Commerce Department imposed preliminary duties averaging 20% on imports of Canadian softwood lumber, used to build houses. Two days later Mr. Trump was about to sign an order to withdraw from NAFTA. He dropped that plan, at least for now.

But the threat remains, and Canada is vulnerable. The United States and Canada traded $635bn-worth of goods and services last year. Three-quarters of Canada's goods exports went to the United States. The reconstruction of trade barriers would put all that in jeopardy.

What hurt American farmers was a deal struck by Canadian farmers and regulators to allow a new lower price for products that compete with ultra-filtered milk. Similar rules protect egg and poultry producers.

These aspects are now part of the much bigger confrontation to renegotiate NAFTA. No one in Canada (or Mexico) knows just what the United States will demand. In March the acting United States trade representative sent a letter to Congress with 40 ideas for revising the agreement. They include eliminating NAFTA's dispute settlement mechanism, which has not been as tough on lumber subsidies and other Canadian practices as the United States wants, and making it easier for public agencies in the United States to buy American.

Mr. Trudeau would rather charm the Trump administration than confront it. Millions of American jobs depend on trade with Canada, which was the biggest buyer of American goods last year.

Canada is bracing for the worst. One response is to diversify trade away from the United States, but that will be hard, given that it is the world's largest economy and on Canada's doorstep.

Whatever happens, Canada will stand up for dairy farmers, a small but influential group in Ontario and Quebec. But Mr. Trump may have changed the game.

Adapted from *The Economist*, April 29, 2017.

1. **dairy farmer:** producteur de laitage
2. **logger:** exploitant forestier

Lexical work

Understanding the key words

→ Find their meanings and their lexical categories (noun, verb, adjective, adverb, etc.): loggers; unruffled; to put in jeopardy; grievances; preliminary duties; murky; to harvest trees; his swipe; bad ties; to withdraw; paragon; to straddle; to stand up for.

→ Now, try to rephrase the title in your own words and write an introduction (source and date).

First track: A step-by-step approach

I Read the text

1. Pick up the main idea(s) in each paragraph.

II Rephrase

2. Rephrase the idea(s) you have found in each paragraph.

III Language

3. The lexical field to describe the economic relation between Canada and the USA is clearly related to war and conflit. Underline the words that belong to it in the following sentences:

a) Trump put loggers on his Canadian enemies list.
b) But the threat remains, and Canada is vulnerable.
c) These aspects are now part of the much bigger confrontation to renegotiate NAFTA.
d) The reconstruction of trade barriers would put all that in jeopardy.
e) Canada is bracing for the worst.
f) Canada will stand up for dairy farmers.

4. Come to a conclusion: How does the journalist describe trade within NAFTA?

IV Train for the exam

5. Use all the information above to report briefly to the class in French.

6. Write an account of the article in English following the guidelines below (200 words):

§1 Introduction (source, date and main idea)
§2 The reasons for renegotiating NAFTA (give figures)
§3 The industries that are targeted and the reasons
§4 Canada's response to Mr. Trump
§5 Other trading partners for Canada
§6 Why it is not such a good idea to endanger this FTA
§7 Conclusion

Second track: A straightforward approach

I Read the whole text

1. Take down notes about what you believe is important.

II Rephrase

2. Organise your ideas and make a plan.

III Language

3. Translate into in English:

a) Les producteurs de laitage qui se plaignent de la concurrence canadienne demandent au Président d'intervenir.
b) Les exploitants forestiers ne savent pas quoi faire.
c) L'accord de libre-échange auquel la plupart des entreprises tiennent ne satisfait pas tout le monde rural.

IV Train for the exam

4. Write an account of the article in French in 200 words.

5. Write a report OR make an oral presentation in English. Investigate further to discuss the following topics:

- What would it mean for the USA and for Canada if the NAFTA was cancelled?
- Why is Canada right in trying to find other economic partners? But why should the USA remain its biggest partner?

Grammaire

▸ Les propositions relatives avec ou sans antécédent

→ Donald Trump, **who** had just heard complaints. → *Donald Trump, **qui** venait d'entendre des protestations.*

→ Trump (…) launched an investigation of imported steel, **of which** Canada is the biggest single supplier.
→ *Trump a lancé une enquête sur l'importation d'acier, **dont** le Canada est l'unique plus grand fournisseur.*

→ **What** hurt American farmers was a deal struck by Canadian farmers.
→ ***Ce qui** a fait du mal aux fermiers américains a été un accord passé par les exploitants canadiens.*

(Voir grammaire p. 204)

8 Video tracks

Common track

→ Before you start watching the video:

1. Give a definition of the term "protectionism" and see how it is related to the closing off of markets.
2. Look at the title and think about what it might mean for a company to deal with protectionist measures.

→ Watch the video:

3. Listen and try to hear and understand the following words: short term; uncertainty; his campaign rhetorics; anti-free trade measures; to pull out of TPP; all corners of the world; a plant; components; CEO.
4. Debrief with the other students and the teacher about their meaning.

Pronunciation work

→ Listen, repeat the following words and record yourself: to backfire; to be competitive – to pursue; a wait – and – see approach; tendencies; policies; facility; expertise; unpredictability.

Video vidéo 31 Nathan live!

Protectionism – closing off of markets Made in Germany

http://newsvideo.su/video/8943597

Deutsche Welle

Word box

- stance: *posture*
- in spades: *en grande quantité (« à la pelle »)*
- world order: *ordre mondial*
- uncertainty: *incertitude*
- upside: *aspect positif*
- tirade: *diatribe*
- harm: *faire du mal*
- deceiving: *trompeur/euse*
- blade: *lame*

First track:
A step-by-step approach

I Watch the first 3 minutes of the video once

1. Write in French what it is about.

II Watch the first 3 minutes of the video a second time

- Watch the first part: (1'47)

2. What does David Winter introduce?
3. What is Donald Trump's motto?
4. How long has the world order been as it is?
5. What do investors hate?
6. What was Donald Trump's first step against globalisation?
7. Who might be harmed?

- Watch the second part: (1'07 → 3'00)

8. What is the name of the company?
9. Where is it located?
10. What is the name of the CEO?
11. What does the company produce?
12. How much of the production goes to the USA?

III Train for the exam

13. **Oral report:** Put together all the information you have collected and report to the class.

Second track:
A straightforward approach

I Watch the first 3 minutes of the video once

1. After the first viewing, you are expected to have understood the general idea(s) exposed in the document. Write a short debrief.

II Watch the first 3 minutes of the video a second time

2. Take notes and focus on how different ideas are connected to one another.

III Train for the exam

3. Write an account of the video. In your conclusion, state your point of view.

Debate

Group A supports free trade and is strongly against protectionism and tariffs.

Group B is in favour of protectionism, against free trade.

Each group prepares its arguments.

The debate is launched under the supervision of a student from each group whose role is to distribute speaking and listening roles equally.

8 Audio tracks

Common track

I Anticipate the topic of the audio

1. Before listening to the audio, look at the visual document and the title and say as much as you can.
2. Find out about Britain and Ireland: their area, their population.
3. Find out more about Northern Ireland and the Troubles.
4. Look at the title and rephrase it.

II Understand the key words

5. Listen and try to understand the following words:
pettiness; stake; a face-off; construe; utterly; Taoiseach; kinship; mighty.
6. Debrief with the other students and the teacher about their meaning.

Audio piste 47 Nathan live!

Lonely Britain versus formidable Ireland

Pronunciation work

→ **Listen, repeat the following words and record yourself:**
Northern Ireland; utterly; kinship; the post-separation border; idiocy; embodiment; changes; Taoiseach.

First track:
A step-by-step approach

I Listen to the whole audio once

1. Write in French what it is about.

II Listen to the first part

2. Collect information about:

a) The names of the journalist and his newspaper.

b) The reasons for such a programme partly devoted to him.

c) His point of view on Theresa May and her government.

III Listen to the second part

3. What does Brexit threaten?

4. What term describes Brexit?

5. What has the early British election brought about?

6. What are the two questions that need answering?

IV Listen to the third part

7. Who is Ireland's Taoiseach or Prime Minister?

8. What does he want for Ireland?

9. Why is Ireland Britain's best friend?

10. What does the British press do?

11. Why is a hard border not the right solution?

12. What has been agreed upon with the December summit?

V Train for the exam

13. **Oral report:** Put together all the information you have collected and report to the class.

Second track:
A straightforward approach

I Listen to the whole audio

1. After the first listening, you are expected to have understood the general idea(s) exposed in the document. Write a short debrief.

II Listen to the whole audio a second time

2. Take notes on how the different ideas are connected to one another.

III Train for the exam

3. Write an account of the audio. In your conclusion, state your point of view.

Role play

Student A and B are British expats living and working in the Irish Republic (Dublin).

Student A is worried about his post-Brexit situation whereas Student B is optimistic about the outcome of Brexit.

Each student prepares his/her arguments before playing the situation.

Record the scene.

Texte

Brexit : les amples concessions de Theresa May

Les expatriés, le chèque de départ et le sort de l'Irlande : un compromis a été trouvé entre l'UE et le Royaume-Uni. La deuxième phase des discussions sur les futures relations commerciales va pouvoir commencer.

Soumise à un ultimatum cassant de l'Union européenne, Theresa May a cédé sur les principaux points en suspens pour pouvoir annoncer, vendredi 8 décembre à l'aube depuis Bruxelles, qu'un accord avait été conclu, permettant une avancée cruciale pour l'avenir de l'économie britannique : l'ouverture des négociations sur les futures relations commerciales avec l'Union européenne.

« Je me félicite vivement du prochain passage à la phase suivante des discussions sur le Brexit, sur le commerce et la sécurité », a déclaré la Première ministre britannique avec un sourire qu'on ne lui avait pas vu ces derniers jours. L'UE avait donné jusqu'à dimanche à Mme May pour faire de nouvelles propositions, après l'humiliation qu'elle avait subie lundi lorsque le Parti démocratique unioniste (DUP) nord-irlandais avait torpillé l'annonce d'un accord.

Mais pour en arriver là, Theresa May a dû passer sous les fourches caudines* de la Commission européenne, non seulement sur la facture du divorce – 50 milliards d'euros au lieu des 20 qu'elle avait acceptés initialement – mais sur l'Irlande et sur la compétence de la Cour de justice européenne (CJUE), même si les Européens ont aussi cédé du terrain sur ce point. « L'accord a exigé des concessions des deux côtés, mais il est dans le meilleur intérêt du Royaume-Uni. Il est juste pour le contribuable britannique et préserve l'intégrité du Royaume-Uni », a-t-elle reconnu.

Le compromis sur l'Irlande est un modèle d'« ambiguïté constructive » chère à l'UE. Il ne tranche pas, et pour cause, l'insoluble équation irlandaise. Londres a décidé de sortir du marché unique, ce qui impose une frontière entre le Nord et le Sud, que les Britanniques prétendent refuser et que les Irlandais rejettent totalement.

Mais le texte ouvre la voie à une possible volte-face britannique : « En l'absence de solutions acceptées, le Royaume-Uni maintiendra un alignement complet sur les règles du marché unique et de l'union douanière. » Outre l'avantage de remettre la solution aux calendes grecques, cette disposition satisfait le DUP puisqu'elle exclut l'établissement d'une frontière maritime entre l'Irlande et la Grande-Bretagne, hantise des unionistes.

Ce point précis est d'ailleurs garanti par un paragraphe ajouté depuis lundi. Il prévoit que l'exécutif et l'assemblée nord-irlandaise, où siège le DUP, décideraient d'un éventuel « arrangement distinct » pour l'Irlande du Nord. Symptomatiquement, le document accepté vendredi par Londres emploie l'expression d'« économie de toute l'Irlande, » qui ravira les républicains et les partisans d'une réunification tout en garantissant, à l'intention des unionistes, que « dans tous les cas », Londres « continuera à assurer le même accès sans restriction pour les entreprises nord-irlandaises à l'ensemble du marché intérieur du Royaume-Uni ».

Vendredi matin, le soulagement était tel à Londres que les plus europhobes des membres du gouvernement May ont semblé se mettre à l'unisson du concert de louanges adressées à la première ministre. « Elle a pris d'importantes décisions dans l'intérêt national », se félicitait Steve Baker, ministre « ultrabrexiter ». Mais déjà, Nicola Sturgeon, Première ministre (indépendantiste) du gouvernement d'Edimbourg, réclame que les « arrangements particuliers pour l'Irlande du Nord soient ouverts aux autres nations » du royaume.

D'après *Le Monde*, 8 octobre 2017.

* **Passer sous les fourches caudines :** expression rappelant la défaite de l'armée romaine en 312 avant J-C, signifiant être humiliée.

Common track

1. Find information on the Irish Republic and Northern Ireland.
2. Which one is part of the UK?
3. Which one will remain part of the EU?
4. What lexical categories do these words belong to (noun, adverb, verb, adjective, pronoun, etc.)?
5. Sum up the main idea of the text in a few lines.
6. What are the English words for:
faire des concessions ; conclure un accord ; une avancée cruciale ; passer à la deuxième phase des négociations ; torpiller l'annonce d'un accord ; céder du terrain ; le contribuable britannique ; chère à ; l'union douanière.

1. Use a dictionary; look up the following words and find equivalents in English:
l'insoluble équation irlandaise ;
une possible volte-face ; remettre la solution aux calendes grecques.
2. Identify the main topic in English.
3. Is the agreement reached between the EU and Britain a good thing?
4. Imagine a title in English for the document.
5. Introduce the text in English.
6. Write one or two sentences in English for each paragraph in your own words (no translation).
7. Use your sentences to write a well organised account of the article in English in 180 words.

Go faster

I **Read the whole document and suggest a title in English.**

II **Write one or two sentences in English in your own words for each paragraph.**

III **Write an organised account of the article in English. Do not forget the introduction and the conclusion. (200 words)**

IV **Branching out: Give your own point of view on the agreement. Who might be opposed to it? Why?**

V **Write a 200 word essay developing what will happen next in the second chapter of the Brexit negotiations.**

Debate

Group A

Students from Group A believe the agreement will enable the EU and the UK to move forward. They list the fields and areas that will be dealt with.

Group B

Students from Group B don't believe in Ms. Theresa May's cabinet's ability to move because of its hard brexiteers. List arguments that will be subject to difficult debates.

8 Tasks

Document 1 piste 48 — Audio

CETA has arrived: how should we feel about it?

Pronunciation work

→ **Listen, repeat the following words and record yourself:**
collapse; investment; remove barriers; opportunities; European; threatened; uncertainty.

Document 2 — Text

South American trade bloc gains strength, misses EU deal

BRASILIA — Leaders of the South American trade bloc Mercosur met on Thursday in greater political unity following the expulsion of Venezuela, but with their biggest goal of a trade deal with the European Union yet to be achieved.

A shift from leftist to right-of-center governments in Argentina and Brazil has given the group, that also includes Paraguay and Uruguay, greater ideological coherence, and it has focused more on trade and less on politics.

Mercosur triggered its democratic clause this year and expelled Venezuela due to authoritarian moves by President Nicolas Maduro such as the delaying of elections and the jailing of opposition leaders.

Mercosur has been re-energized by recovering its original purpose as a trade bloc based on democratic principles, its leaders said. Mercosur will start trade negotiations with Canada early next year, and then with Singapore and South Korea.

Negotiations with the European Union gained speed and were almost concluded this month after nearly two decades of wrangling, but stumbled on an EU delay in presenting improved offers for imports of Mercosur beef and ethanol.

"There is very little left to do. We are very close," Brazilian Foreign Minister Aloysio Nunes said.

Nunes has made it clear, however, that the ball is in the European court and Mercosur awaits an EU reply after the South Americans presented an offer covering 90 percent of goods traded.

A proposal by Uruguay to negotiate free trade with China was rejected. Nunes said such an accord would have an overwhelming impact on Mercosur economies and needed careful study.

Ministers on Wednesday overcame Paraguayan resistance and reached agreement on a common policy for government procurement of goods and services, Temer said.

Uruguay's tariffs on other Mercosur countries will rise to 3 percent from 2 percent while goods from non-Mercosur nations will have tariffs of 5 percent instead of the current 3 percent.

Uruguayan Foreign Minister Rodolfo Novoa said it was a temporary measure to close a budget deficit of nearly 4 percent of gross domestic product. He said the other three nations now understood it was not protectionism.

Adapted from *The New York Times*, December 21, 2017.

Word box
- government procurement: *marchés publics*

Document 3 vidéo 32 — Video

The China-Australia free trade agreement

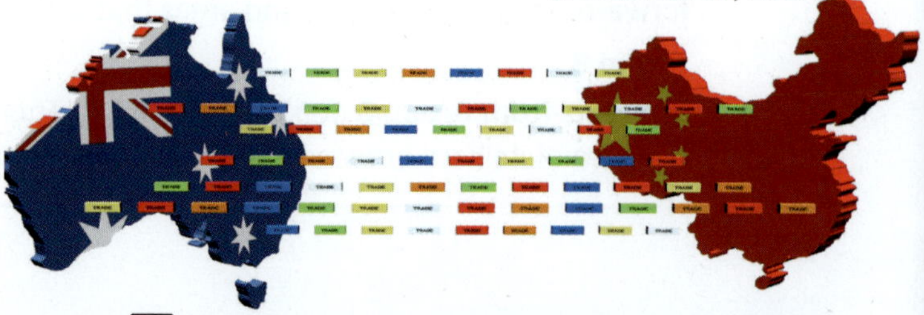

https://www.youtube.com/watch?v=gew37so4S2E

Task 1 Audio

Listen to the audio

1. Explain what CETA is, when it came into force, the countries that are involved.
2. What is Donald Trump's policy regarding FTAs?
3. What are the reasons for CETA to come into force so rapidly?
4. What is not in this bilateral agreement?
5. Organise all the information you have collected.
6. Write a report.

Task 2 Text

Read the whole text

1. Which countries mentioned in the text belong to Mercosur?
2. Why was Venezuela expelled from Mercosur?
3. Why has the EU-Mercosur free trade not yet been reached?
4. How long have the talks been going on?
5. What does the free trade agreement entail?
6. Which countries would Mercosur like to reach a FTA with?
7. Organise your ideas and make a plan.
8. Write an organised account of the article in English.

Task 3 Video

1. Anticipate from the title.

Watch the whole video

2. Collect key words, key data, key ideas.
3. Write an organised report.

Task 4 Put in common

Each group studies the three reports referring to the three documents.

1. Making a plan: See how the three documents are related to one another.
   - Audio: the main ideas are...
   - Text: the main ideas are...
   - Video: the main ideas are...
2. How are the ideas from each document related?
3. Each group writes a final report which is a synthesis of the three documents.

The ups and downs of globalisation, or fortune and misfortune of a global trading era

The term "globalisation" has been in the news for the last 30 years and seemed to introduce the world to a new trading era especially with China and India. The term was used to refer to more goods being manufactured in low-cost countries and being sold everywhere but especially in the western world. Consumers were certainly happy to have access to cheaper goods and businesses were applauding at having access to a low-cost labour force.

Now globalisation also means that components are made in several countries and assembled in another. It is true of Honda in the UK, which has car components made in several European countries. But it is also true of Airbus and many other big companies.

The tools to make exchanges faster and cheaper were Free Trade Agreements (FTAs). At its peak, the WTO, or World Trade Organisation, with its 164 members promoted multilateral agreements. With the 2008 crisis, negotiations stalked and regional and bilateral agreements emerged.

NAFTA between the USA, Mexico and Canada was introduced in 1994 to ease trade exchanges between the three countries. It is now questioned by the Trump administration.

The EU is an economic and political community started in 1957 with the Treaty of Rome and has kept expanding to new members to promote economic exchanges and stability in the region. Here again the Brexit referendum held in the UK on June 23, 2016 questioned the existence of free trade.

The Association of South East Asian Nations (ASEAN), a 10-member international body that represents more than 500 million people living in the region, was created in 1967. Its purpose is to ease travel between the Southeast Asian countries, promote co-operation and fight terror threats.

Mercosur, set up in 1991, tries to achieve the same cooperation for the countries in South America.

CETA is the latest FTA that was signed in 2016 between the EU and Canada and came into force on September 21, 2017.

A widespread backlash has followed the FTAs

Many agreements, among which TPP (Trans-Pacific Partnership Agreement) and TTIP (Transatlantic Trade and Investment Partnership), might never come into existence because of the US President's America First policy. Existing deals such as NAFTA are also questioned by the USA.

On the other side of the Atlantic, Brexit is also the sign that the economic partnership between the EU member states is seen as not being fair.

So here we can see that two forces are opposed and globalisation, that was seen as the key to economic growth, is now perceived as responsible for joblessness.

Free trade is described as the exchanges of goods without quotas, tariffs or other constraints. However, some are saying that FTAs are far from being fair.

Here are some reasons:

- They have sent jobs overseas.
- They benefit larger businesses at the expense of small and medium-sized companies.
- They encourage processed food and industrial farming.
- They do not advocate for fairer labour legislations between trading countries.
- They do not deal with pollution laws.

The future will reveal if there is aviable economic alternative capable of reconciling both sides.

Question time

1. Is the word "globalisation" recent?
2. What is the WTO?
3. Which countries are involved in NAFTA?
4. Why is globalisation rejected today?
5. Is the UK still part of the EU? Why?

➥ Vocabulary p. 198

Trends

Brexit

Brexit: How it started and what has happened since, and what might be in store for the EU and for the UK.

1. The Referendum

It was scheduled on June 23, 2016. David Cameron, Prime Minister, had promised 100 MPs from the Conservative Party that he would organise a referendum in 2017 if reelected. David Cameron had been hard pressed by Eurosceptic members of parliament from his own party and the UKIP gaining political ground. As he was reelected in May 2015, Cameron called the referendum.
He saw it as a calculated gamble, aimed at silencing the Eurosceptics in his own party for a generation.
The results:
51.9% (17.410.742 votes) were in favour of leaving the EU against 48.1% (16.141.241 votes) who wanted to remain within the EU. Scotland and Northern Ireland were opposed to leaving the EU whereas England and Wales favoured a move away from the EU.

2. Consequences

David Cameron resigned from his position and was replaced by Ms. Theresa May as Prime Minister on July 13, 2016. As David Cameron's successor, Ms. May had to negotiate the terms of Britain's exit – and to trigger Article 50 of the Lisbon treaty, which begins the formal process of withdrawal. In March 2017 Article 50 was triggered as Ms. May was urged to do so much earlier than planned originally.
What Article 50 started was a new round of talks that ended on December 15, 2017, with an agreement on the rights of EU citizens in the UK, on the exit bill, that amounts to £50 billion and on how to avoid a hard border between Northern Ireland and the Republic.

Now chapter two or act two of the Brexit negotiations can start. It focuses on trade terms. Some see Brexit with no deal as a disaster that must be avoided at all cost. A no-deal Brexit would damage Britain first and other European countries second. Indeed, the EU accounts for 43% of Britain's goods exports and half its imports. In services, which represent 80% of British GDP and almost half its exports, the EU market is paramount. Moreover, leaving with no deal would mean not having an easy access to 60 countries the EU has free trade deals with. What is more, Britain would not longer be part of all EU organisations such as Euratom, the European Medicines Agency (EMA), the REACH chemicals directive, the European Aviation Safety Agency, etc.
A no-deal Brexit would also imply tariffs on 90% of British goods exports. Customs would also take much longer with customs declarations to check. Prices of British goods exports would increase, industries would want to relocate to continental Europe to avoid red tape: 80% of the cars made in Britain are exported and half of them to the EU. So Honda would not see any incentive in remaining in the UK.

3. To conclude for now

Dealing with European countries on WTO terms is not even to be considered: indeed, Britain would have to resume full WTO membership and that would take time as the WTO proceeds by consensus among its 164 members. In any case, the EU does not deal on WTO terms as it has bilateral agreements to trade more easily. So it will certainly be of great interest to see if hard brexiteers will win over soft brexiteers. Whoever wins, trade talks have started and will need time and good faith.

Questions

- 1. When did the referendum on Brexit take place?
- 2. Who organised it?
- 3. Why was it organised?
- 4. What are the two possible types of Brexit?

SWOT

An analysis of a global economy

Favourable | Unfavourable

Internal

Strengths

- A low-cost and efficient labour force
- Emerging global competitiveness
- Modern new plants and modernised plants
- Providing jobs and creating a middle class that has a better revenue
- Bringing about a new industrial culture
- Having access to infrastructures such as electricity with solar panels to less affluent countries

Weaknesses

- International labour legislation is more difficult to implement
- Working conditions might not be up to the standards of developed countries
- Dependence on imports
- Highly dependent on markets if economy based on single crops or/and raw materials
- Not developing one's own potential
- Not designing high added-value services or/and goods

SWOT

External

Opportunities

- Tapping new markets
- Providing goods at lower prices
- Rapid urbanisation
- Developing infrastructures
- Increasing demand for goods at affordable prices

Threats

- Terrorism and wars
- Charging more as patents are owned abroad
- Environmental issues
- Governance issue: economic growth is not evenly spread
- Growing gap between the rich and the poor
- Relying on multinationals and their investments
- Global economic slowdown

Test yourself

After having studied this unit, you must be able to answer the following questions:

1. What does TPP stand for? How many members are there?
2. Where is Saskatchewan?
3. Where is Denso from? What does it produce?
4. Why has it moved to Thailand?
5. Why have the Highlands in Scotland always been represented as economically backward?
6. When did it change and why?
7. How many people were there in 2011 in the Highlands?
8. What does NAFTA mean? How many members are there?
9. What is a free trade agreement?
10. Who is targeted by Mr. Trump's policy regarding Canada?
11. What does Fintan O'Toole think of the British Prime Minister in relation to the Brexit negotiations?
12. Why was the British election a flop?
13. Why is the Northern Ireland border a difficult issue in the Brexit negotiations between the EU and the UK?
14. How much will the UK pay to leave the EU?
15. What is CHAFTA?
16. Which member countries do you know who belong to Mercosur?
17. Which FTA was not reached in 2017?
18. What does CETA stand for?
19. When was the referendum on Brexit?
20. Who was Prime Minister in Britain before Ms. Theresa May?

An economist's bleak view of the future of globalisation

Global cooperation is collapsing just when it is most needed.

GLOBALISATION is not new. In the late 19th century capital moved freely across the world and goods crossed national borders (despite tariffs) with the help of cheap transport. People, too, migrated across the oceans on a proportionately far bigger scale than they do today. All that came to a dramatic end with the outbreak of the first world war.

Trade did not recover its share of world GDP until the 1960s. But after the Berlin Wall fell in 1989, it became tempting to believe in a kind of "Whig theory of globalisation" with economies growing ever more linked thanks to the internet and the spread of liberal capitalism. Perhaps the world is due for another change of trend. That is the view of Mr. King, an economist at HSBC, which, as it happens, is one of the most global of banks.

In "Grave New World" Mr. King argues that economic progress that reaches beyond borders is not "an inescapable truth". Technology may have boosted globalisation until now, but it may not do so in future. Companies may decide to replace cheap labour in the developing world with robots at home, causing global supply chains to collapse. The internet has also increased inequality within economies, as skilled workers have reaped the most benefits, creating a division between the "haves" and the "have nots".

A resurgence in migration has also caused a political backlash, on both economic and cultural grounds. Populist politicians have gained voters, and even power in some countries. And there may be even greater migrant flows to come, as Africa's population grows and its citizens seek to escape from failed states, or the consequences of climate change, and to enhance their economic opportunities. The developed world may place more restrictions on inflows, as America did in the early 20th century, barring both Asians and those who could not pass a literacy test.

Geopolitical shifts will also make a difference. After 1945, America was globalisation's leading architect and its main sponsor. But its authority is now being challenged on a number of fronts. China is asserting itself in the Pacific; Russia is doing so in eastern Europe and the Middle East. Western Europe no longer backs America on all issues and takes a sharply different view from Donald Trump on climate change. The election of Mr. Trump proves that domestic voters have become tired of the country's global responsibilities and want to put "America first".

The result, says Mr. King, is that "cooperative arrangements between nation states will be increasingly hard to come by. Conflict—at least in the economic sphere—will become ever more frequent." National governments are turning their backs on global institutions and focusing on their domestic interests.

So what is the answer? The irony is that likely solutions require international cooperation, the very thing that populism makes more difficult. Mr. King looks at ideas such as breaking up the euro, a global organisation to reconcile capital flows between countries or even a borderless world, and concludes they either will be insufficient or are unlikely to happen.

The author ends with a mock campaign speech from a Ms. Trump in 2044, which looks back at the collapse of the EU and America's withdrawal from NATO. For an optimistic economist, it is a surprisingly bleak way to end a well-written and thought-provoking book.

Adapted from *The Economist,* May 25, 2017.

I Compréhension de l'écrit

Après une lecture attentive du texte, vous en ferez un compte rendu en français et ferez apparaître les idées essentielles en 200 mots (+/−10 %). Indiquez précisément le nombre de mots.

II Expression écrite

"If we are to believe Mr. King, globalisation is dying."

Comment this statement, give arguments to support your view. Come up with examples. (200 words)

III Interaction écrite

Rédigez une lettre commerciale en anglais selon l'usage commercial courant en tenant compte des informations ci-dessous.

Expéditeur : Madame Marceline Bataille, directrice commerciale
de la Société Excelsior, 22 rue du Mont-Blanc
74000 Chamonix, France

Destinataire : Monsieur Charles Wayne, Directeur Produit chez Modular Furniture, 88 Stilton Road, Bristol B4 9NG, U.K.

Date : le 23 avril 2018

Objet : Réponse à une réclamation pour retard de livraison.

Corps de la lettre :

- Accuse réception d'un courrier du 20 avril 2018 pour retard de livraison de la commande N° 678905.
- Le retard est regrettable et elle présente ses excuses.
- Le retard n'est pas imputable à l'entreprise, mais à la société de transport : une grève surprise des routiers français n'a pas permis d'effectuer les livraisons comme prévu.
- Un courrier a été envoyé à cette entreprise de transport et le respect des livraisons de nos prestataires sera surveillé plus étroitement.
- Renouvellement des excuses et compréhension.
- Salutations d'usage.

➥ Voit Tools p. 214

1 Why reversing globalisation may not be a good idea?

After the 2008 global financial crisis, global leaders pledged to avoid protectionist measures in order to speed up economic recovery and boost growth. However, protectionism has been rising since. Is a retreat from globalisation possible? If not, what is the way forward?

Throughout history, countries have used a range of protectionist measures to limit imports or promote exports. While many economic arguments favor free trade and trade liberalisation, protectionism is still widely practiced by almost all countries for any or all of the following reasons: to protect their strategic and infant industries, deter competition that is perceived as unfair, safeguard jobs in certain industries or for specific workers, protect the environment, and for political reasons. What has changed over the years is that industrialised nations have gradually moved toward using different deterrents to trade, such as non-tariff barriers, instead of resorting to more direct protectionist methods, such as imposing tariffs.

After the 2008 global financial crisis, G20 leaders signed a pledge in November 2008 to avoid protectionist measures in order to speed up economic recovery and boost growth through increased trade. Ironically, protectionism has witnessed a worrisome rise since then. The year 2016 witnessed the traditional champions of open government and free trade – the United States and the United Kingdom – yielding to populists, while China staunchly defended globalisation.

Advancements in transport, technology and communications and an increasing pool of talent and skills post 1980 led to rapid economic integration through trade and financial flows. Greater integration, increased competition, efficient use of resources, and improved productivity benefited all economic entities: nations benefited as economic growth accelerated; businesses profited from the access to cheap raw material, increased labour supply, and markets to sell finished products; consumers gained because of the availability of the wide variety and lower price of goods, and many workers got exposure to new jobs and skills.

While it is true that globalisation opportunities have not come without costs, that doesn't seem to be a sufficient reason to erect trade barriers and reverse the entire process.

Adapted from *Global Economic Outlook*, 2017.

2 Number of protectionist measures implemented since November 2008

Number of protectionist measures implemented since novembre 2008

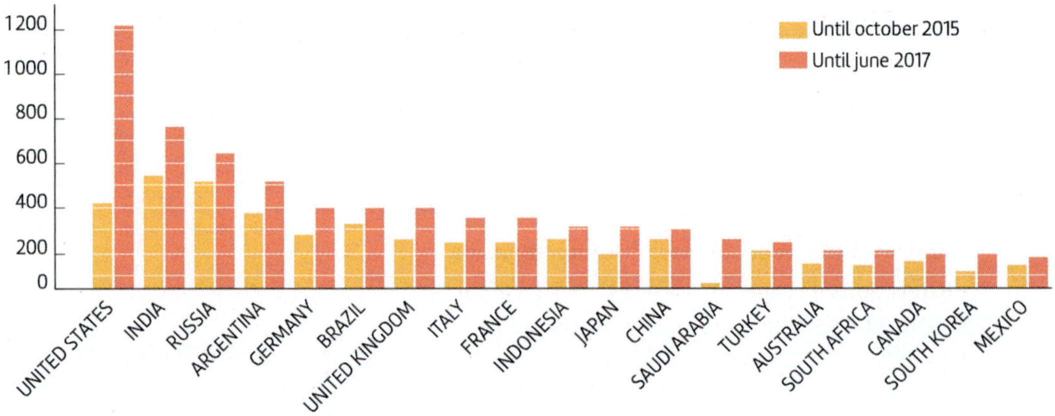

Source : Center for Economic Policy Research, April 2015 and April 2017

I Compréhension de l'écrit

Après une lecture attentive de l'article, vous en ferez un compte-rendu structure en français en tenant compte du graphique. (150 mots +/–10 %)

II Expression écrite

a) Use the chart in the document to account for the reversing globalisation trend.

b) Do you think this trend is here to stay?
Give an your point of view with arguments. (200 words +/–10 %)

3 China pushes global influence through trade

vidéo 33 Nathan live!

https://www.youtube.com/watch?v=8fbvhuvvsSQ

III Vidéo

1. Watch the video twice and take notes.
2. Take 10 minutes to prepare an oral report.
3. Report and discuss with the examiner.

Vocabulary

bilateral and/or multilateral agreements (n): *accords bilatéraux/multilatéraux*
Border (n): *frontière*
cap exports (vb): *mettre un plafond/limiter les exportations*
CETA (Comprehensive Economic and Trade Agreement) : *Accord Économique et Commercial Global*
CHAFTA (China Australia Free Trade Agreement): *Accord de libre échange entre l'Australie et la Chine*
competitive (adj): *compétitif/ve*
confrontation over tarde (n): *confrontation au sujet d'échanges commerciaux*
customs (n): *douane*
dispute (n): *conflit*
dutyfree (n): *sans taxes douanières*
expel (vb): *expulser*
exploratory talks (n): *négociations exploratoires*
flow (n): *flux labour legislation (n): législation du travail*
FTA (Free Trade Agreement) : *accord de libre échange*
government procurement (n): *marché public*
growth (n): *croissance*
implement (vb): *mettre en place/implanter*
impose duties on imports (vb): *imposer des taxes à l'importation*
incentive (n): *incitation*
lawsuits (n): *actions en justice*
Mercosur: *Marché commun du Sud (Amérique du Sud)*
MP (Member of Parliament (UK)): *député*
NAFTA(North American Free Trade Agreement): *ALENA Accord de Libre Échange Nord Américain*
protectionist measures (n): *mesures protectionnistes*
pull out of a deal (vb): *se désengager*
put in jeopardy (vb): *mettre en danger*
quotas (n): *quotas*
remove (vb): *retirer ; enlever ; ôter*
scrap (vb): *se débarrasser de*
stand up for (vb): *soutenir ; militer pour*
step out of a deal (vb): *se retirer d'un accord*
strike temporary deals (vb): *arriver à des accords provisoires*
subsidiaries (n): *subventions*
surplus of (n): *surplus, excédent*
tariffs (n): *taxes douanières*
top end provider (n): *fournisseur haut de gamme*
TPP (Trans Pacific Partnership): *Partenariat Trans-Pacifique*
trade (n) : *commerce*
trade barriers (n): *barrières douanières*
trade negotiations (n): *négociations commerciales*
TTIP (Transatlantic Trade and Investment Partnership): *Partenariat transatlantique de commerce et d'investissement*
UKIP: *parti politique britannique d'extrême droite*
underlying disagreement (n): *désaccord sous-jacent*
withdraw from (vb): *se retirer de*
WTO (World Trade Organization): *OMC Organisation Mondiale du Commerce*

Grammar

1 • Le superlatif

a) Le superlatif de supériorité = le plus

- ***The* + adjectif court + *-est* ou *The* + adjectif terminaison en *y* + *iest***

→ *It is the **largest** company in the world.*

→ *New York is **the busiest** city in the USA.*

- ***The* + *most* + adjectif long**

→ *One of **the most successful** entrepreneurs of our age.*

- **Les adjectifs irréguliers (à connaître)**

good / well → the best; bad → the worst;
far → the farthest / the furthest

→ *They had **the best** results of the year. **The worst** is yet to come. This is **the furthest / farthest** we can go.*

b) Le superlatif d'infériorité = le moins

***The least* + adj**

→ *The product was abandoned by the brand because it was **the least successful**.*

→ Le produit a été abandonné par la marque car c'était le moins réussi.

c) Le superlatif avec *ever* + *present perfect*

→ *He is the best manager the company **has ever had**.*

→ C'est le meilleur dirigeant que l'entreprise n'ait jamais eu.

2 • Le *pluperfect* (ou *past perfect*)

- **Construction : sujet + *had* + participe passé**
- **Emploi :**

a) Le *pluperfect* s'emploie dans un contexte passé. Il sert à marquer une antériorité par rapport à une action exprimée au prétérit.

b) Le *pluperfect* + *-ing* est l'équivalent du *present perfect* + *-ing*, mais dans un contexte passé. Il sert à mettre l'accent sur l'activité décrite.

c) Au style indirect, le prétérit comme le *present perfect*, sont transformés en *pluperfect* au style indirect passé.

3 • Le discours rapporté

- **Emploi :** le discours rapporté s'emploie pour rapporter les propos d'un tiers.
- **Construction :**

a) Lors du passage du **discours direct au discours rapporté**, il faut faire attention **aux pronoms susceptibles de changer et à la concordance des temps.**

→ **Discours direct :** *The manager said: "We don't see it as necessary to change our policy."*

→ **Discours rapporté :** *The manager said they **didn't** see it as necessary to change **their** policy.*

b) **Pour les phrases interrogatives,** l'ordre des mots n'est pas celui de la question directe : le point d'interrogation disparaît.

→ *"When will they recover from the disaster?" experts asked.*

→ *Experts asked when they **would** recover from the disaster.*

4 • Les noms et les adjectifs composés

- **Les noms composés sont très fréquents en anglais.** Ils se construisent de plusieurs façons : **nom + nom** *(air fresheners)*, **adjectif + nom** *(bottled water)*, **verbe + nom** *(cooking oil), mais aussi* **nom + particule adverbiale** *(a take-off)*, **participe passé + particule adverbiale ou verbe + particule adverbiale**.

a) Ils prennent parfois un tiret entre les deux termes (*name-brand*). La marque du pluriel se porte sur le dernier élément, quelle que soit sa nature grammaticale.

b) Le dernier élément est celui qui porte le sens principal, le premier ayant valeur d'adjectif. Il est d'ailleurs invariable (*a ten-dollar-bill*) → pas de *s* de pluriel → *a dollar*, car il a valeur d'adjectif.

c) Les adjectifs composés se forment sur les schémas suivants : **nom / adv + V-*ing*** *(an air conditioning device)*, **nom / adv + V-*ed*.** *(politically-involved activitist ; electrically-powered spacecraft).*

d) Les adjectifs composés d'un **nom+ V-*ed*** *(battery-powered aircraft; sun-powered house ; water-powered factory).*

5 • Les comparatifs

a) Les comparatifs dits de « supériorité » = plus … que

- **Les adjectifs courts + *-er … than***

→ *Europe is **smaller than** America.*

- **Les adjectifs en *y* + *-ier … than***

→ *London is **rainier than** Paris.*

- **Les adjectifs longs : *more* + adjectifs longs + *than***

→ *Cars are **more** expensive in France **than** in Germany.*

- **Les adjectifs irréguliers (à connaître) :**

→ *good / well → better … than;*

→ *bad → worse than…*

→ *than far → further / farther … than.*

→ *Roads are **better** now **than** 50 years ago. Los Angeles is **farther / further than** Chicago.*
→ *Pollution is **worse** today **than** in the last century.*

Remarques :
Pour indiquer un accroissement progressif, on utilise :
→ *Prices are **higher and higher** / goods are **more and more** expensive.*
→ Les prix sont de plus en plus élevés / les produits sont de plus en plus chers.
Ces formes peuvent être remplacées par l'adverbe ***increasingly*** : *Prices are **increasingly** high / goods are **increasingly** expensive.*

Pour indiquer un accroissement parallèle :
→ *Some consumers think that the more expensive an item is, the better it is.*
→ Certains consommateurs pensent que plus un article est cher, meilleur il est.
Attention à l'ordre des mots qui diffère dans les deux langues.

b) **Les comparatifs dits d'infériorité = moins … que** ***less*** **+ adjectif +** ***than*** : quelle que soit la longueur de l'adjectif. C'est la même construction pour les adjectifs irréguliers : → *Silver is **less expensive than** gold.*

Remarque :
Le comparatif d'infériorité est moins utilisé en anglais qu'en français. On préfère en anglais dire ***smaller*** (plus petit) que ***less tall*** (moins grand).

c) **Les comparatifs dits d'égalité = aussi … que** ***as*** **+ adjectif +** ***as*** : la forme est identique pour tous les adjectifs, irréguliers compris. Par contre, ***as*** se substitue à ***than*** : → *India will soon become **as** rich **as** China.*

Remarque :
→ *Prices are **the same** (as before).*
→ Les prix sont **les mêmes** (qu'auparavant).

6 • Le gérondif (la forme en *-ing*)

On utilise la forme en *-ing* (gérondif) :

a) **Pour remplacer une subordonnée relative ou traduire un participe présent (français).**
→ *The biggest factor **deterring** customers from refill is cost.*
→ Le facteur le plus important qui dissuade/dissuadant les clients de réutiliser les emballages est le coût.

b) **Après les verbes indiquant un début, une fin, une continuité :** *start, begin, stop, continue, keep on, go on, etc.*
→ *This supermarket chain has **begun selling** new products.*

c) **Après les verbes dits d'appréciation :** *like, love, enjoy, prefer, hate, dislike, can't bear, can't stand, etc.*
→ *Before, customers **didn't like buying** that product. They **preferred buying** another brand.*

d) **Après les prépositions :** *in, by, with, without, after, before, etc.*
→ *We have a challenge finding a solution. They have made profit **by changing** targets.*

e) **Pour transformer un verbe en nom :**
→ ***Paying** a premium has become necessary.*

Remarque :
- Certains noms se terminent par ***-ing*** : *packaging, advertising, marketing, etc.*
- Un grand nombre d'adjectifs également : *tiring, surprising, shocking, interesting*, etc. On notera qu'ils se traduisent en français par la terminaison **-ant** : fatigant, surprenant, choquant, intéressant, etc.

7 • Le passif

a) **La voix passive** permet de **mettre en valeur les actions subies par le sujet** alors que la forme active sert à mettre en valeur ce qui est à l'origine de l'action.
→ *The new look was inspired by global research.* (forme passive) *Global research inspired the new look.* (forme active)

b) La forme passive est reconnaissable en anglais par la présence de ***be*** suivi du participe passé du verbe. **Attention :** il n'existe aucune exception à cette règle.

c) Le complément d'agent, quand il est exprimé, est introduit par la préposition ***by***. Le passif est rarement suivi d'un complément d'agent car, lorsqu'il s'agit de préciser qui fait l'action, on a recours à la voix active.

d) **La forme passive s'utilise à tous les temps :** présent, passé, futur, etc. C'est ***be***, et lui seul, qui marque le temps.
→ *Coffee is exported / will be exported / was exported / has been exported / had been exported / would be exported, etc.*
→ Le café est exporté / sera exporté / a été exporté, etc.

Rappel :
Le passif n'est pas un temps, c'est une forme, une manière d'exprimer une action (comme en français).

e) L'anglais ne possédant pas de pronom indéfini « on » à proprement parler, les tournures impersonnelles en anglais sont exprimées par le passif.
→ *I was given a day off to take my driving licence.*
→ On m'a donné un jour de congé pour que je passe mon permis de conduire.

8 • L'expression du futur

a) **Le futur se construit en général avec l'auxiliaire** ***will*** **:** sujet + ***will*** + base verbale.
→ *The market **will** double by 2025.*
Il peut aussi se construire avec ***be going to*** (le locuteur est sûr que quelque chose va arriver).

b) **Plusieurs expressions sont utilisées dans un contexte futur :** *in the next year, in the years to come, in the long run… when, as soon as, as long as, until/till, unless…* (conjonctions de temps pour introduire une subordonnée temporelle)

Attention : à la concordance des temps dans les propositions subordonnées temporelles : ***when*** + présent simple (proposition subordonnée) → ***will*** (proposition principale).

9 • Le prétérit simple et continu

• **Construction du prétérit simple**

a) Le prétérit des verbes réguliers se forme en ajoutant *-ed* à la base verbale.

→ *The store **opened** 7 years ago.*

b) Beaucoup de verbes ont un prétérit irrégulier. Il faut les apprendre.

c) **Une phrase négative se construit sur le type :** ***did*** + ***not*** + *base verbale.*

→ *The store **didn't open** in January.*

d) Pour poser une question, utilisez soit : auxiliaire + sujet + BV (pour les *yes/no* questions), soit : *wh-* + *word* + ***did*** + sujet + BV? (pour les *wh-* questions).

• **Emploi du prétérit simple**

Le prétérit (ou *simple past*) est utilisé pour quelque chose qui est complètement terminé et sans lien avec le présent. De ce fait, le prétérit est toujours associé (soit dans la phrase même, soit dans le contexte sans que cela ne soit exprimé) a une expression qui ramène à un moment précis du passé :

→ *5 years ago, yesterday, last year, on 22nd January 1957, when I was at school…*

• **Construction du prétérit continu**

a) **Le prétérit en *-ing*** se construit avec ***be*** au prétérit + V-***ing***

→ *I **was going** to the market when I met you.*

b) **Une phrase négative**

→ *You **were not working** at your office when your sales assistant arrived.*

c) **Pour poser des questions,** soit : aux + sujet + V-***ing*** soit : ***wh-*** + aux + sujet +V-***ing***

→ ***Were you working** at your office when your sales assistant arrived?*

• **Emploi**

Le prétérit en *-ing* s'emploie souvent en lien avec le prétérit simple. Il souligne que l'action est présentée dans son déroulement et souvent interrompue par une autre action passée montrée dans sa brièveté.

→ *She **was preparing** a report when she received an email in which she was told to start preparing a business trip.*

→ Elle travaillait sur un rapport quand elle reçut un courriel lui demandant de préparer un voyage d'affaires.

10 • L'auxiliaire modal *may*

• **Construction**

May obéit aux particularités de tous les auxiliaires modaux : ni suivi ni précédé de ***to***, pas de ***-s*** à la 3e personne du présent simple, prend la marque de la négation et se place à la 1re place dans une phrase interrogative.

• **Emploi**

Comme de nombreux autres modaux, ***may*** peut être utilisé de deux façons différentes (comme ***must***) :

a) Avec ***may***, on marque l'autorisation, dans une langue soutenue. On peut également utiliser le modal ***can*** pour la permission.

b) Pour parler des chances de réalisation d'une action. Avec ***may***, la probabilité est moyenne. Dans ce type d'utilisation, on peut marquer que l'action a des chances de se réaliser (***may*** + BV), qu'elle est peut-être en train de se réaliser (***may*** + V ***-ing***), ou bien qu'elle s'est probablement réalisée dans le passé (***may*** + ***have*** + ***ed***). Si l'action n'a que peu de chances de se réaliser, on utilisera l'auxiliaire modal ***might***.

→ *It **may boost** the sales/**may be boosting** the sales/**may have boosted** the sales.*

Remarque :

May + BV peut se remplacer par : ***is likely*** + ***to*** + verbe.

→ ***It's likely to boost** the sales.*

11 • L'article défini : *the* ou ø ?

Quand on emploie un nom dans son sens général, on n'utilise pas d'article en anglais, au singulier comme au pluriel. Par contre, si on veut parler d'une notion en particulier, ou si l'on connaît précisément la personne ou l'objet dont il est question, on utilise ***the***.

→ *People work more today than a decade ago.*
≠ *All **the** people I saw in this company work a lot.*

Remarques :

- Certains noms sont presque toujours employés avec ***the*** car ils sont uniques : *the Sun, the Earth…*
- Les noms de pays ne prennent pas d'article, à quelques exceptions près :

→ ***The** USA; **the** UK.*

- Pour les titres, si l'on donne le nom de la personne, on supprime le ***the*** :

→ ***The** President of the United States / ø President Trump.*

12 • Le present perfect

- **Le *present perfect* simple (*have / has* + participe passé) s'emploie pour :**

a) Se référer à un événement, fait ou action qui n'est pas daté et qui n'a pas d'occurrence précise dans le passé.

→ *They **have chosen** a new manager.*

Attention : s'il y avait eu un repère temporel : *two years ago, during the war, etc.* le prétérit aurait été obligatoire.

b) Se référer à une action / un fait commencé dans le passé et qui perdure jusqu'à maintenant.

→ *He **has worked** with them since 1998.*

→ Il travaille avec eux depuis 1998.

Attention : ce cas précis d'emploi du *present perfect* se traduit par du présent de l'indicatif en français.

- **La différence entre *for* et *since* dans les phrases au *present perfect* :**

→ *He has worked with them **since** 1998.*

→ *He has worked with them **for** many years.*

On utilise ***since*** devant une date, un point de départ précis dans le passé.
On utilise ***for*** devant l'expression d'une durée.

- **Le *present perfect* progressif (*have* + *been* + BV-*ing*)** est utilisé pour donner plus de relief à la phrase. Avec le *present perfect* progressif, l'intention / l'implication du locuteur (celui qui parle / écrit) change.

→ *He **has worked** with them for many years.*

→ Il travaille avec eux depuis de nombreuses années.

→ *He **has been working** with them for many years.*

→ Cela fait de nombreuses années qu'il travaille avec eux.

13 • Les quantifieurs

a) **Différencier *much* et *many* = beaucoup**
Les noms indénombrables (au singulier) sont précédés de ***much*** → ***much** money.*
En anglais, les noms dénombrables (au pluriel) sont précédés de ***many*** → ***many** employees.*

b) **Différencier *a little* et *a few* = peu**
Les noms indénombrables (au singulier) sont précédés de ***a little*** → ***a little** money.*
Les noms dénombrables (au pluriel) sont précédés de ***a few*** → ***a few** employees.*

c) D'autres adverbes et expressions adverbiales sont utilisés pour **exprimer une grande quantité** et sont utilisés indifféremment avec les noms dénombrables et indénombrables : *a lot of / lots of / plenty of.*

d) **Comparer des quantités**
Plus de : ***more*** + nom… → ***More** companies are involved in sustainable development today.*
De plus en plus : ***more and more***
Moins de : ***less*** + nom indénombrable (singulier) → ***less know how***
Fewer + nom dénombrable (pluriel) → ***fewer** applications*
De moins en moins : ***less and less/fewer and fewer***
Autant de : ***as much as*** ou ***as many as***

→ *You can have **as many** friends **as** you want on Facebook, but will you get **as much** real friendship?*

Remarque : *too much / too many* = trop

→ ***too much** money* → trop d'argent

→ ***too many** people* → trop de gens

14 • Les propositions infinitives (avec et sans *to*)

a) **Construction du verbe *want* (vouloir)**
- ***Want***, lorsqu'il précède un verbe, est toujours suivi de ***to***.

→ *He wants to be the best.* → Il veut être le meilleur.

- ***Want* + CO + *to* + verbe :**

→ *He **wants** his company **to** improve to be the best.*

- Contrairement au français, qui utilise une subordonnée complétive (Il veut que son entreprise s'améliore pour être la meilleure), l'anglais utilise une proposition infinitive.

Remarque :
La 2e partie de la phrase, ***to be the best***, est aussi une proposition infinitive exprimant un but. Le français le traduit par : « pour être la meilleure ». Ne pas traduire « pour » par ***for*** en anglais. Le ***to*** suffit à exprimer le but.

b) **Construction avec *would like* (voudrait / aimerait)**
Would like est une formule atténuée de ***want*** qui se construit de façon identique :

→ *He **would like** his company **to be** the best.*

c) **Construction du verbe *allow* (autoriser)**
- ***Allow*** se construit toujours avec ***to***, comme ***want*** : ***allow*** + CO + ***to*** + verbe.

→ *We do not **allow** certain products to be sold in some shops.*

- ***Allow*** se construit fréquemment au passif.

→ *Some shops **are not allowed** to sell this product.*

d) **Construction particulière du verbe *make* (faire)**
***Make* + CO + verbe** signifie faire faire quelque chose à quelqu'un.

→ *The aim of the law is to **make shops stop selling** those products.*

e) **Construction du verbe *let* (laisser, permettre)**
Let se construit sans ***to*** : ***let* + CO + verbe.**

→ *We shouldn't **let shops sell** those products.*

15 • La phrase concessive

Elle est introduite soit par ***although***, ***in spite of***, ***despite***, ***though*** (bien que, en dépit de, quoique).

→ ***Although** he missed his train, he arrived on time.*

→ ***Despite** heavy rains, the region was not flooded.*

→ ***In spite of** her hard work, she was not able to pass her exam.*

→ *She passed her exam with flying colours **though** she did not work hard.*

16 • Les principaux suffixes

On peut ajouter un suffixe à un nom, un verbe ou un adjectif, de façon à créer un mot dérivé. Les principaux suffixes sont les suivants :

-ful (plein de, caractérisé par) : ***powerful*** → puissant.
Ce suffixe s'écrit avec un seul « *l* » à la fin !
-less (sans, dénué de) : ***childless*** → sans enfant.
-y ou *-ly* (pour marquer une qualité) : ***wealthy*** → riche, ***friendly*** → amical.
-ish (pour marquer quelque chose de négatif) : ***selfish*** → égoïste.

17 • L'expression de la fréquence

a) Pour connaître la fréquence à laquelle un tiers pratique une activité, l'anglais utilise ***how often*** :
→ ***How often*** *do you visit your family?*
→ ***How often*** *do you watch tv/entertain your friends/go to the doctor's?*

b) Les réponses à ce type de questions vont exprimer la fréquence à laquelle l'activité est pratiquée.
→ *Once / twice / three times a year / a week / a month…*
→ une fois / deux fois / trois fois par an / par semaine / par mois…

c) Pour donner plus de détails sur la durée de cette activité, on utilisera des expressions telles que :
→ *one hour a week / two hours a month…*
→ une heure par semaine / deux heures par mois…

d) Pour exprimer une action qui se répète à intervalle régulier, on utilise ***every*** :
→ *They visit their family* ***every*** *two weeks.*
→ Ils rendent visite à leur famille toutes les deux semaines.
→ ***Every*** *second, a new child is born.*
→ Un enfant naît toutes les secondes / chaque seconde.

Rappel :
Pour dire tous les jours / mois / ans, etc., on emploie ***every*** : *everyday / every Christmas / every evening.*
Pour dire à chaque fois, on utilise ***everytime*** :
→ ***Everytime*** *someone is one minute late, he's fined.*
→ Chaque fois que quelqu'un est en retard d'une minute, il est mis à l'amende.
Pour dire n'importe quand, on emploie ***whenever***.
→ ***Voir p. 206.***

18 • Les temps des verbes

Présent et passé
Il n'y a pas d'exacte équivalence entre les temps des verbes en anglais et en français.

a) **Le présent**
- Activité en cours → **présent :** ***be + -ing***
- Activité récurrente, vérité intemporelle → **présent simple**
- Bilan au moment présent d'une activité commencée avant mais toujours valable → ***present perfect***

b) **Le passé**
- La notion d'imparfait ou de passé composé n'existe pas en anglais. La question à se poser est : l'action est-elle finie (prétérit) ou bien a-t-elle des répercussions dans le présent (*present perfect*) ?
- Il faut faire attention aux marqueurs temporels, certains ne sont possibles qu'avec le prétérit (*ago*) et d'autres qu'avec le *present perfect* (*in the past three years*).

Remarques :
- Pour traduire **depuis** : verbe au ***present perfect*** + ***for*** avec une durée (*he's been there for three hours*) et ***since*** avec une date (*I've lived here since 1990).*
- ***During*** ne s'emploie qu'avec un événement spécifique et signifie « au cours de ».
→ ***During*** *the week, I start working at 9:00 a.m. / I work eight hours a day.*
- Pour parler d'un événement antérieur à un fait déjà exprimé au prétérit, on utilisera le *pluperfect* : sujet + ***had*** + participe passé.

c) **La forme en *-ing***
Quel que soit le temps auquel elle est associée, cette forme, appelée « aspect du verbe », met l'accent dans la plupart des cas sur l'activité dont on parle.

19 • L'expression du conseil

a) ***Should*** **+ verbe**
Le modal ***should*** s'utilise pour donner un conseil, pour exprimer une projection probable dans le futur qui n'engage que la personne qui le donne ou qui l'exprime.
→ *We* ***should*** *listen to our employees.*
Should est comme les autres modaux : il est suivi du verbe sans ***to***. Il se traduit en français par la forme conditionnelle du verbe **devoir** : devrais (-ait, -ions, -iez, -aient).

b) ***Ought to*** **+ verbe**
Ought to permet d'exprimer un conseil davantage fondé sur un usage général, admis, qu'il convient de respecter. C'est en cela qu'il se distingue dans l'usage de ***should***.
→ *Citizens* ***ought to*** *respect their countries' institutions :* c'est la bienséance, la morale qui le prescrit.

c) ***Had better*** **+ verbe /** ***'d better*** **+ verbe**
Une autre manière de donner un conseil :
→ *You* ***had better find*** *a solution quickly.*
→ Vous feriez mieux de trouver une solution rapidement.

d) ***Advise*** **+ COD +** ***to*** **+ verbe**
Pour conseiller à quelqu'un de faire quelque chose.
→ *Governments* ***advise people to get*** *ready for further sacrifices.*

Remarque :
Changement d'orthographe entre le nom *advice* et le verbe ***advise*** (conseiller).

20 • Les propositions relatives

- **Emploi**
  Les propositions relatives peuvent être ou non encadrées par des virgules. Il existe deux types de propositions relatives : certaines sont déterminatives, c'est-à-dire essentielles à la phrase, les autres sont dites non-déterminatives (ou appositives), car elles ne sont pas essentielles, mais donnent une information complémentaire.

→ *Mr Smith, **who** joined our chain in May 2010, said…*

- **Construction**
  La proposition relative est introduite par un pronom relatif. Pour choisir le bon, il faut prendre en compte deux paramètres concernant l'antécédent : la nature (humain ou objet / idée) et la fonction (sujet /complément).

Remarques :
- Quand on annonce quelque chose, la proposition relative en début de phrase commence par ***what***.
- Quand on veut reprendre tout ce qui a été dit dans la proposition précédant la virgule, on utilise ***which***.

→ ***What** I mean is that more sales are expected.*
→ *More sales are expected, **which** means that…*

- Pour les relatives exprimant la possession (dont), on utilise le pronom relatif ***whose***.
- Il y a aussi les adverbes relatifs (utilisés comme pronoms) : ***where, when, why***.

→ *The place **where** I was born.*

Antécédent	Fonction du pronom relatif		
	Sujet	CO	Complément du nom
humain	***who, that***	***who(m), that***	***whose***
non humain	***which, that***	***which, that***	***whose, of which***

21 • *To be to*

a) L'expression ***to be to*** peut exprimer :
- **Ce qui est déjà prévu**

→ *The plane **is to** take off at 6:00.*

- **L'obligation**

→ *You**'re not to** leave until I say so.*

- **L'hypothèse, au prétérit modal**

→ *If the authorities **were to** do that, the UN would react immediately.*

b) D'autres expressions assez proches permettent de parler de ce qui est imminent (***to be about to***), de ce qui va inévitablement arriver (***to be bound to***), de ce qui est susceptible d'arriver (***to be (quite) likely to***).

→ **L'expression du futur, p. 200.**

22 • Le présent (simple et continu)

a) **Le présent simple (*the simple present*)**
Il s'utilise pour exprimer une vérité générale, une caractéristique, une action habituelle, itérative (répétée).

→ *China still **dominates** the business → La Chine domine toujours le commerce (comme par le passé et comme vraisemblablement dans le futur).*
→ *It **supplies** nearly half of the European Union's garment imports*
→ La Chine fournit presque la moitié des imports de vêtements de l'Union européenne (comme par le passé et comme dans le futur).

Rappels :
- Seule la 3ᵉ personne du singulier modifie le verbe avec l'ajout du ***-s*** ou du ***-es*** suivant la terminaison du verbe :

→ *China supplies half of the European garment imports.*

- La forme négative et la forme interrogative se caractérisent par la présence de l'auxiliaire ***do*** pour toutes les personnes, sauf à la 3ᵉ personne du singulier pour laquelle on emploie ***does***.
- **Attention à l'ordre des mots dans les questions :**

→ *How much of the European garment imports **does** China supply?*

- **Attention aux formes contractées à la forme négative:**

→ *China **doesn't** supply 100% of the European garment imports.*

b) **Le présent continu : *be + -ing***
Le présent en ***be + -ing*** peut être utilisé pour décrire un événement qui continue au moment présent.

→ *But more orders **are shifting** to lower-wage economies such as in Cambodia and Vietnam, where garment factories **are mushrooming**.*
→ Les commandes se tournent en ce moment même (***are shifting***) vers des pays aux salaires plus bas, d'où les usines de textiles qui poussent comme des champignons en ce moment même (***are mushrooming***).

Rappel :
Le présent en ***be + -ing*** se forme avec les trois formes du présent du verbe ***be*** : ***am / is / are*** + **BV *-ing***.

23 • Les subordonnées introduites par *if*

- **Le conditionnel présent et passé**

a) *If* +présent simple + principale au futur :

→ *If they **drive** slowly, they **will consume** less gasoline.*

→ S'ils conduisent lentement, ils consommeront moins d'essence. Les conducteurs ont le choix, et on ne sait pas pour quelle solution ils opteront.

b) *If* + prétérit + principale au conditionnel présent :

→ *If she **had** an electric car, she **would drive** to Geneva.*

→ Si elle avait une voiture électrique, elle irait jusqu'à Genève. Elle n'a pas de voiture électrique pour l'instant, mais peut-être que quelqu'un lui en prêtera une. On appelle ce conditionnel **irréel du présent**.

c) *If* + *past perfect* + principale au conditionnel passé :

→ *If she **had had** an electric car, she **would have driven to** Geneva.*

→ Si elle avait eu une voiture électrique, elle serait allée jusqu'à Genève.

→ Elle n'a pas pu se rendre à Genève faute de voiture électrique.

Cette phrase exprime un regret, que l'on appelle aussi **irréel du passé**.

Remarque :

On notera que proposition introduite par ***if*** est suivie de ***had*** + participe passé (*pluperfect/past perfect*) et que le conditionnel passé se forme avec un modal (***would / should/could*** ...) + ***have*** + participe passé.

24 • Les pronoms personnels

a) Les pronoms personnels sujets *I, she / he / it, you, we, they.* *He* et ***she*** ne peuvent être utilisés que pour se référer à des êtres humains, hommes ou femmes, voire des animaux familiers. Le pronom personnel sujet ***it*** se réfère au non humain.

→ *The company is developing but some analysts doubt **it** is as profitable as **it** claims.*

Dans l'exemple, les deux it se réfèrent à la compagnie.

b) Les pronoms personnels compléments *me, you, him, her, it, us, them.* Ils n'ont qu'une seule forme quelle que soit leur fonction.

c) Les déterminants possessifs *my, your, his, her, its, our, their*.

Attention :

Vous noterez que ***his*** a deux valeurs.

→ ***His** notebook is missing* (adjectif/déterminant possessif, ici le propriétaire est masculin).

→ *This table is **his*** (pronom possessif, cette table est la sienne).

d) Les pronoms possessifs *mine*, *yours*, *hers*, *his*, *ours*, *theirs*

→ *The responsibility is **theirs**, not **ours**.*

→ La responsabilité est la leur, pas la nôtre.

e) Les pronoms réfléchis *myself*, *yourself*, *himself*, *herself*, *itself*, *ourselves*, *yourselves*, *themselves*

→ *Big brands consider **themselves** to be everlasting.*

→ Les grandes marques se considèrent éternelles.

À ne pas confondre avec les pronoms réciproques : ***each other / one another***.

→ *As soon as they met, they started arguing with **each other**.*

→ Dès leur rencontre, ils ont commence à se disputer (l'un avec l'autre).

→ *Companies compete with **one another** in order to increase their market shares.*

→ Les compagnies se concurrencent (les unes les autres) dans le but d'augmenter leurs parts de marché.

25 • Les adverbes

a) Les adverbes sont des mots invariables qui sont utilisés pour modifier le sens d'un verbe, d'un adjectif, d'un autre verbe ; ils peuvent également servir à nuancer une phrases entière. Il existe une grande variété d'adverbes : **de manière, de temps, de lieu, de degré, etc.** Leur place peut varier suivant leur nature.

b) Certains adverbes sont formés à partir de l'adjectif auquel on rajoute la terminaison ***-ly*** :
***financial** → **financially**; **increasing** → **increasingly**; **angry** → **angrily**.*

→ *They can't make ends meet **financially**...*

Attention aux adjectifs en ***-ly*** qui, eux, ne sont pas des adverbes : ***lovely***.

Rappel :

Les adverbes dits de fréquence (***often, sometimes, always, never***) sont toujours placés entre le sujet et le verbe ou entre l'auxiliaire et le verbe.

Les adverbes de temps (***yesterday***, ***tomorrow***...) sont généralement placés en fin ou début de phrase.

Attention aux faux amis : ***actually*** → en réalité ; ***hardly*** → à peine ; ***eventually*** → pour finir, finalement ; ***currently*** → en ce moment.

26 • Les noms indénombrables

a) Les noms indénombrables sont généralement les mots que l'on ne peut pas compter : liquides (***water***, ***milk***...), aliments, matières (***iron***, ***air***...), certains noms abstraits (***love***, ***happiness***...) ou concrets (***equipment***, ***fruit***...). Ils ne prennent jamais de ***s***, ni d'article ***a / an***, et le verbe est toujours au singulier.

→ **Retenez bien :** voici quelques noms indénombrables usuels à bien connaître : ***abuse, advice, business,***

***equipment*, *furniture*, *garbage*, *hair*, *information*, *luggage*, *news*, *progress*, *weather*...**

b) **L'article utilisé est : *some*** (phrases positives), ***any*** (phrases négatives / interrogatives) or ***no***.

→ *They don't do **any** publicity. He wants **no** advertising for his product. Can I give you **some** news about the teaser campaign?*

c) **Vous pouvez rendre dénombrable un nom indénombrable en lui donnant une quantité :**

→ *The market information is interesting.*

→ *He's got a **new piece of information**.*

Ou en utilisant un nom composé :

→ *The **product placement software** is efficient.*

→ *Can we buy a **new software program**?*

Dénombreurs usuels : *a piece of (advice), a glass of (water), a pair of (jeans, scissors)...*

27 • Les particules adverbiales

a) **Les particules adverbiales modifient le sens du verbe.** Il ne faut pas les confondre avec les prépositions qui servent à introduire le complément.

→ *A new firm has taken over.*

to take = prendre, mais ***to take over*** = enlever, prendre la suite.

b) **À l'impératif, la particule adverbiale reste *(Take it off!)***, alors qu'une préposition n'est présente que lorsque le complément intervient (*He listened to me / Listen!*).

28 • L'auxiliaire modal *must* et *have to*

- **Construction**

Must obéit aux particularités de tous les auxiliaires modaux : pas de ***to*** à l'infinitif, pas de ***s*** à la 3e personne du présent simple, prend la marque de la négation et se place à la 1re place dans une phrase interrogative.

- **Emploi**

Comme de nombreux autres modaux, (***may***) ***must*** peut être utilisé de deux façons différentes :

a) Quand le locuteur veut faire pression sur celui dont il parle. Avec ***must***, on marque une obligation.

Attention :

- ***Mustn't*** marque l'interdiction. Pour dire : «Je ne suis pas obligé de...», on utilisera l'expression ***I don't have to...***
- ***Must*** n'existe pas au prétérit (on utilise alors ***had to***) ni au futur (on utilise alors ***will have to***).

b) Pour parler des chances de réalisation d'une action. Avec ***must***, la probabilité est très forte.

→ *They **must** have changed something in their programme, it doesn't run any longer.*

Dans ce type d'utilisation, on peut marquer que l'action a de grandes chances de se réaliser (***must*** + **BV**), qu'elle est certainement en train de se réaliser (***must*** + **verbe *-ing***), ou bien qu'elle s'est certainement réalisée dans le passé (***must*** + ***have*** + **participe passé**).

29 • Le cas possessif

a) **Le cas possessif ou génitif**

→ *The government's response.*

→ La réponse du gouvernement.

Cette forme de complément du nom, **appelée génitif ou cas possessif**, marque ce qu'il est convenu d'appeler la possession. Le « possesseur » peut-être un nom propre ou un nom commun. Attention à la place des mots dans cette structure. Au pluriel, le ***s*** disparaît, seule l'apostrophe demeure.

→ *Governements' difficult choices.*

→ Les choix difficiles des gouvernements.

b) **Nom + *of* + nom**

On évite le cas possessif lorsque le nom du possesseur est trop long ou quand on veut créer un effet (insistance, suspens...) :

→ *And the name of the winner is...*

→ Et le nom du gagnant est...

Remarque :

Le ***'s*** du génitif disparaît parfois avec l'usage en formant des noms composés. Le premier nom jouant alors un rôle de déterminant par rapport au second :

→ *air quality* → la qualité de l'air

→ *unemployment rate* → taux de chômage

→ *staff turnover* → rotation du personnel

→ *football match* → match de football.

30 • *Whatever, whoever, whichever*

Les pronoms composés en ***-ever*** se construisent à partir des mots en ***wh-*** et siginifient «peu importe, qui que / quoi que...»

Un équivalent en anglais moins formel serait :

no matter what / who / where...

whoever : peu importe qui, qui que ce soit

whatever / whichever : quoi que ce soit

whenever : n'importe quand

wherever : n'importe où, quel que soit l'endroit

however : quelle que soit la façon dont...

→ *You can do **whatever** you want with a machine like this!*

Remarque :

Ne pas confondre ***however*** + adjectif ou ***however*** + proposition avec l'adverbe ***however*** qui signifie «cependant».

1 Faire un CV (CV and/*or resume*)

Un CV (curriculum vitae) est un document qui se modifie au fil des années et qui se modifie aussi en fonction de l'entreprise à qui vous le soumettez. Il doit permettre d'être lu rapidement et de montrer votre expérience professionnelle ainsi que vos qualifications. N'oubliez pas les activités périscolaires qui priment chez les employeurs anglo-saxons.

Your name
Address
Country
Phone
Email

Career Objective
To obtain an entry-level position in international trade utilising my language skills in Spanish and Russian

Education
2018-2020: Victorine H Business School, France
BTS CI (2-year technical diploma in International Commerce)
2015-2018: Lycée XXXXX, France
Economics and Social Studies Baccalaureate (A-level/High School Diploma)

Work Experience
2019: A 2-month work placement at Louis Vuitton, NYC. Prospecting clients in the USA by mail and phone; designing a leaflet for the summer season and writing a questionnaire for retailers in American department stores to improve our visibility.
2018: A 2-month summer job at the local bakery. Handling the cash register, taking orders and organising delivery at weddings, summer festivals.
2017: A 2-month summer job at a summer camp that enrolled children and managed recreational facilities. Managing a team and programming activities.

Languages
French: Mother tongue
Spanish: Mother tongue
Russian: European Level B1 (intermediate)

IT skills
Excel, Word, PowerPoint and Sage

Interests
Sports: Aikido instructor
Volunteer work as a firefighter, reading, cinema and drama (in a drama club for 10 years)
References available upon request

Info

Dans votre CV :
- pas de photo ;
- pas de nationalité ;
- pas de date de naissance.

Tips

➡ Le CV donne les grandes lignes de vos activités professionnelles. Notez que vous utiliserez des verbes en -ING pour introduire les tâches accomplies, ex : *handling customer queries, scheduling activities according to age groups.*

2 Rédiger une lettre de demande de stage ou de candidature spontanée

Pour mettre toutes les chances de votre côté, il faut, au préalable, faire un travail de recherche sur l'entreprise à qui vous allez envoyer votre lettre. Dans votre courrier, vous joindrez votre CV et vous indiquerez pourquoi cette entreprise vous permettrait de mettre en pratique vos connaissances. Vous montrerez que vous connaissez l'entreprise, que ce courrier n'est pas un hasard.

My ADDRESS
Phone number
Email address

DATE

COMPANY'S ADDRESS

Name of the person you are writing to
Her/his title
Name of the company

Dear Mrs O'Leary/Dear Sir/Madam,

LOOKING FOR A WORK PLACEMENT

I am a first/second year student preparing a post-baccalaureate degree specialised in small and medium-sized companies at the Lycée .... in Gennevilliers. Part of the curriculum is based on a work placement that I have to carry out from the beginning of May to the end of June.
I would like very much to gain work experience with a local company that would give me the opportunity to use my skills.
Your company appeals to me as you are a small, progressive firm where there may be opportunities to work as part of a team on various projects. A student from our school recommended your company where she was fortunate to obtain a placement in the past. She spoke highly of her work placement and mentioned that your company gave her the possibility to use and develop her skills.
As you will see from my enclosed CV, I believe I have the necessary skills to contribute to your company.
Previously I had a summer job at the company................................ where I learned to supervise a team.
I believe it has enabled me to learn communication and organisation skills.
I am available for an interview to discuss my qualifications in relation to a potential placement with you.
I thank you in advance for considering my application.
I look forward to hearing from you.

Yours sincerely/Yours faithfully,

Name

3 Rédiger un rapport de stage et le présenter oralement

Part 1

A. How I found the company where I carried out my work placement

- It took me quite a lot of time to find a company that was interested in having a trainee.
- I was helped in my internship search by my teacher.
- I secured a work placement interview and met with my tutor.
- The job interviewer wanted to find out if I would be a keen trainee.

Part 2

B. Presenting the company

- The company is located in (place).
- It is a small company run by the (name) family.
- The company was founded in (year) by (name).
- The company activity is to provide hospitals, clinics and pharmacies with medical equipment.
- Their main supplier is located in Switzerland.
- The company has specialised in (name of items).
- The CEO is (name), Mr/s (name) is the human resources manager ; etc.

Word box

Work placement ; internship ; training: *j'avais pour mission / j'étais chargée des...*

Part 3

C. The tasks I was responsible for

- I was in charge of setting up appointments with suppliers and clients.
- My task was to double check that orders placed by our customers had been forwarded to our transport company to be delivered on the date stated on the order form.
- One of my assignments was to go through the emails answer the most urgent ones, and forward the others to my mentor.
- Sorting out the mail when it arrived and bringing it to the departments responsible by the request was a daily activity.
- Once I had to organise a meeting with the heads of every department to draw up a work schedule for a special project that needed to be completed within three weeks.
- I had to deal with angry clients or unhappy suppliers.
- I had to call companies that had not settled their invoices.

Part 4

D. Point of view

- I like the company where I was a trainee. First, my colleagues were very helpful; second, they let me take initiatives and third, I could interrupt them, they would always listen to my inquiries.
- However, it was sometime a little dull as I started the day with the emails, then I sorted the letters, and I really started working on my project late in the morning.
- I wish I had had an extra week to finish my project.

Tips

- ➡ Faites un plan en quatre grandes parties que vous suivrez.
- ➡ Ajoutez des documents de l'entreprise.
- ➡ Votre présentation doit durer 2 minutes.

4 Faire un compte rendu oral ou écrit en anglais à partir d'un document écrit en anglais

How should firms deal with a "toxic employee"?

When Simon realised he had to deal with a "toxic employee", he knew he needed to act fast. Simon, the boss of a small firm in New York, says the man in question had been wrongly trying to claim credit for other's new business wins, and was deliberately ignoring members of his team. At the same time the employee was said to be rebelling against the company by forming a clique, and threatening to start his own business.

"We needed to show our company that one person does not stand above the team," says Simon. And so the alleged rabble-rouser was sacked.

Simon adds: "The money and time we spent handling this situation... well, it could have been a lot worse if he had stayed on. The internal politics would have been terrible. I don't know if we'd even have a company now." Most of us have had to endure a corrosive fellow member of staff on one or more occasions during our working lives, whose bad behaviour - everything from selfishness, bullying, rudeness, being overtly-domineering, or even just being constantly too loud and opinionated can have a devastating impact on staff morale. In academic circles, such a problem employee is now more often described as "toxic". Numerous studies have shown that they cost a business or government department money, due to the productivity of other workers plummeting, or people taking sick leave or even resigning.

One 2015 report by Harvard Business School estimated that keeping a toxic worker on the payroll can cost an average firm more than $12,000 (£9,400) a year. This is more than double the £5,000 of increased annual productivity it says a good employee can provide.

A separate study said that the annual financial impact of a toxic employee could be even more onerous. The 2012 survey of 2,700 firms by jobs website Career Builder found that a quarter of respondents put the figure at more than $50,000, while 41% said the number was around $25,000.

Prof Dylan Minor, co-author of the Harvard report, says that what can be frustrating for managers is that toxic employees "are usually very productive, because overconfident workers can be successful." He adds: "But employers have to think about the other dimensions, the toxicity." But with employment law in many countries making it far from easy to get rid of a damaging worker, how can companies best deal with the problem without necessarily seeking the termination of the toxic employee? And how can firms best avoid such people in the first place? Also, could the existence of toxic employees be blamed on the company itself, and a bad working culture that enables such people to behave the way they do in the first place?

Bruce Tulgan, a US management expert, says that company leaders need to be clear about what is permissible within the firm, and identify "low performers", which is what he calls toxic employees. He suggests meeting with the difficult employee to "make the behaviour explicit, and break it down, monitor and measure it, and offer course-corrected feedback." Mr. Tulgan adds: "A lot of time that can correct the [bad] behaviour."

But if those corrected measures don't improve the employee's conduct, he recommends firing them "since you are paying them and they aren't following instructions, and that is insubordination."

Adapted from *BBC Business*, December 8, 2016.

I Introduction

Comme l'épreuve est orale, le niveau de stress peut être élevé. Pour vous donner de l'assurance, rédigez votre introduction et donnez votre plan.

Vous devez obtenir une introduction semblable à celle-ci :

The text is from BBC Business posted on BBC website on 8 December 2016. The main idea is toxic employee. So clearly we shall start by defining what a toxic employee is and how to solve the problem.

II Plan

Le temps est compté : vous n'avez que 20 minutes pour préparer votre plan en trois parties.

A. Faire la liste des arguments qui définissent "the toxic employee".
B. Faire la liste des conséquences à l'intérieur de l'entreprise.
C. Faire la liste des solutions.

III Reformuler

Une fois les listes faites, il faut apprendre à reformuler. Voici quelques exemples :

A. ☐ **Selfishness:** a toxic employee is selfish or acts selfishly. The other members of the team do not count in his eye.
☐ **Rudeness:** a toxic employee is rude. He or she might not say hello or thank you. He or she considers he/she deserves the help of his/her co-workers.
☐ **Overly domineering:** he or she wants to be right all the time. He or she is bossy.

B. ☐ **The company loses money.** Employees are sick so they are absent on leave more often. Employees resign, which means that they leave the company for a job elsewhere.
☐ **Productivity is down:** employees are less productive.

C. ☐ **The company needs to say what is permissible.** A set of rules or a code of conduct must be defined by the company.
☐ **The company must meet the toxic employee.**

IV Citer le texte

Vous pouvez citer le texte pour asseoir vos arguments.
Exemple : He suggests meeting with the difficult employee "and speak frankly".
This sentence shows that a way to find a solution is to talk to the toxic employee.

V Conclusion

Ne pas oublier la conclusion ; ici, qui est responsable du "*toxic employee*".
L'entreprise qui a embauché le mauvais salarié ou une situation de travail qui génère ce comportement.

VI *Branching out*

- **Comment enrichir le sujet à partir de vos connaissances ?**
L'approfondissement du sujet dépend des connaissances que vous avez acquises sur la problématique présentée dans l'article. Ici, il s'agit du monde du travail. Vous pouvez donc partir de la problématique de l'employé(e) toxique pour vous exprimer plus largement sur la thématique du travail.

Deux exemples d'enrichissements possibles :
- Today the work place has changed thanks to new technologies; the possibility to work from home may preserve employees from the bad impact of a toxic atmosphere at work.
- Managers should be able to anticipate tensions in a team by separating people who cannot work together. They should treat every employee equally and try to highlight their qualities rather than insist on their flaws. Although competitiveness can be encouraged, it mustn't turn into a counterproductive confrontation of egos.

- **Votre examinateur peut également vous emmener vers des problématiques plus larges en vous demandant par exemple d'exprimer votre opinion sur :**
- le télétravail ;
- l'open-space ;
- la discrimination au travail ;
- les droits des salariés (avantages sociaux, etc.).

→ **Toutes ces pistes se trouvent dans les chapitres 3. Companies et 4. Work.**

5 Faire un compte rendu écrit en français à partir d'un texte anglais

State of play: Toymakers bounce back in the land of adult nappies

They have become pioneers in how to adapt to a rapidly ageing society

WILLIAM ELLIOT GRIFFIS, an American educator who travelled to Japan in the 1870s, noted that in the previous two and a half centuries, "the main business of this nation was play." He described toyshops filled as full as Christmas stockings and plenty of grown-ups.

Griffis would have found it familiar walking today around Hakuhinkan Toy Park, one of the largest toy stores in Tokyo. Teens, office workers and grandparents are mostly to be seen perusing its 200,000-odd knick-knacks across five floors. Its director, Hiroyuki Itoh, says he wants the store to be a place where everyone can play. After work, suited salarymen come to spend ¥200 (under $2) for a five-minute whizz around a 36-metre slot-car racetrack. In another corner a group of university students fiddle with displays of toys from their childhoods.

Playthings aimed at the over-20s make up 27% of Japan's domestic toy sales, according to figures from Euromonitor, a market-research firm. That grown-up portion of the market has been crucial for Japan's three biggest players, Bandai Namco, Takara Tomy and Sanrio, as the country's birth rate has slumped. Since the 1970s the proportion of under-15s has halved, to 12% of the population. By 2060 it is likely to be 9%.

Fumiaki Ibuki of Toy Journal, a 114-year-old trade magazine, says Japanese toy companies are pioneers in adapting to ageing. Despite a slow economy, the sector has, in the past two years, done its best in a decade: in the fiscal year ending in 2015, sales in core categories (excluding video games) rose by a tenth on the previous year, to over ¥800bn. Mr Ibuki says toymakers are taking a "borderless" approach: selling to a wider age range, and teaming up with trend-driven sectors like tech and fashion.

When Bandai's Tamagotchi, virtual pets housed in an egg-shaped toy, were booming in the mid-1990s, women in their 20s and 30s were big buyers. The same age-group snapped up Licca-chan, Japan's answer to Barbie, made by Takara Tomy. The firm now has an adult range: its "Cappuccino One-Piece" doll, sells for ¥12,000.

A stigma against adults having fun, strong in the aftermath of the second world war, has faded. Many want to recapture their youth, not so much by playing, but by collecting and displaying toys, says Harold Meij, the boss of Takara Tomy—so, for its premium Tomica model-car range, the company uses vintage designs that adults admired as boys. Having only one child later in life, as more Japanese now do, means that parents have more to spend on their offspring. Children are said to have "six pockets": two from their parents, and four from their grandparents.

During the global financial crisis of 2008, cheap impulse-buy toys took off, such as trading cards and coin-operated machines that dispense capsules of small toys—usually of well-known characters from Japanese comic books and television series.

The big themes in the toy industry are collectability and intellectual property (IP). A recent hit was a watch branded "Yo-kai", after the word in Japanese for supernatural spirits, by Bandai. It exemplifies a popular strategy: Yo-kai, whose hero wears the watch, began as a cartoon series in 2013, was adapted for TV and made into a hit video game.

The model is known as "media mix" in the industry. Bandai has partnered with Dentsu, an advertising giant, to promote anime, a word defining Japanese animation.

But when the story of a character catches on, toy- and film-makers end up splitting fat profits. It all makes for a sizzling recipe.

Adapted from *The Economist*, Feb. 23, 2017.

En général, il vous est demandé de faire en français une synthèse d'un texte en anglais, c'est-à-dire que votre compte rendu doit être plus court, et faire le tiers en général du texte initial.

Comment procéder en temps limité ? Il vous faudra quatre ou cinq paragraphes distincts : introduction (source, date, idée principale), développement en deux ou trois parties et conclusion.

I Introduction

L'article de *The Economist* du 23 février 2017 relate le succès des entreprises japonaises de jouets dans une société vieillissante. Quelles sont les raisons de ce succès ?

II Développement

I. Un paradoxe : les entreprises de jouet japonaises sont prospères dans une société avec de moins en moins d'enfants.

- Noms des entreprises mentionnées dans le texte : Hakuhinkan Toy Park à Tokyo sur cinq étages, Bandai Namco, Takara Tomy et Sanrio.
- Les clients sont des adultes de plus de 20 ans et leurs achats représentent 27 % des ventes sur le marché national.
- Les acheteurs collectionnent et exposent.
- La plupart des Japonais n'ont qu'un enfant, souvent assez tard.
- Parents et grands-parents contribuent à maintenir les ventes de jouets pour enfants.

II. Des sociétés ont adapté leur stratégie

- Une population vieillissante.
- Des jouets qui rappellent l'enfance.
- Des partenariats avec des secteurs de la mode et du Hi-Tech.
- Pendant la crise, des jouets peu chers sont proposés.
- Acquisition de droits de marchandisage, un modèle dit « media mix ».

III Conclusion

La culture du jouet liée à des partenariats avec les médias génère des profits. Le ralentissement économique général au Japon n'a pas de prise sur les industries du jouet qui ont augmenté leurs ventes de 10 % en 2015 par rapport à l'année précédente.

LES PIÈGES

- Évitez les mots anglais.
- Ne pas prendre en compte le paragraphe anecdotique en début d'un article, accroche pour le lecteur.
- Ne pas citer tous les exemples. Ils ne sont là que pour illustrer un propos.
- Pensez en termes abstraits : ainsi « *adult nappies* » est relancé dans le sous-titre par « *ageing society* ».

6 Rédiger une lettre commerciale ou un courriel

Vous rédigerez un courriel en anglais en respectant les consignes suivantes :

Vous êtes Camille Germain, assistant/e de gestion dans l'entreprise « Des antennes au Plafond », 21 rue Pierre Brosolette, 33000 Toulouse.
Email : camillegermain@gmail.com
Vous répondez à votre cliente Jamie Tackle, directrice des achats chez« Genuine Bookstore for kids » par courriel à l'adresse : jamietackle@gmail.com.

- Vous la priez d'accepter vos excuses pour le retard dans la livraison.
- En effet, Genuine Bookstore for kids, 22 Winston Street Birmingham C342970, vous a passé une commande de jeux pour enfants (de 3 ans à 13 ans) le 27 mars 2018.
- La livraison devait être effectuée le 10 avril 2018.
- Vous n'avez pas pu livrer car votre entrepôt a été inondé et la marchandise (jeux de cartes, jeux de société, jeux de construction, puzzles) a été abîmée.
- Vous ne pourrez livrer que dans 15 jours.
- Vous faites un geste commercial : une réduction ou autre.
- Vous vous excusez à nouveau pour la gêne occasionnée.
- Vous espérez que la relation commerciale ne sera pas modifiée.
- Salutations.

Word box

- board games: *jeux de société.*
- construction set: *jeu de construction.*
- deck of cards: *jeu de cartes.*
- jigsaw puzzle: *puzzle.*

To: jamietackle@gmail.com
From: camillegermain@gmail.com
Subject: Apologising for a late delivery
Date: 10 April 2018

Dear Mrs Tackle,

We really would like to apologise for not delivering the games on time. Genuine Bookstore for Kids placed an order for board games, construction sets, and decks of cards on 27 March 2018.
However, we were unable to deliver the goods on 10 April 2018 because our warehouse where we stock our merchandise was flooded. Board games, decks of cards, jigsaw puzzles, etc. were damaged.
We will be able to deliver your order in two weeks' time only. We do hope that it will not cause too much inconvenience.
As a gesture of goodwill, we would like to offer you 10 units of our new board game Dixit.
We hope our business relationship will not suffer from this incident.
Once again accept our apologies for the inconvenience caused.

Yours sincerely,
Camille Germain
Personal Assistant

Tips

1. Ne confondez pas destinataire et expéditeur.
2. Vérifiez que vous connaissez les termes administratifs et usuels. La gêne occasionnée : *inconvenience caused* ; un geste commercial : *a goodwill gesture* ; livrer : *to deliver* ; la relation commerciale : *the business relationship* ; être abîmé : *to be damaged.*
3. Faites des paragraphes en fonction des idées qui vont ensemble.
4. Vous connaissez par cœur les deux formules de politesse, même si les courriels sont souvent moins formels.

7 Négocier

- **Il y a deux grandes phases de négociation :**
  - **Première phase :** prise de contact et découverte des besoins.
  - **Seconde phase :** récapitulation des besoins et vérification, traitement des objections, conclusion avec la commande et ses modalités, et enfin, prise de congé.

- Vous aurez la première ou la seconde partie à jouer. Il est entendu que vous saurez qui est votre prospect, les produits que vous voulez lui vendre, l'entreprise et l'activité de votre prospect. Bien sûr, lors de la première rencontre, vous essaierez d'obtenir le plus d'informations possible pour cerner ses besoins.

- Le prospect est classé selon le profil SONCASE. En fonction des raisons pour lesquelles il/elle désire ce produit, ou encore en fonction de la relation commerciale qu'il/elle veut instaurer. Ainsi, le prospect est perçu comme à la recherche d'un produit de prestige, d'un produit nouveau, ou encore pour une relation commerciale simple et donc, le qualificatif «confort» peut décrire ce qu'il/elle recherche.

Info

SONCASE
- **Sécurité:** *security*
- **Orgueil :** *pride*
- **Nouveau :** *novelty*
- **Confort :** *comfort*
- **Argent :** *money*
- **Sympathie :** *sympathy*
- **Environnement:** *environment*

Phase 1 : Rencontre avec le prospect + découverte des besoins

- **Prise de contact :** I am Mrs NAME, the Sales Manager from COMPANY. And I have an appointment with Mr/s NAME at 1 o'clock. Could you, please, let her/him know that I have arrived?
- ***Small talk*:** Mr/s NAME, nice to meet you. I hope you had a good trip to London. Is it your first time?
- **Découverte des besoins (*needs appraisal*) :** I met with a colleague of yours at the Fair in Hannover last November. That's right and and I was told that you were interested in some of our products. Could I ask you a few questions to find out what your needs are? May I take down notes?
  Vous avez besoin de bien comprendre les besoins de votre prospect en lui posant des questions afin de cerner ses besoins. Vous n'oublierez pas de récapituler pour vérifier qu'il n'y a pas de malentendu, que vous avez bien compris ce que votre prospect désire.

Phase 2 : 2e rencontre avec le prospect pour finaliser la vente

Récapitulation des besoins : Last time we met, you told me that you were interested in having 100 bottles of a specific fragrance. You had not yet decided the size of the bottles you wanted. You were not quite sure if you only wanted 100 ml bottles or also 50 ml bottles.
Vous vérifiez que votre négociation redémarre bien sur les mêmes bases. Il est clair que le prospect peut revenir sur des choix préalables.

Traitement des objections :
Can you ensure me that the delivery will be two weeks after placing the order?
Votre prospect, s'il ne vous connaît pas, a besoin d'être rassuré sur le bien-fondé de son achat. Vous devez le rassurer sur les conditions de livraison, etc. Vous aurez prévu les objections et serez préparé/e à y répondre. N'hésitez pas à apporter un échantillon pour montrer la qualité du produit, etc. Si le contrat n'est pas signé à cause d'une objection, reprenez contact un ou deux jours plus tard pour apporter une réponse à l'objection.

Conditions de paiement et transport :
I guess you would like to pay in pounds, that is fine with us. As for the shipping of the fresh produce, we will start every other day and if you feel it should be every day, we will organise it to be a daily delivery.
Les Incoterms auront été évoqués, choisis, et la vente doit se conclure sur le sentiment que les deux partis ont obtenu un contrat équitable. Votre prospect reviendra vers vous s'il a le sentiment que la relation commerciale est juste. Le fameux « gagnant-gagnant » est votre objectif dans cette négociation.

Conclusion et prise de congé :
It was a delight to do business with you. If you have any questions, please, do not hesitate to contact me. You have my business card. Good bye.

8 Préparer un entretien d'embauche

La préparation (15 minutes) permet de limiter le stress et de se sentir plus à l'aise. Préparer, c'est anticiper les questions qui vont vous être posées. Savoir mettre en avant vos qualités et les points positifs (imaginaires) de l'entreprise auprès de laquelle vous postulez. Vous saurez être réactif(ve), et montrer de l'enthousiasme et de l'intérêt. Présentez vous en tenue professionnelle. **Attention, vous devez faire preuve de réactivité et ne pas vous laisser déstabiliser par l'offre d'emploi car votre examinateur ne connaît pas non plus l'entreprise qui recrute. Vous avez le droit d'imaginer vos questions/réponses de toute pièce, à condition de ne pas être en contradiction avec ce que dit le document.**

Gordon Food Service

Are looking for a Sales representative

Location: Houston, Texas

Job: permanent

Salary $40 *OTE + bonus

Benefits: health and dental care, low-cost benefit options for your family, health, and future.

Perks: company car, laptop and cell phone.

We are looking for a **Food Sales Representative** with Gordon Food Service. You will have the opportunity to **cultivate relationships, develop new business, and provide innovative solutions** to our customers, helping them to achieve their goals and, in return, yours. An internal support system.

The ideal candidate should have:

A qualification in sales and management.

You should have at least 1 year of prior **sales, business, or food service experience.**

You must maintain a valid state driver's license and a safe driving record.

*OTE: On Target Earnings: basic salary + commissions

Word box

- update a customer data base: *mettre à jour des données client;*
- door-to-door prospection: *prospection en porte à porte;*
- answer customers' complaints: *répondre aux réclamations des clients;*
- take appointments/arrange meetings: *prendre des rendez-vous;*
- use professional softwares: *utiliser des logiciels professionnels;*
- be hardworking: *travailler beaucoup;*
- have good interpersonal skills: *avoir un bon relationnel;*
- team spirit: *esprit d'équipe;*
- establish and maintain customer loyalty: *fidéliser la clientèle et maintenir la fidélisation;*
- enrich the portofolio: *enrichir le portefeuille (clients);*
- carry out missions/tasks: *entreprendre des missions/effectuer des tâches;*
- writing skills: *aisance rédactionnelle.*

Pendant les 15 minutes de préparation, vous veillerez à noter et à récapituler l'essentiel des informations présentes dans le document afin de les reformuler lors de l'entretien avec votre examinateur/recruteur. Vous postulez obligatoirement pour une fonction de commercial(e). Vous avez vos deux années de BTS pour vous entraîner à utiliser le vocabulaire spécifique aux missions commerciales.

I Voici un exemple de début d'entretien :

Job interviewer: Good morning/afternoon, I'm NAME the Human Resource Mmanager for Gordon Food Service. First, could you introduce yourself, and tell me about your qualifications and work experience?

You: Good morning/afternoon. Pleased to meet you. Thank you for having me. I am NAME. I am here for the position of sales representative advertised on your website. I was able to secure a job interview after my phone call with your assistant, Mr/s NAME.

I have just graduated from my school where I prepared a two-year post-baccalaureate degree specialised in marketing. During my studies, I had to carry out two internships: the first one was at Whole Foods, NYC, and the second one was at Cyril Lignac Cuisine Attitude.

II Vous pouvez au cours de l'entretien également vous inventer un parcours professionnel fictif afin de vous valoriser en montrant un profil dynamique de quelqu'un qui souhaite enrichir son expérience professionnelle.

You: I'm currently working for another food company as a sales rep, but I would like to join your company because it is much larger and I would appreciate a new challenge.
→ *En ce moment, je travaille en tant que commercial(e) au sein d'une autre entreprise spécialisée dans l'alimentaire, mais je souhaiterais rejoindre votre équipe car elle est beaucoup plus importante et que je suis à la recherche de nouveaux défis.*

III Comme pour les autres jeux de rôle, vous pouvez anticiper ou inventer ce qui n'est pas précisé dans le document de départ, du moment que vous ne faites pas de contresens. D'autre part, l'entretien d'embauche vous demande de savoir formuler les questions, puisque vous serez amené à en poser au recruteur du type :

You: What salary can I expect? What are the working hours? Do you offer any benefits *(avantages sociaux)* and perks? *(avantages en nature)* When will you give me your answer? etc.

IV Ensuite vous décrirez vos missions qui doivent révéler vos compétences commerciales, en vous aidant du vocabulaire ci-dessus. En fin d'entretien, n'oubliez pas de demander quand vous aurez une réponse, de remercier et de prendre congé.

9 Préparer l'entretien de vente – Vente de produit

Comment préparer l'entretien de vente d'un produit ?

I Avant de commencer l'entretien

Le candidat est face à face avec un examinateur qui jouera le rôle du **client**. Il s'agit dans la majorité des cas d'un entretien en **B to C (Business to Consumer)**.

Ce n'est pas une épreuve de négociation, il s'agit d'une épreuve où **l'anglais et les capacités de communication sont évalués**. L'étudiant devra faire preuve de réactivité et de professionnalisme tout en ayant **le champ libre pour argumenter sur le produit, à condition de ne pas être en contradiction avec le document d'origine.**

Pendant la préparation (15 minutes), il est conseillé de **noter les points forts du produit, d'anticiper les objections, de donner les informations demandées même si elles ne figurent pas dans le document de départ** (exemple : si la durée de garantie n'est pas précisée, anticipez la question).

RRP: £449.00
Price: £353.34 & FREE delivery in the UK.
You Save: £95.66 (21%)
1850 W
15 Bar
Black
Energy Class A

Only 14 left in stock (more on the way).
Want it delivered by Monday, 12 Feb.?
Order within 5 hrs 20 mins and choose One-Day Delivery at checkout

- Gift-wrap available.
- Removable Respiro* brew Unit
- Plastic Body
- **Milk Frother
- Ceramic ***grinder to retain the purity of the coffee aromas
- LED Interface with Buttons

*Brew unit: unité chauffante
**milk frother: appareil pour faire mousser le lait
***grinder: moulin (à café)

II L'entretien (15 minutes)

→ **Pour commencer, saluez et présentez-vous au client :**

Ex: Good morning, I'm (first name/name) and I am a **sales representative** for Respiro, the famous **kitchen appliance** company. I'm here today because I know you are interested in buying a new **state of the art** coffee machine, etc.

ATTENTION : Les exemples ci-dessous sont donnés à titre indicatif, il y a un grand nombre de formulations possibles ; il est fortement conseillé à chaque étudiant(e) de trouver lui-même/elle-même la façon de s'exprimer qui lui convient le mieux. D'autre part, il s'agit d'une ébauche d'entretien, le candidat devra se montrer beaucoup plus exhaustif.

→ **N'oubliez pas de ménager des temps de pause, de manière à laisser la parole à votre client.**

Vous lui présentez le produit, en faisant apparaître ses avantages et en les reformulant. Vous évitez de mentionner les caractéristiques que vous ne comprenez pas. En effet, vous n'êtes pas censé connaître la technologie de tous les produits dans le commerce.

Ex: This new coffee machine includes the **latest technology**, allowing you to drink the best coffee on the market. It is both **energy efficient** and **easy to use**.

→ Ici, vous n'avez pas beaucoup de détails sur le produit. Par conséquent, vous pouvez imaginer d'autres caractéristiques.(différentes couleurs, etc.)

Ex: The Dolce comes in several colours: blue, red white and black, all for the same price.

→ Vous pouvez également décider, pour enrichir l'entretien et démontrer votre réactivité, de proposer une couleur particulière comportant un surcoût :

Ex: We also propose the Silver Dolce for an **additional cost** of $20.

→ Que vous pouvez justifier par :

Ex: The material used to get this colour is more expensive, but your machine becomes also **ornamental** and can be placed in your living room.

→ Pour encourager le client à vous commander le produit, vous mentionnez le fait qu'il n'en reste que très peu en stock et que le prix que vous offrez est inférieur au prix en magasin (RRP : *recommended retail price*).

Ex: The price we offer is **$95 lower than the normal price**. It is a **special offer**, which means limited in time. So **I advise** you to profit from this **unique opportunity**.

→ La somme finale étant conséquente, $353, vous pouvez proposer des modalités de paiement flexibles, en insistant sur la gratuité de la livraison et sa rapidité.

Ex: We can **deliver you** at your home within 24 hours, **for free**. As for the **terms of payment**, you can pay in **several installments** (en plusieurs versements).

→ Au cas où le client ne serait pas satisfait du produit, vous lui proposez le remboursement.

Ex: If you are not satisfied with our product, you can **get a full refund within 7 days**.

III Fin de l'entretien

- Hypothèse 1 :

Votre client achète le produit :

→ Vous récapitulez le modèle choisi et la quantité voulue, avant de passer à la commande et de rappeler les modalités de paiement.

Ex: So, you would like to order one blue Dolce. All right, so if you don't mind we will fill the bill of order together. As for the terms of payment, you have chosen to pay in three installments. So can you sign here please?

→ Ensuite, vous prenez congé du client en le félicitant pour son achat et en insistant sur votre disponibilité en cas de problème ou de question.

Ex: Thank you for your trust, you have made a great purchase and I'm quite sure you won't regret it. Do not hesitate to contact me by phone or email in case you need further information, or if you meet a problem with the delivery or with the product itself. Good bye, and enjoy your Dolces!

- Hypothèse 2 :

Votre client n'achète pas le produit parce qu'il a besoin d'un délai de réflexion, de consulter un conjoint, etc.

Ex: I understand you cannot make up your mind right now, but I advise you to do it as fast as you can since we have only 14 Dolce left in stock. You can call or email me as soon as you have decided to buy the product. Good bye for now, I do hope to hear from you soon!

Info

- Il faut être capable d'interagir pendant 15 minutes avec un client en anglais. Plus vous enrichirez l'échange, meilleure sera votre prestation.

10 Préparer l'entretien de vente – Préparer une vente de voyage

Comment préparer l'entretien de vente d'un voyage ?

→ Afin d'être efficace dans sa préparation, le candidat **devra noter et récapituler** toutes les **informations connues et inconnues** sur le voyage proposé en les **hiérarchisant : destination/durée/périodes/prix/prestations incluses/non incluses/inconnues**

→ De même que pour la vente de produit (voir tools 9), **les informations manquantes devront être suppléées par le candidat.**

→ De même que pour l'entretien de vente, le candidat n'est pas supposé connaître tout de la géographie mondiale. Certains sites risquent de vous être complètement inconnus ; dans ce cas, il est fortement conseillé d'éviter de citer les noms géographiques que vous ne maitrisez pas car vous allez les déformer et entraver la communication.
Vous vous rabattrez sur des phrases du type : You are going to visit many beautiful/famous sites/landscapes/cities.

Voici un exemple d'entretien :

Vous observerez particulièrement les aspects du voyage que le candidat (*sales rep*) a été obligé d'anticiper :

Sales rep: *Good morning/afternoon. We have an offer which you may find interesting. It is an* ***all inclusive trip*** *in Italy. How many people would travel?*

Client: *I will travel alone, but yes, Italy sounds appealing; but I need to know the trip length and of course its price and if it is* ***available all year round****.*

Sales rep: *it is a 10-day trip in the most beautiful and famous* ***sites*** *in Italy for $1,593 per person if you choose to travel between February and April.*

Client: *You mean that the package isn't available the rest of the year?*

Sales rep: *No, it is available all year round but with a premium price during the* ***peak seasons****.*

Client: *Oh, I see, and how much would it cost if I chose to travel in June?*

Sales rep: *Well, there would be an* ***additional cost*** *of $100, I'm afraid.*

Client: *I see. I suppose the prices are for one person?*

Sales rep: *Yes, of course. But you should bear in mind that this offer includes a great number of services well beyond the basic transport and* ***accommodation fares****.*

Client: *Would you mind telling me exactly what is included in the price?*

Sales rep: *Not at all! The* ***return flight*** *from London Heathrow to Rome, as well as a* ***5 star accommodation*** *all along the 10 ten-day trip are included. The hotels you will have the privilege to stay in are all of* ***the highest standards****, with spacious rooms all equipped with a private bathroom and full breakfast.*

Client: *All right, I see. But are all the other* ***meals*** *included?*

Sales rep: *Most of them are, but some lunches during the stay are not included in order to allow more flexibility in the* ***schedule****. You do not wish your visits to be interrupted by a mandatory lunch break, do you? And I must add it is part of our policy to let our clients enjoy the opportunity to discover local food while visiting the sites. Moreover, our tours are* ***escorted,*** *which means that there will always be a professional tour operator around to* ***advise*** *you.*

Client: *What about local transport? From Rome to Pompei for example? Are they part of the* ***package****?*

Sales rep: *Of course they are: bus fares, train fares and even boat fares are included; only taxi fares aren't included when you spend some time on your own.*

Client: *Are the visits always done with an English-speaking guide?*

Sales rep: *Of course. All the visits in our program are guided visits, with an English-speaking specialist of the site.*

Client: *What are the* ***booking terms****?*

Sales rep: *If you choose this package, I advise you not to* ***delay*** *your booking, especially if you wish to travel in June, because we are almost full already. When you book, you must pay a* ***down payment*** *corresponding to 20% of the total* ***amount****. You are expected to have paid the total amount one week at most before* ***departure****. You may of course, choose to pay in several installments, from the day of the booking to one week before the travel.*

Client: *I understand. It is a significant amount of money, and I would like to know if you have a* ***refunding policy*** *in case I have to* ***cancel*** *my trip.*

Sales rep: *When you book your travel, we offer you to* ***subscribe*** *a* ***cancellation*** *insurance for $20 per person. As for travel insurance, in case you fall ill during the travel, you should first ask your insurance if it covers you* ***abroad****. If not, you'll have the possibility to subscribe a travel insurance for $5.*

Client: *I see. The package you offer sounds interesting; but I cannot choose the dates without having made arrangements with the company I work for. Can I call you back as soon as I know about the exact dates?*

Sales rep: *Yes, please do! I advise you not to delay your answer too much as I mentioned previously, as our bookings are almost already full.*

Client: *All right, I'll come back to you as soon as I know the answer.*

Sales rep: *It is my pleasure, I hope to hear from you soon! Good bye.*

Info

Les compétences requises pour la vente de voyage sont pour la plupart identiques à celles exigées pour la vente de produit (voir tools 9 pages 218-219). La différence réside dans la connaissance du vocabulaire propre au voyage et au tourisme.

Le candidat confronté à une vente de voyage préparera son entretien à partir d'un document généralement publicitaire, proposant un séjour dont les détails seront donnés de manière plus ou moins complète.

11 Préparer un jeu de rôle commercial

Objectifs

Être capable de s'exprimer oralement en langue vivante étrangère de façon pertinente et intelligible à partir d'un support qui sera la base d'une négociation de vente. Vous aurez à mettre en œuvre soit la première partie de la négociation, soit la seconde.
La première est constituée de la prise de contact, de la découverte des besoins. La seconde porte sur la récapitulation des besoins, du traitement des objections et de la conclusion de la vente et prise de congé. Cet échange peut se décliner en six étapes (voir ci-dessous).

Déroulement de l'épreuve

Temps de préparation : 20 minutes ; **temps de l'épreuve :** 20 minutes.

Sujet: You work for the Energy Saving Trust in Scotland. Today you are meeting a potential customer to persuade him or her to buy solar panels for his or her home.

Solar electricity: Generate cheap, green electricity from sunlight
Solar electricity systems capture the sun's energy using photovoltaic (PV) cells. The cells convert sunlight into electricity, which can be used to run household appliances and lighting. PV cells don't need direct sunlight to work – you can still generate some electricity on a cloudy day.

The benefits of solar electricity

- **Cut your carbon footprint:** Solar electricity is green, renewable energy and doesn't release any harmful carbon dioxide (CO2), or other pollutants.
- **Cut your electricity bill:** Sunlight is free, so once you've paid for the initial installation your electricity costs will be greatly reduced.
- **Sell electricity back to the Grid:** If your system is producing more electricity than you need, or when you can't use it, someone else can use it – and you could make a bit of money. Read more about feed-in tariffs and selling electricity.
- **Store electricity for a cloudy day:** If your home isn't connected to the national grid you can store excess electricity in batteries to use when you need it.

Is solar electricity suitable for my home?
To tell if solar electricity is right for you, there are a few key questions to consider:

- **Do you have a sunny place to put it?** You'll need a roof or wall that faces within 90 degrees of south, and isn't overshadowed by trees or buildings.
- **Is your roof strong enough?** Solar panels are not light and the roof must be strong enough to take their weight, especially if the panel is placed on top of existing tiles.
- **Do you need planning permission?** In England, Wales, Scotland and Northern Ireland, you don't need planning permission for most home solar electricity systems, as long as they're below a certain size.

Cost, savings and maintenance
An average system (2.2kW) costs around £12,000 (including VAT at 5%).

Need more advice? Call us on 0800 512 012 for free impartial advice.

http://www.energysavingtrust.org.uk

Méthode

1. **Prendre connaissance du document et l'analyser :** il s'agit d'une situation de vente en général.
2. **Situation de communication :** situation de négociation-vente.
    - Vous accueillez le prospect.
    - Vous posez des questions pour découvrir ses besoins.
    - Vous récapitulez pour vérifier que vous avez bien compris.
    - Vous récapitulez la demande et vous traitez les objections.
    - Vous concluez la vente.
    - Vous prenez congé.

Role play

→ Conversation between a consultant for the Energy Saving Trust, a green group, and a potential customer at the Energy Fair in Scotland.

Your role: Consultant for the Energy Saving Trust in Scotland.

Examiner's role: A company manager interested in cheap and clean energy.

Your task: Convince the visitor to buy solar panels for his or her house.

You will start the dialogue: The document should help you to ask and answer questions during the exchange.

- **1st stage:** get to know your potential client.
- **2nd stage:** find about the clients' specific needs.
- **3rd stage:** rephrase your client's needs and explain how your product can answer his/her needs; be ready to answer his/her questions and objections.
- **4rd stage:** talk about the price, explain what services are included in it and be open to negotiation.
- **5th stage:** conclude the sale, thank the client for his/her trust and make sure that you are available for him/her at any time for further information or claims.
- **6th stage:** take your leave.

Info

Les Tools 9 et 10 peuvent vous aider.

Crédits photographiques

Couverture : © monamis/ADOBE STOCK PHOTO/FOTOLIA.

7 ht © Patrick Lefevre / Belpress / Andia ; 7 bas DR ; 8 ©PeterVandenbelt/SHUTTERSTOCK ; 9 bas ©elenabsl/SHUTTERSTOCK ; 10 ©Nomad_Soul/SHUTTERSTOCK ; 12 ht ©Pe3k/SHUTTERSTOCK ; 12 bas ©canon_shooter/SHUTTERSTOCK ; 14 ©prizma/SHUTTERSTOCK ; 16 g DR ; 16 d ©singh_lens/ SHUTTERSTOCK ; 18 ©annanahabed/ADOBE STOCK PHOTO ; 20 DR ; 22 Baloo Rex May/CARTOON STOCK ; 23 ©konradbak/ADOBE STOCK PHOTO ; 25 ht ©Lenscap Photography/SHUTTERSTOCK ; 25 bas ©Niloo/SHUTTERSTOCK ; 25 m ©Joe Seer/SHUTTERSTOCK ; 29 ©AHMAD FAIZAL YAHYA/ SHUTTERSTOCK ; 29 ©AHMAD FAIZAL YAHYA/SHUTTERSTOCK ; 31 ht DR ; 31 bas DR ; 33 ht © Carpenter, Dave / CARTOON STOCK ; 33 bas DR ; 35 ©Michael Moloney/SHUTTERSTOCK ; 36 DR ; 38 DR ; 40 ©Nezabudkina/SHUTTERSTOCK ; 41 ©barneyboogles/ADOBE STOCK PHOTO ; 44 g ©Tero Vesalainen/SHUTTERSTOCK ; 44 d DR ; 47 ©Yorkman/SHUTTERSTOCK ; 55 bas DR ; 56 © Lee Jin-man / AP / SIPA PRESS ; 57 ht DR ; 57 bas ©wowomnom/SHUTTERSTOCK ; 58 ©rainbow rays/SHUTTERSTOCK ; 62 DR ; 64 ©360b/SHUTTERSTOCK ; 64 ©Christopher Penler/ SHUTTERSTOCK ; 64 ©Eric Broder Van Dyke/SHUTTERSTOCK ; 67 ©Takashi Images/SHUTTERSTOCK ; 68 ht DR ; 68 bas DR ; 71 DR ; 73 d ©Christopher Penler/SHUTTERSTOCK ; 73 g DR ; 73 d DR ; 73 g DR ; 77 ©Yann Bohac/SIPA ; 79 g DR ; 79 d DR ; 80 DR ; 81 ht DR ; 81 ht DR ; 81 bas ©kalpis/ADOBE STOCK PHOTO ; 83 ©Guy Bell/Shutterstock/SIPA ; 86 DR ; 88 DR ; 92 DR ; 97 d DR ; 97 bas g DR ; 97 ht g DR ; 103 ht ©JoeyCheung/SHUTTERSTOCK ; 103 bas DR ; 104 DR ; 105 DR ; 110 ©Masyanya/ ADOBE STOCK PHOTO / FOTOLIA ; 112 ©MISHELLA/SHUTTERSTOCK ; 116 DR ; 116 DR ; 119 ©GERARD BOTTINO/SHUTTERSTOCK ; 121 DR ; 123 ht ©Masyanya/ADOBE STOCK PHOTO / FOTOLIA ; 123 bas g ©joseph_hilfiger/ADOBE STOCK PHOTO / FOTOLIA ; 123 bas m ©Boris Stroujko/ADOBE STOCK PHOTO / FOTOLIA ; 123 bas d ©Beboy/ADOBE STOCK PHOTO / FOTOLIA ; 125 ©Maksimilian/ SHUTTERSTOCK ; 127 ht DR ; 127 bas DR ; 129 bas DR ; 131 ©hakule/SHUTTERSTOCK ; 134 DR ; 136 ht DR ; 136 bas DR ; 140 DR ; 145 ©lightrain/SHUTTERSTOCK ; 149 DR ; 151 ht © Supriya07 / SHUTTERSTOCK ; 151 bas DR ; 152 ht DR ; 155 ©testing/SHUTTERSTOCK ; 158 DR ; 160 ©phil Holmes / SHUTTERSTOCK ; 164 DR ; 167 ©Elauqelat/SHUTTERSTOCK ; 169 DR ; 173 DR ; 175 bas DR ; 175 ht ©michal812/SHUTTERSTOCK ; 176 ©chsherbakova yuliya /SHUTTERSTOCK ; 177 bas DR ; 177 ht ©gualtiero boffi/SHUTTERSTOCK ; 179 ©Rainer Lesniewski/SHUTTERSTOCK ; 182 ©Rainer Lesniewski/ SHUTTERSTOCK ; 182 DR ; 184 g ©nito/SHUTTERSTOCK ; 184 d DR ; 188 ©Stephen Finn/SHUTTERSTOCK ; 191 DR ; 193 ©northallertonman/SHUTTERSTOCK ; 197 DR ; 218 © M.studio/ADOBE STOCK PHOTO / FOTOLIA ; 220 ©Sergii Figurnyi/ADOBE STOCK PHOTO/FOTOLIA.

N° de projet : 10260757 _Graph'M
Dépôt légal : décembre 2019 - Imprimé en Italie par Bona SpA